OCR

RECOGNISING ACHIEVEMENT

AS Media Studies for OCR

Tanya Jones, Julian McDougall, Jacqueline Bennett and Julian Bowker

Edited by Richard Harvey

Hodder & Stoughton

A MEMBER OF THE HODDER HEADLINE GROUP

The authors and publishers would like to thank the following for permission to reproduce copyright illustrative material:

Aquarius Library for photographs from *The Simpsons* on page 183, *Hollyoaks* on page 13, *Crouching Tiger, Hidden Dragon* on pages 4 and 87; BBC for the photograph of *The Weakest Link* on page 85 and the BBC logo on page 19 and the photo from *EastEnders* on page 256; BFI for the photograph from *Thelma and Louise* on pages 99 and 255, *A Clockwork Orange* on pages 96 and 248, *Fight Club* on pages 92 and 158, *Double Indemnity* on page 18, *Starsky and Hutch* on page 237, *Dixon of Dock Green* on page 238, *Inspector Morse* on page 237, *Prime Suspect* on page 238, *The Little Tramp* on page 16, *Schindler's List* on page 259, *Alien* on page 260, *Citizen Kane* on page 260, *Coronation Street* on page 257; Corbis for the three photos of Princess Diana on pages 101 and 263; Channel 4 for the photo of *Big Brother 2* on page 188; The Kobal Collection for the photograph from *Blade Runner* on pages 102 and 268 and *Psycho* on page 259; LWT for the photo from *Blind Date* on page 84; The Moviestore Collection for the photos from *Gladiator* on pages 91 and 107, *I Know What You Did Last Summer* on pages 46 and 90, *The Simpsons* on page 93, *The Blair Witch Project* on pages 46 and 90, *The Matrix* on pages 96 and 244; The Ronald Grant Archive for the photo from *The Flintstones* on page 93 and 180, *Titanic* on page 94 and 198, *Crouching Tiger, Hidden Dragon* on pages 21 and 89, *The Sixth Sense* on pages 100 and 258, *Sleepy Hollow* on pages 98 and 254, *The Simpsons* on page 180, *Halloween* on pages 12 and 88, *Scream* on pages 95 and 243, *Lawrence of Arabia* on page 46; Sony for the Sony logo on page 19;

The authors and publishers would like to thank the following for permission to reproduce copyright material:

BBC for the 'BBC R & D Annual Review 1997-1998' page 193; BBC Online for DVD News on page 202; *The BFI London IMAX Experience Magazine* for 'Now The Ultimate Cinema Experience' on page 205; *The Big Issue* for the cover on page 134; *The Daily Express* for the front page on page 145; *The Daily Mirror* for the front page on page 145; *The Guardian* for 'Now: TV Ads Just For You' on page 192, 'Net Takes Safety Away from CDs' on page 196, 'It's the BBC But Not As We Know It' on page 196, 'All Eyes On The Movies' on page 217, 'The AOL/Time Warner Deal' on page 224, 'CNN Unveils European Strategy' on page 230, Big Brother Boost For Channel 4 Ratings' on page 230; *Hello! Magazine* for the cover on page 134; *The Times* for 'Is The Game Over For Online Players' on page 207; *Sight and Sound Mediawatch 2000* for 'Spinning The Net' on page 189 and the AOL Time Warner diagram on page 227.

Orders: please contact Bookpoint Ltd, 130 Milton Park, Abingdon, Oxon OX14 4SB. Telephone: (44) 01235 827720, Fax: (44) 01235 400454. Lines are open from 9.00 – 6.00, Monday to Saturday, with a 24 hour message answering service. Email address: orders@bookpoint.co.uk

British Library Cataloguing in Publication Data
A catalogue record for this title is available from The British Library

ISBN 0 340 801301

First published 2001
Impression number   10 9 8 7 6 5 4 3 2
Year   2005 2004 2003 2002

Copyright © 2001 Richard Harvey, Julian McDougall, Tanya Jones, Jacqueline Bennett and Julian Bowker

Typeset by Fakenham Photosetting Limited
Printed in Great Britain for Hodder & Stoughton Educational, a division of Hodder Headline Plc, 338 Euston Road, London NW1 3BH by Martins the Printers Ltd, Berwick upon Tweed.

Contents

Section 5   Audience and Institutions   185

Preface

When the Government announced that it wanted to broaden the curriculum at A level by introducing the new four-subject AS system in September 2000, it assumed that an extra subject in the Sixth Form would be a science or Maths for those studying the Arts, and a Language for those studying Science. Not surprisingly, students had other ideas, and Media Studies was one of a number of newer courses which saw its numbers increase dramatically. From the first A level course in 1990 which had just 60 candidates nationally, Media Studies has grown to a cohort of 25,000 at AS in 2001, itself double the A level entry for the year 2000.

The most popular Media Studies A level has always been the OCR course, which, until now, has never had a textbook devoted to it. There have been general Media textbooks and books aimed at A level, but they have all tried to cater for a number of different possible courses; *this* book is designed entirely for the OCR AS specification.

Many Sixth Formers may not have previously undertaken any specialised media work; they may well have chosen Media Studies as a fourth subject. It is often, however, the one which they will put first for their A2 options because they have enjoyed it so much. An ever-increasing number opt to continue with it at university.

Media Studies offers an unusual space in the education system, bringing opportunities to discuss the things students would choose to consume anyway – magazines, websites, CDs, films, computer games, radio and television programmes. With practical work, it also brings the chance to develop skills of teamwork, organisation and planning alongside the particular skills developed on the equipment used. There are few things more exciting for students than seeing something they have produced shown to an audience; the systematic tips given in the section devoted to production work should enable them to make the most of this opportunity so that what they produce is *worth* showing !

This book offers a clear set of key terms which act as a working dictionary for student analysis of media texts. There are sections on each of the course units, where the authors describe a number of possible options for the two OCR exams which should serve as a solid framework for students, encouraging them to look further. They will be pointed towards the use of media resources such as newspapers, the Internet and video material, as a book can only be a foundation for the wider study they will undertake. Media Studies is a living and ever-changing subject and keeping up-to-date is crucial for success!

Hopefully taking Media Studies will have some impact upon students' media consumption outside the course – not to make them change what they enjoy but to make them think about it in different ways and to be more aware of the significance of the media in their lives. I hope this book will help in that aim.

Pete Fraser (Chief Examiner, August 2001)

Section 1

Introduction

It has become a cliché of the modern world that we all live in societies that are media-saturated, yet few of us are fully conscious of the forms that this 'saturation' takes. It is too easy to say that we simply rely upon the mass media for information and entertainment. It can be powerfully argued that our understanding of the world in which we live, and of ourselves, is constructed by the media we consume. Certainly the media in the 21st Century dominates our lives as never before. Books, magazines, newspapers, advertisements, radio, television, computer games, the Internet, films, videos, DVDs, records, tapes and CDs are, to a lesser or greater degree, central to our lives and provide an ever-expanding quantity of entertainment and information. To keep up with the constant stream of media available for consumption, it is necessary for citizens of the 21st Century to develop a degree of **media literacy**. Just as through the 18th and 19th Centuries it was considered absolutely essential that everyone should be able to read and write, and great strides were taken in education to ensure that basic literacy was available to ordinary people, so it is now seen as a necessity to be able to 'read' media texts – it is recognised as an essential skill for personal development.

As long ago as 1982, the UNESCO Declaration on Media Education set out that, '*We live in a world where the media is omnipotent: an increasing number of people spend a great deal of time watching television, reading newspapers and magazines and listening to the radio. Children already spend more time watching television than they do attending lessons in school. We need to accept the impact of the media and appreciate their importance as elements of culture in today's world. Arguments for the study of the media as a preparation for responsible citizenship are formidable now and with the development of communications technology, ought to be irresistible.*

[We need] to develop the knowledge, skills and attitudes which will encourage the growth of critical awareness . . . and should include the analysis of media products, the use of the media as a means of creative expression and effective use of and participation in available media channels.'

In 1993 David Buckingham asserted that, '*We are currently living in a period, like earlier periods such as the Renaissance, where the pace of change appears to be accelerating. Any contemporary definition of literacy must therefore inevitably include the understanding and competencies that are developed in*

1

relation to "new" media technologies as well as older technologies such as writing and print.'

(*Changing Literacies: Media Education and Modern Culture*; Institute of Education Paper, 1993.)

If these views were significant then, how much more relevant are they at the beginning of the third millennium?

So, what is your involvement in different media forms? What do you 'consume' throughout the day?

ACTIVITIES

Throughout a 24-hour period, jot down all the times that you are aware of consuming media texts. Include texts that you do not specifically choose to consume, that is, texts that do not involve primary involvement. Note briefly what they are. Before you begin, refer to the explanations below of the different levels of consumption.

Media Studies terms and analysis

It is worth reminding yourself here that in Media Studies certain terms mean slightly different things than in everyday usage. Most people, for instance, when they use the term **text** mean something that is written or printed. In studying the media the term refers to any media product: it might be the written or printed word, but it could also refer to visual images (moving or still), complete films or television programmes, sound 'texts', such as music CDs, or even computer games or websites.

It is possible to make distinctions between different forms of **media consumption** depending upon the attention that is given to the text by the consumer.

Primary involvement refers to the times when you are exclusively focused upon one activity. It might be watching a film at the cinema, watching a television programme, reading a magazine or newspaper, listening to the radio or playing a computer game.

Secondary involvement refers to those occasions when media consumption occurs whilst you are engaged in another activity. This might be listening to the radio or music while doing other forms of work, or playing a CD on your computer while using it for surfing the web, a game or even homework.

Tertiary involvement is the weakest and most passive category. It occurs when the consumption of the media texts is merely incidental background to your other activities. This might be when you are vaguely aware that the television or radio is on in the background or in another room in the house.

It is possible to shift from one category to another. Glancing at advertisements on hoardings as you travel to and from school or college, flicking casually through a newspaper or magazine whilst listening to the radio, or glancing at the television while waiting for a particular programme to start would all be considered a tertiary level of involvement. However, if you stopped to look at the advertisement more closely, or paused to read an article in the magazine or newspaper, or settled to watch the television your level of involvement would change.

Although Media Studies is concerned with developing the skills of media literacy so that you are able to make informed judgements, it is also about enjoyment. Significantly, the word appears in the principal aims of the OCR specifications where it states that they: '*are designed to facilitate the development of media literacy skills to enable candidates to achieve critical independence in their knowledge, experience and enjoyment of the media.*'

Media Studies, therefore, enables you to combine serious analysis with enjoyment, but it is sometimes hard to know exactly where the enjoyment of media texts ends and the analysis of them begins. To ask you suddenly to stop enjoying an action movie and put on a serious, academic hat instead would be ridiculous. But this serious hat, believe it or not, will fit you just as well for studying *Crouching Tiger, Hidden Dragon* as it will for the plays of Brecht or the paintings of Salvador Dali. All involve narrative and spectacle, the construction of meaning, representation of people and issues and, most importantly, acts of interpretation by their audiences.

Equally, it is possible to dislike a game show just as much as you did before whilst applying critical theory to deconstruct it. What Media Studies gives you is the ability to investigate the reasons for your reactions to texts, and that is a skill that will serve you far beyond the classroom and the examination room. For example, it would be difficult for any current or ex-Media Studies student to watch *Big Brother* without considering realism, institution, technology and conventions. In fact, it is not the greatest of leaps to move from such discussions to more philosophical questions about the nature of reality, the concept of celebrity within popular culture and the psychology of voyeurism.

Some students express concerns that they may have their enjoyment of media texts spoiled by theoretical discussion and analysis, but the ability to understand and comment critically on how and why texts are constructed makes the consumption of media texts an infinitely more satisfying and rewarding experience. Someone who understands the workings of a car won't find driving any less enjoyable.

Some students report a sceptical reaction from their parents the first time they analyse media texts such as *EastEnders* for homework, whereas a Dickens novel is considered a perfectly acceptable text. Here we are drawn into the 'High Culture–Low Culture' debate, where popular culture is often dismissed as entertainment and 'serious' culture as educational. You will discover, however, that the distinctions are not at all clearly defined. Dickens wrote most of his novels in a serialised form and they were published in popular magazines. The cliffhangers at the end of each episode were just as melodramatic as contemporary soaps, and just as eagerly awaited by their audience. It is far too easy to make stereotypical value judgements. Media Studies encourages you to question these labels and categories, and to look for the reasons behind these notions of 'quality'.

There is much to be learned from investigating how people react to different kinds of media text in different ways, and to question what influences these different responses, rather than to assume there is one shared response for everyone. This doesn't have to be a long, deep research project. Start by simply asking family and friends for their reactions to particular texts and then ask for reasons. Analysing these responses will show you that meaning is not the same for everyone – interpretation is central to meaning, and interpretation is influenced by life experience.

A scene from the film
Crouching Tiger,
Hidden Dragon.
See page 87, figure 1.

For much of the course you will be analysing texts that you already consume for enjoyment outside of the classroom. In this way, Media Studies invades your life and your living room. In many ways you are your own expert. You will be able to bring your own experience and expertise into the classroom. The teacher is an expert on analytical concepts, media production, theory and the economic/historical/social/political contexts with which you need to be familiar. The teacher will

also relate these theories to chosen texts, but you will be able to apply
your new-found understanding to additional objects of study, which may
be may films, television programmes, music, computer games, magazines
or websites with which you are more familiar.

You may also be experienced with DTP software or web design, or you
may have a camcorder at home which you use all the time. How might
this work on the AS course? Well, perhaps for the Foundation
Production unit you might be able to design a webzine from your own
knowledge of entertainment sites, with your teacher's theoretical
guidance, or perhaps you might be able to bring your own passion for
science fiction to the study of American Cinema and Social Class/Status,
or your own knowledge as a consumer of DVD or digital TV to the
New Technologies case study. This is what makes Media Studies an
exciting and significant subject to study. You will learn to investigate and
analyse media texts, and the teacher's job is to arm you with the
analytical, practical and theoretical tools with which to do this, not to tell
you all the answers.

Deconstructing yourself

The term **deconstruction** comes from French critical theory and, put
simply, it describes the process of analysing a text to understand the
different kinds of meanings that might be produced by it and, more
importantly, by the audiences who receive it. This means the emphasis is
put on the viewer/listener/reader. The term **reader** is another of those
common expressions that have additional significance in the study of the
media. It means that you are making sense of a text, even if you are
listening to music or watching a film. If this is confusing, think of the
expressions 'to read the situation', 'I can read you like a book' or 'he
reads the game very well'.

Throughout your AS course you will have been put in the position
where you have had to question your own response to texts, and all of us
can become very defensive when doing this. There is always a tendency
to believe that we like things because we think they are good. It is
perfectly possible to enjoy texts and at the same time realise that they are
not very good, in the same way that we can dislike a text while being
aware of the qualities that make it a text of significant quality.

The following activity prepares you for your AS work by helping to you
to deconstruct yourself as a consumer of media. It may be preparation for

forming your own opinions about media issues and debates at A Level, or
it may just empower you to be active in your response to media texts in
daily life.

ACTIVITIES

1. Work through the following exercise to describe your own television viewing habits/tastes
   and your attitudes towards different kinds of programmes.

   a) Using the grid below, show how much time you spend on each type of activity in an
      average week.

	Up to 1 hr	1 hr–2 hrs	2 hrs–5 hrs	over 5 hrs (please state how many)
Watching television programmes				
Reading newspapers				
Watching films at the cinema				
Listening to radio				
Going to the theatre				
Listening to CDs				
Reading magazines				
Watching films on video/DVD				
Watching films on TV				

   b) In the first column of the grid overleaf 14 different types of television programmes are
      listed. In the second column rank the 14 different types of television from 1–14 based
      upon how often you watch each type of programme. Rank the programme you watch
      the most as number 1. In the second column indicate the viewing context in which you
      usually watch the programmes: write A for alone and fully engaged; B for with other
      people, but still fully engaged; C for alone but with the programme on, whilst you do
      other things; and D for with other people, whilst the television is on, and whilst you
      talk or do other things.

Programme type	Viewing frequency rank 1–14	Viewing context A–D
News/news programmes		
Soap opera		
Documentary (all kinds)		
Sitcom		
Comedy shows		
Quiz shows		
Game shows		
Chat shows/discussion programmes		
Music programmes		
Arts programmes		
TV drama		
Programmes about sport/sports coverage		
Adaptations of novels/plays		
Other (please state)		

2. Now describe in two or three words your feelings towards the following programmes (e.g. 'big fan' or 'can't stand it').

Who Wants to Be a Millionaire? ....

Ali G ....

EastEnders ....

Friends ....

Hollyoaks ....

Changing Rooms ....

Airline ....

7

TFI Friday ....

The Bill ....

NYPD Blue..

ER ....

3. Next, get together with a few other students who have worked through this exercise and discuss the following three questions. The points you make and disagreements you might have will raise some useful and, perhaps, enlightening issues about the nature of teaching and learning.
   a) How do you think your television viewing habits/preferences differ from 'typical' Media Studies AS students?
   b) To what degree do you think that your own television viewing habits/preferences would make any difference to your ability to assess students' analysis of television programmes? Please give reasons for your answer.
   c) Do you think that Media Studies teachers are able to distance themselves from their own tastes when teaching/assessing? If so, how do they do this?
4. Finally, make some notes about how this exercise has made you think differently about your own television viewing and Media Studies as a subject.

Supplementary activity

This is one that you can undertake at any stage of your course. Keep a diary of your consumption of the media for one week. Make a note of all your primary consumption. Consider on your own or in group discussions whether your consumption has changed and the reasons why it has or has not.

Production

We have already quoted one of the principal aims of the OCR Media Studies specifications (the development of media literacy skills). The second might be considered to be almost as important, and may well be one of the main reasons that you chose to do Media Studies in the first place. It states that the '*specifications are designed to facilitate the development of technical and creative production skills to encourage imagination and aesthetic activity in media contexts.*' In other words, you should be able to produce your own texts with flair and imagination. Your ability to deconstruct and analyse media texts and understand the technological and institutional context will enhance your production skills.

How to use this book

This book is clearly focused upon the specifications for OCR AS Media
Studies, but the help and guidance available and the skills learned by using
this book are equally applicable to any other AS Media Studies course.

Although the book is an ideal whole-class textbook, it is also designed so
that you can work through the course using it for independent study.
The first two sections serve as introductions, and the rest follow the
course outline.

- Section 2 covers the key concepts that you will encounter throughout
  the course.
- Section 3 offers clear guidance on the processes of production for the
  Foundation Production briefs.
- Section 4 covers Textual Analysis, both Section A – Unseen Moving
  Image Analysis, and Section B – Comparative Textual Study. The
  content of this part of the book covers both the current topics and the
  new topics for 2003 and 2004.
- Section 5 deals with case studies (audience and institutions), and covers
  both Section A – New Technologies and Section B – Media
  Ownership.
- Section 6 looks in detail at how the study of AS Media Studies covers
  the principal areas of Key Skills. However, if you do not have to work
  on activities specifically aimed at key skills then this section offers
  additional help with the topics of Representation, Genre, Audience,
  New Media, Mise en Scène, Photojournalism and Sound.
- Section 7 helps you to look back at what you will have learned
  throughout the course and also looks forward to your next stages of study.

Throughout the book you will find a variety of clearly defined suggested
activities and most of them can be undertaken on your own at any time.
However, there are some areas of discussion where you will find it
helpful to work with others.

Section 2
The Key Concepts of Media Studies

Introduction

Your Media Studies course will include various areas of study. You might focus on a particular film, television programme, print publication or piece of practical production work. You will build up not only critical analysis skills, but also an understanding of institution and production practices. In order for you to be able to make connections between the different elements of your course, you need to have a clear understanding of the Key Concepts within Media Studies. These concepts encourage you to discuss the wider implications of the media and provide you with a more comprehensive view of what the media is and how it works. This section aims to introduce you to the Key Concepts and explains how they relate to the OCR Media Studies specifications.

PART ONE
Media forms and conventions

Form

The term **form** can best be explained in relation to the shape, structure or skeleton of a text, and in this way is often linked to **narrative**. Narrative provides a basic shape to the media text. Indeed, structuralist analysts, such as Tzvetan Todorov, have argued that all stories told contain the same basic structure: the initial equilibrium of the story world is disrupted during the body of the story by opposing forces, but is re-established at the end as a new, revised equilibrium. Obviously, individual media texts will represent this basic structure in a way that is individual to them. For example, the form of soap operas necessitates continuous, multi-stranded story lines, with individual episodes frequently ending with a cliffhanger. On top of this basic structure are placed the elements that make the text even more distinctive.

Style

Style refers to the distinctive 'look' of a media text. In film you can frequently identify the individual style of a particular director. He or she might use distinctive *mise-en-scène*, lighting, music, camera angles, movement, framing and editing. In print media such as magazines it might be said that particular texts have a house style. These can be identified by the use of colour, typography, graphic design, layout and tone of written text.

Genre

If a group of media texts have a similar form/structure or pattern of elements, then this might be due to a link in **genre**. Westerns, for example, have common structural elements which make them recognisable as a specific genre: they often end with a final gunfight and resolution to the problems established at the beginning of the film. *Unforgiven* and *Once Upon a Time in the West* both have characteristics of form which define them as Westerns, but individual elements which make them distinct. Films of the same genre have distinctive characteristics or conventions.

A German poster for Halloween H20. See page 88, figure 2.

Film genres can sometimes be subdivided into smaller but distinctive categories called sub-genres. The James Bond films are a sub-genre of the spy thriller genre. There are also occasions when a film might be said to be a combination of more than one genre. These are called hybrids. *Alien* is a hybrid of both science fiction and horror.

Conventions

In order to be able to identify media texts within particular categories or genres, you will need to analyse a text for the codes and **conventions** it uses. The characteristic 'ingredients' of a particular genre, and the elements which make it recognisable, can be defined as conventions. Conventions provide a common link between, for example, a group of films, television programmes or types of newspaper. These conventions may be connected to form, language, theme or visual elements. Tabloid newspapers share styles of language, composition, image and content which make them distinct from broadsheet newspapers. Horror films share styles of lighting, camera work, character profile and music which differentiate them from other genres.

Television soap operas all contain a series of conventions that help to distinguish them from other programmes, such as documentary programmes or news broadcasts. Soap operas contain, for example, rolling story lines, recognisable characters and consistent settings. They often tackle social issues, and will have a series of episodes which build towards climaxes. Soap operas are also set in small community areas, with defined meeting places.

The cast of Hollyoaks.

Conventions are not always used in an obvious or literal way in media texts. They might be subverted or revised in order for the creator to make a specific point. Modern horror films tend to end with the final female character confronting the force of evil which has eradicated the other characters: *Halloween* is a classic example of this. Many very recent horror films, however, have created final scenes which do more than merely pit the heroine against the killer. *The Blair Witch Project* has its final female character alone with a video camera, unable to confront what is frightening her and waiting to die. *Se7en*, which is a horror/thriller hybrid, allows for no such final confrontation because the final female character has been killed before the film's climax; she is evident in the scene, but only because her head is delivered in a box!

Conventions provide recognisable elements for the audience to use as an indication of the intention and potential meanings evident within the text they are viewing, listening to or reading.

To show your understanding of form, style, genre and conventions in analytical and practical work, try to concentrate on three areas:

- How form and style are used in each medium to generate meaning.
- What effects form and style have upon the audience.
- How media texts are organised in categories or genres.

PART TWO
Media languages

Media languages can be **written**, **verbal**, **non-verbal**, **visual** and **aural**. Most texts that you study will include a range of media languages and will use them to generate different effects and responses.

Written language

The most obvious place for **written** language is within print-based media. Newspapers and magazines all have a particular style and presentation of language which is specific to their genre and audience. The language of print-based media is evident in the articles you read, but also in text such as the captions for photographs, mastheads (the title of the publication) and advertisements. Written language is also an essential element within silent films and works to 'fix' or anchor our reading of the visual elements in the same way that a caption does in a newspaper.

The text within print publications is often referred to as **copy**. It is carefully selected in order to create an identity for the particular publication, and as a means of engaging the particular target audience. The language chosen generates meaning as it helps to form our understanding of the ideological stance, intention and values of the particular publication. For example, a caption for a photograph will help to fix the way the audience looks at the image. Captions allow the publication to present the story in a particular way. By looking at the way the publication tries to shape our understanding of the image through the caption, we can understand more about the intention of the magazine or newspaper.

Verbal language

Verbal language is evident in many media areas such as films, television programmes and the radio. The choice, delivery and context of the language used are important factors in the way meaning is generated for the audience. A television news item, for example, will be delivered using language that creates a sense of the importance of the story in the mind of the viewer. This in turn might link with images shown in order to shape that importance further.

Non-verbal language

Non-verbal media language is often defined in terms of body language: gestures, stance and mannerisms. We can read meaning into a scene in a drama, for instance, by the way in which the actor uses his or her body. Silent films are perhaps the best example of a medium in which non-verbal language is essential. They include captions in order to help explain the action we see, but it is from the obvious and subtle movements, gestures and mannerisms of the actors that we understand fully what the scene is about.

Visual language

Many of the media texts you will study as part of your course will be visual, for example, films or television programmes. In order to study them effectively you will need to be able to discuss **visual** language. An analysis of the visual elements of a film will include technical areas such as **camera work**, *mise–en–scène* and analytical readings using analytical frameworks such as **semiotics**. What you see on the film or television screen, or in the piece of photojournalism, has been chosen in order to generate a series of effects and meanings.

A film director, for example, when planning a particular scene, will choose to use certain camera angles and movements in order to tell the story of the scene. A **tracking shot** (sometimes called a **dolly shot** when the camera moves on a dolly around a scene) might be used to introduce the audience to the film's setting, and thus establish the setting as having an important role within the film.

A **point-of-view shot** (where the camera is placed in the scene as if it were one of the characters) might be used in order to position the audience within a scene and to allow them to experience some of the thoughts and emotions of a particular character.

Camera angles and positioning are technical devices that help construct the film or television programme.

A scene from the silent film The Little Tramp.

Another important area of study within visual language is *mise-en-scène*. Literally meaning, 'put into the shot or scene', *mise-en-scène* also includes lighting, props, location, costumes and set design. If you freeze frame a film or television programme and analyse the constituent elements of the still, looking at all of the elements of *mise-en-scène*, you will then be able to make comments on the genre of the piece, its intention and the meanings it is attempting to produce. You might freeze frame a film and notice the use of shadows and light. This might then help you to define the film in terms of its style. Examples of **film noir**, for instance, can often be identified by their distinctive visual style.

Semiotics

The term **semiotics** (the study of signs and symbols) can often be confusing, but at its simplest it is a way of discussing both the literal and the potential meanings of the images we see on the screen. It was Roland Barthes (see bibliography) who developed notions of signification in his analysis of the way signs work in culture. Barthes identified two orders of signification, **denotation** and **connotation**.

Denotation is the term applied in Media Studies to indicate literal or obvious meaning. This can be referred to as a simple description of what is physically seen or heard.

Connotation is the term used to indicate potential or suggested meaning. A cross, for example, is a sign which has many different literal and potential meanings. Depending on the context in which it is placed it can be a literal indication of a mathematical plus sign or a crossroads. Given another visual context, the cross might become a crucifix, which is understood by most societies to indicate or **denote** Christianity. This is the literal level of the sign's meaning. The potential meanings of the crucifix, or its **connotations**, are more varied. It might conjure up images of suffering or oppression or sacrifice.

When you are discussing visual language remember to analyse all that you see and all that is implied on the screen or in the image. Look at the images, the composition, the colours that are in front of you, but also remember to identify what helps to construct the visual – the camera angle.

Aural language

Aural language is an important area for study within media texts. We have looked at written and visual language, but you also need to be able to discuss what you hear. Media texts often include a mixture of sounds, all of which help to generate meaning for a text. This includes spoken language, but also any sound within the world of the programme or film (**diegetic** sound) or on the soundtrack (**non-diegetic** sound). Radio is an interesting medium because it is purely aural. It cannot rely on images to help root (or **anchor**) the sounds we hear. In a film or a television programme we might hear the diegetic sounds of traffic or animals or the weather and this will help in our construction of environment, atmosphere and mood. If a city is saturated with sounds of cars, building work, radios, and so on, it can create the impression that the setting is

A scene from Double Indemnity, *a classic film noir.*

chaotic and oppressive. If a building is devoid of sound we might perceive it as isolated or isolating. The non-diegetic sound within media texts can be in the form of music or any other noise that is added in post-production. The aural language of a media text (both diegetic and non-diegetic) can help us also to define the genre of a piece. A horror film, for example, might include non-diegetic heartbeat sounds or chants in order to provoke a response in the audience.

PART THREE

Media institutions

Definition

For the purposes of this Key Concept, try to think about media institutions in terms of the people who have a role in the production process of media texts, the companies/organisations they represent and the processes of production, distribution and marketing in which both are involved.

The roles within the media production process are many. Depending on the medium you are studying they may include, for example, directors, editors, producers, script and screenwriters. A discussion of institutions may begin with identifying issues of ownership, and you will need to conduct research into who owns companies such as Time-Warner, Sony or Ginger and what their area of production is. The last area of importance within this Key Concept asks you to look at processes of production. You may look at a specific media product and analyse how it has been produced, what its distribution breadth is and what strategies are being used to market it.

To show your understanding of institutions you will need to be able to discuss:
- Media texts as products of institutional, economic and industrial processes and how this affects the text, which is produced.
- The production, distribution, exhibition and consumption of media texts.
- The advancements in media technologies and how this affects the processes of production and consumption.

Any media text, whether it is a film, newspaper, television or radio programme is produced within an institutional context. A television drama, for example, will begin life as either a piece of commissioned or non-commissioned work. Once the drama has been written, a production company will produce it. The production company will, in turn, offer the programme to a television station for broadcast. The process seems simple, but it is often lengthy and fraught with difficulties. If the drama has not been commissioned, the writer(s) will have to approach an appropriate production company. This is likely to be one that either has a history of producing this type of drama, or one that is willing to speculate

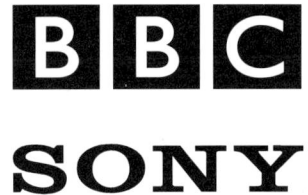

on the success of the product. (The insecurity of this stage can be bypassed if the writers or presenter of the programme own the production company. Chris Evans, for example, was able to produce *TFI Friday* through Ginger Productions.) Once the drama has been produced it has to be sold to a television station, and again the success of the sale will depend on factors such as the station's history of broadcasting this type of programme, audience desire for the product and even whether or not there is an available and appropriate scheduling slot.

Any new media product will have to prove itself in economic terms. If the production costs outweigh the potential return, either in terms of revenue or viewing figures (which make the profile of the institution more secure), then the product is unlikely to begin production. Generating financial backing for a product is often extremely difficult. Often funds have to be generated through asking investors to speculate on its potential success.

The industrial processes behind a media text are those which create it. A pop video, for example, will have been created using camera and editing technologies. With the advent of digital processes, most video production has left analogue methods behind. When you look at a media text, as well as considering what you see in front of you, try to consider what kinds of technology produced it. The type of industrial process used to create a media product will affect the text produced, because it will have an impact on the potential contexts in which the text can be consumed and the way the audience will be able to consume it.

As an extension to some of the points we have just looked at, the Key Concept of Media Institutions also asks you to study production and distribution. Production extends what we looked at within industrial considerations and includes research into the roles within the production process. For each of the media you study you will need to know the nature of each role and the place of that role within the production process. Also consider what technology each person is required to use, and the control they have over the 'look' of the final product. Production processes use people and technology together. A newspaper editor, for example, will liaise with advertising managers, art directors and the publisher to ensure that the product is cohesive. The technology that each of these people uses comes together to produce the final product. You will need to consider the production process as a unified whole. Economic, institutional and industrial concerns should also be considered fully within a discussion of the production process.

Distribution, consumption and exhibition

The **distribution** of a media text is a vital element in its success. The distributor of a product will need to consider issues such as the context(s) for the product's exposure and access to the target consumer. (For a film, the context in which it is screened is its **exhibition**.) For a film distributor, for example, choices will have to be made concerning where the film is first screened or premiered, whether the place in which it is screened allows for **consumption** by the target audience, or whether the film is worthy of cinema release or goes straight to video. The marketing of a media product is also an important consideration, and institutions have to consider such areas as posters, trailers, teaser campaigns, Internet sites and so on.

Media technology has advanced at an incredible rate and this has had an effect on both the texts produced and the way in which they can be consumed. We have already identified a shift in film editing from analogue processes to digital, but the digital explosion extends into most of the mediums you will study. Radio, television, the music business and print media can all now take advantage of digital technology. Most households are now saturated with new media technologies: mobile telephones, computers with Internet facilities and games consoles to name but a few. We can watch a film on video, DVD or digital television. We can listen to music on CD, mini disc, DAT or from an MP3 file downloaded from the Internet. The technology available, and therefore the ways in which we can consume the media around us, are more varied than they have ever been. What you, as students of the media, will need to consider is the effect of all this choice on the consumer. Does our mode of viewing, listening or reading change because there is so much choice? News stations such as CNN, and music television channels such as MTV, offer bite-sized chunks and do not demand consistent or continuous viewing. The question has to be asked: are we now used to a more fragmented viewing practices? We now have greater access to information, but does this necessarily breed a greater understanding of the world around us?

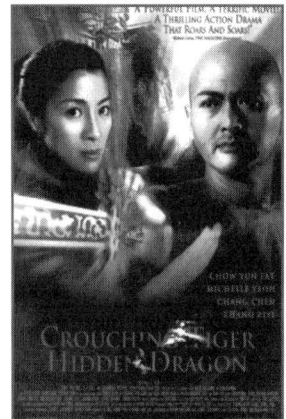

A poster advertising the award-winning film, Crouching Tiger, Hidden Dragon. *See page 89. Figure 3.*

PART FOUR
Media audiences

Definition

The audience for any media product is the group that consumes it. The target audience is the group at whom a product is specifically aimed. Some media texts will aim to engage a wide or **mass** audience, and others might aim at a specific or **niche** group. Each audience (and indeed individual member of an audience) will consume the media product in a different way. In order to be able to target the most appropriate audience the producers of a media text will research using categories, which include age, gender, socio-economic group, sexual orientation and consumption history or preference.

Media language and audiences

The various languages (discussed previously) media texts use to generate meaning are chosen to provoke specific responses in the audience. Media products all have a target audience, which could be defined by many things, including age, gender and demographic group. We will explore the concept of an audience in more detail later in this section, but language is one of the ways in which a media product can shape audience responses. Different audiences and different individuals within the same audience will engage with and understand the language they are offered in varying ways.

To show your understanding of media audiences you will need to be able to discuss:
- The fact that all media texts have a target audience.
- The various ways in which both institutions and producers research and target the audience.
- The ways in which the audience responds to representation in media texts.
- The means by which individuals learn to consider their role within an audience.
- The consumption of media texts by the audience.

Whether you are studying a lifestyle magazine, a piece of animation, a chat show or any other media text, each has a defined target audience. When you are discussing the Key Concept of Audience you must show an awareness that these audiences are different and that a product has been constructed to be consumed by that particular audience.

In order to be able to target an audience effectively, media institutions and producers use various methods of research in order to discover the preferences and expectations of that audience. One useful way of defining research types is by categorising them as either **qualitative** or **quantitative**.

Qualitative research methods aim to discover the opinions and preferences of the target consumer, and one good example of this mode of research is the **focus group**. The producers of a product will select a group which has the profile of their target audience, and will show them the product. This can be done pre-release, or post-release if the product is not performing as successfully as anticipated. The response of the focus group is then used by the producers to alter, completely rethink, or even confirm the look and content of the product.

Quantitative research concerns itself with data. It can be used either by the producers of a product or by the institution which is selling it. Television companies use **BARB** (Broadcasters' Audience Research Board) data to analyse viewing figures, and Radio stations use **RAJAR** (Radio Joint Audience Research) statistics to check listening figures. Qualitative and quantitative methods are used in parallel in order to research the habits and preferences of the target audience.

In order to define the profile of the audience, institutions and producers might look at existing demographic models (definitions based on socio-economic or lifestyle profiles), or they may try to construct a new audience for their product. Constructing a new audience is much harder to achieve and a producer will have to create a product which is attractive to those that feel there is a gap in their product market, or bring a group of individuals together who all aspire to a new social phenomenon.

Once a profile of the target audience has been established the product producers will target the audience by using a carefully constructed campaign of promotion. The product might be advertised in magazines that the target consumer reads, on Internet sites which are popular with that group, or feature on a commercial between preferred programmes.

Reading a text

It would be a mistake to assume that audiences for media texts are passive consumers of what they see, hear or read. The text they are in the process of consuming might include a **preferred**, **oppositional**, or **negotiated** reading – or a combination of all three. There may also be an **aberrant** reading.

A **preferred** reading (or **dominant system of response**) is a way of understanding a text that is consistent with the ideas and intentions of the producer or creator of that product. This may lead to an acceptance of the dominant values within the text.

With a **negotiated** reading (or **subordinate response**) the individual has a choice as to whether or not they accept the preferred reading as their own. Audience members might read the text through a filter of their own personal agenda. Although there may be a general acceptance of dominant values and existing social structures, the individual might be prepared to argue that a particular social group may be unfairly represented.

In an **oppositional** reading (or **radical response**) individual members of an audience might reject completely the preferred reading of the dominant code and the social values that produced it.

An **aberrant** reading is where an entirely different meaning from that intended by the maker will be taken from a text. This could be when individual members of the audience do not share, in any way, the values of the maker of the text. A famous example of this was the television series *Till Death Us Do Part*. The character of Alf Garnett was created by Johnny Speight as a figure of fun. His extreme and bigoted views were, however, admired by some of the audience of this popular series: clearly aberrant readings of Speight's text.

Just as audiences are often prepared to question information they receive or representations of social groups, individuals frequently consider their own place within a particular audience. For example, if an individual were to refer to himself or herself as a *Guardian* reader, they might also be considering what this indicates about their interests, political orientation, socio-economic status and educational experience. Some audience members might derive status from the audience group of which they consider themselves to be part. Some might feel a sense of social responsibility and others might use the defined group in which they place themselves to engender a feeling of community or security.

When you are discussing media audiences, remember that as individuals we often define ourselves through the groups within which we are included. Fans of different types of music will often define themselves in relation to their musical tastes. They may dress in a way which presents them as connected with a genre of music, or create a website or magazine/fanzine through which they contact other fans.

It is clear, therefore, that audiences consume the media texts with which they are presented in differing ways: they may accept, reject or negotiate a response to a preferred textual reading and will often be extremely active within the consumption process. The impact of a text on the target audience can come in many forms and we should not forget that analysis is often a secondary response. An audience will often respond emotionally to what they are consuming: it might repulse them or give them pleasure. These emotional responses should be considered as important factors in how the audience encounters a text. We might also have a particular ideological position that is being engaged by the media text. Remember that whether we read something from a dominant, negotiated or oppositional perspective it is intrinsically linked to whatever personal experience or detail the text encourages us to reflect upon.

When discussing theories of audience consumption, you should try to refer to certain theorists to substantiate or explain points you are making. Australian researchers Hodge and Tripp, and British researcher David Buckingham, for example, have conducted extensive studies into the nature of children's consumption of television. Their findings point to an active model of consumption, within which children have the capacity to decode what they are seeing and form coping strategies to deal with problematic material. The active model of audience consumption is countered by American researchers, such as Donnerstein and Linz, and Bushman whose findings point towards passivity in the audience. The American theorists' model uses the case of media violence to promote the idea that an audience will be directly and negatively affected by watching violent images. Bushman conducted studies in which he sought to prove that exposure to violent images encourages violent behaviour. Whichever theorists you use within your own debate, remember that their arguments can be challenged!

5 PART FIVE
Media representations

Definition

The different modes of reading a text are important when considering how an audience tackles the issues of **representation**. Representation is the process by which images, words or sounds are used to indicate issues or debates beyond what they literally mean. The most common form of representation is that of social groups, and debates arise that analyse both the positive and negative aspects of representation. Of course, the notion of positive and negative representation is subjective, and different members of a social group might have opposing views of what is or isn't a positive/negative representation. Debates arise when a **stereotype** is either explored or exploited.

> **Stereotype** – This is an oversimplified definition of a person or type of person. It is to place a person into a narrow definition that allows little no opportunity for change. Stereotyping is frequently, though not always, a result of prejudice.

A film character, for example, has importance because of their place within the story world, but we could also extend their importance by defining the social, political or racial group of which they are part and then begin to discuss how that group is being treated within the film and society. Audiences will often respond to different representations actively and bring their own thoughts about society and the world to that response.

To show your understanding of media representations, you will need to be able to discuss:
- the processes through which representation occurs;
- the ways in which these representations can be analysed;
- the ways in which the media analyst or student can engage with the processes of representation in order to be able to analyse its use within media texts.

Media texts use representation to varying degrees and for various purposes. It might be the intention of a particular text to discuss the representation of a certain social group, or a text might contain representational debate almost unintentionally. In order to understand the processes through which representation occurs, we will look at two examples: the use of characters within soap operas and the use of photojournalistic images within newspapers.

The representational potential of a soap character can be established in a number of ways.

- If the character is of a different ethnic minority than others in the soap opera, or is part of an ethnic group, the issues concerning the depiction of ethnic minorities might be debated. As with all of these examples, you will need to remember that representation does not solely deal with *negative* stereotypes. *Positive* representations may also be constructed. It is essential to be aware of just who it is that deems the stereotypes on display as *positive* or *negative*.
- The focus of an episode or a series of episodes might be the sexuality of a particular character and may deal with the responses of other characters to that sexual orientation.
- The gender of a character might be highlighted in an episode by the experiences they have and the treatment they receive, thus encouraging the viewer to consider the depiction of men or women.
- A character's age might be a focus and their attitudes or behaviour contrasted with those of other age groups. From this we might consider the treatment of different age groups within society.
- Social class is another area of possible representational debate, and discussion may ensue from the problems characters have that are connected with their socio-economic status.

Discussions concerning issues of representation should include the profile of the character, the position they are given within the programme and how they link to wider social debate. Remember, however, that an individual character or group of characters does not have to be part of a minority in order to warrant representational debate.

If we now look at the processes of representation connected with an image within a newspaper, we can broaden our knowledge of the processes of representation. Any piece of photojournalism, even before it has been placed within a newspaper, will have potential representational qualities, but the discussion can be extended when we consider the factors below.

- The caption added to any image within a newspaper aims to fix the audience's potential reading of that image. The caption will help us to consider not only the basic representational qualities of the image, but also what the newspaper wishes us to understand from it.
- An image will be chosen to highlight a particular aspect of the story it

has been chosen to illustrate, and we can use the text of the story to extend any discussion of the representational debate evident in the image.

- The specific newspaper in which we see the image is also important and should be remembered when discussing image representation. The newspaper's political or socio-economic leaning will have an impact on the way images are used within it and will therefore inform our consideration of representation.

- The position of the image on the page or within the newspaper is an essential factor to consider. Newspapers are composed through a hierarchy of importance, with the lead story on the front page. The importance of the image and, by extension, the representational debate which it explores, can be understood when this positioning is analysed.

These factors, alongside the content of the image, help us to consider not just what is being debated, but also how it is being debated.

We can analyse these processes of representation by considering all of the factors that surround an image, sound or word. Remember to consider where something has been placed, how it has been composed, the type of publication, programme or film which is its context, the media institution that has produced it, the current social debate surrounding it, and also your own response to the way in which something is being represented.

PART SIX
Ideology

Definition

Ideology is often referred to as an unconscious set of ideas, values and beliefs that a group, society or an individual believe to be true or important, and provide a framework for a particular view of the world. The values and beliefs perpetuated by the majority within a society may be described as the **dominant** ideologies. Within a society there might be different ideologies at play representing different sets of social interests, but powerful institutions such as religion, the family, education, government, the law and the mass media may influence dominant ideologies. Dominant ideologies may also be hidden in terms such as 'common sense' or the common sense view. Such a consensus view of society is achieved with the consent or agreement of the majority of a particular society as a whole, and this consensus is referred to as **hegemony**. Hegemony is, however, subject to renegotiation and redefinition, and the consensus may be broken as the ideologies of subordinate groups come into direct conflict with dominant ideologies.

Within an analysis of a media text you will need to consider how people, places or things have been represented historically, and how/why that representation has changed. There will have been shifts in ideas, values and beliefs, which mean, for example, that a group now has a differing representation. Consider the way in which the police have been represented over the years and you can examine how this representation reflects the social and political attitude current at any given time. You might also discuss in groups how renegotiations in hegemony have been reflected in media representations of women, homosexuality, ethnic minorities and family in recent years.

Summary

As we have seen through this discussion of Media Studies Key Concepts, they exist in relation to each other. When you are analysing texts, consider not only what needs to be discussed for each one, but also how they can be discussed together. The key conceptual areas have been defined in order to help you to understand and explore all of the areas necessary to produce a comprehensive media analysis.

Section 3
Foundation Production

Introduction

Practical work is probably the main reason why students undertake a Media Studies course, but you will be spending a considerable amount of time learning about, amongst other things, 'reading' the media, institutions, audiences, ideology and representation. Then, when you undertake the production element of the course, there is suddenly a reason to it all and a chance to demonstrate skills, understanding and creativity.

This section is designed to help you prepare, organise, create, edit and analyse your work within the confines of an A Level specification.

In some ways it might be said that creating a practical project for an examination is an artificial exercise. After all, we know that Spielberg does not sit down and define all the character roles in a forthcoming movie according to academic theorists before the screenplay is completed. We also know that a television programme will be defined by its scheduling and by the channel on which it is broadcast, and that these can be highly significant factors from inception onwards. In other words, the institutional and audience factors are fundamental for all but the most art-house of pieces.

At the beginning of your Foundation Production you will probably think that you have plenty of time before your piece is due for completion and there is ample time for thinking before you begin work. It is best to avoid this dangerous train of thought as it implies too much 'inspiration time' before any real work gets done. In this scenario everything becomes a rush job, everything is done at the last minute and the finished piece frequently does not do the student justice.

This section focuses principally on the six set briefs in the OCR specification, suggesting preparatory exercises to develop competency. The exercises will give you an opportunity to develop your creative skills in your chosen medium. There are suggestions for various ways to approach planning and research, construction and evaluation for the final projects, and some pointers are given for improving artefacts along the way.

31

This section will focus on the four media required for these briefs:
- moving image (film and television);
- print (newspapers and magazines);
- radio;
- new media (websites, multimedia, interactive media, digital media).

Although the section is aimed primarily at the OCR A Level specification, the comments, suggestions and exercises would be equally valid for all Media Studies A Level specifications with a production unit, since the principles of assessment remain constant across the various awarding bodies for practical work.

Context of Foundation Production

In the OCR AS Media Studies specifications the purpose of the production module is defined as follows:

The purpose of this unit is for candidates to demonstrate a range of technical skills and understanding of media concepts by the construction of a media text of their own production. Candidates also record and monitor the production process and demonstrate evaluation, from planning to outcome, in the Production Log.

Ways of approaching practical work

There are usually a series of stages for any project to go through, from the original idea to final production, but the most important factor when planning a project is to remember that production work usually takes far longer than you anticipate. Given that you also should allow 'fall-back' time when preparing for a project, the time soon evaporates – what seemed well organised, under control and on schedule can easily become a last minute panic, resulting in disappointing work.

Obviously the availability of technical equipment will depend to a large extent upon the facilities at your school or college, although you may have access to your own or friends' equipment. Of course, the other significant limiting factor is technical expertise in the use of the equipment, which is why this is assessed as part of the project. Skilled work on low-tech equipment can often be far stronger than work done by those using sophisticated equipment with limited technical competence. This is why there are preparatory exercises suggested for each of the major mediums specified here to allow you to gain competence before you begin the project. It is strongly recommended that you complete at least one of these tasks, and ideally all of them, before actually beginning the project itself. There is a world of difference between theory and practical work and you cannot develop your practical skills adequately without practical experience. It is common to discover that groups who have never used video cameras or non-linear editing facilities before, and thus cannot make creative use of the equipment, have made poor quality artefacts. Equally, there is usually a significant difference between the first web page produced using a particular software package and a later production once greater technical competence has been developed. It is essential to practise basic competencies first so that your creativity will not be hampered.

Competency

For each of these media there is a list of specific competencies given in the specification. These are regarded as the basic skills you need to demonstrate in your practical work to show that you have learnt how to work within that medium appropriately.

It is easy to see how to use these competencies in theory, but the trick comes in ensuring you have thought carefully about each aspect when making your artefact. You might rightly argue that George Lucas does not think explicitly about 'have I demonstrated an ability to use appropriate framing for my shots' when making the latest *Star Wars* epic, but he will automatically frame his shots (in conjunction with his team of course) in an interesting, appropriate and varied way for each scene, because he is a skilled practitioner. Only by explicitly making yourselves debate the best framing and **mise-en-scène** for a key shot, for example, can you hope to develop the kind of competence necessary for it to come naturally. Just as when you started to read, you started with little words and spelt them out slowly when you were not sure what they were, so you must now learn to communicate using this new vocabulary of moving image, print, audio or new media competence. At the beginning of your AS course you probably needed to learn how to 'read' the screen, audio track or printed page in detail and be able to identify how the different elements were used to communicate to a reader/viewer on many levels, and create a defined context in which the text could be interpreted. Now you must do the same in order to learn production skills.

Preliminary research

The principal difference between this unit and the other two units for AS Level is that this is practical. This may seem to be a ridiculously obvious statement to make, but the truth is a little more complex than that.

For the Textual Analysis unit the objective is for you to understand the key theories and debates relating to the texts that you study: to '*assess candidates' media textual analysis skills using a short unseen moving image extract and to assess their understanding of the concept of representation using two texts.*' (OCR Specifications). Your research may be conducted individually or in a group, the texts may be mainstream or *avant garde* and the institutional context significant or secondary, but the overall intention is that you should analyse existing texts and, in effect, pass judgment on them.

The purpose of the Audience and Institutions case study is to develop your '*knowledge and understanding of media institutions, production processes, technologies and related issues concerning audience consumption and reception.*' (OCR Specifications).

The practical production unit allows you to reverse these procedures and become the creator, and allows you and others to construct (and also deconstruct) your creation. The danger with this unit is that you will either abandon all the theory and principles that you have so painstakingly learnt and construct an insubstantial piece fairly quickly, or produce a piece which is so complex and meticulously structured that it becomes self-indulgent and obscure. Just as the professionals do, you have to strike a balance and produce something that is marketable and credible.

Form

The form of your piece is largely dictated by the chosen brief. If you are creating an opening sequence for a film, the form of your piece is substantially different to the form of a series of television adverts, for example. This is a crucial starting point for your project. So to create an opening sequence you will need to research a number of thriller film openings and note the general principles about their form. For instance:
● How are characters introduced?
● How is the mood set?
● How is the sound used?
● How are the titles and opening credits integrated?

Style

Form and style cross over substantially, but you should ensure that for style you have observed:

- the type of shots used in similar opening sequences or advertisements;
- use of fonts in moving image, print and new media material;
- the jingles for radio, which will always directly reflect the nature of the station and especially the context of the particular programme or element, e.g. traffic news;
- the language used, as this is a very clear signifier about the text itself – you would not expect to read an article in *The Sun* written in the style of *The Times*, for example, or an interview with Britney Spears written in the style of *Loaded* appearing in *Woman's Own*. This crosses over with content and theme, but is fundamental when defining the style of an artefact.

Audience segmentation

In your studies on audience you will have learned that audiences can be 'segmented', or divided up in different ways and may be identified with different texts and different contexts. Some of these divisions are explicit. If your movie is classified as a 15 or 18 you are aware that there will be some language or actions in the movie that necessitated it being given its particular classification. Some of the divisions are implicit. If you like a particular style of music and follow local bands, for example, you are likely to be a member of a target audience for a new radio station playing that type of music and giving exposure to local bands. Newspapers and magazines are carefully constructed to appeal to a very particular audience, whether that is a fairly broad target audience or a niche audience.

Defining a project

Having prepared yourself by doing some detailed relevant research, you need to start preparing for your chosen project. **For OCR AS Media Studies the MAXIMUM number allowed for a group is four.**

It may be best to apportion specific jobs to each member of the group from the beginning. Not only does it make the organisation much easier if tasks can be allocated among the group, but it also allows group members to develop a speciality very quickly and to have a specific focus for their production log. Since it is essential for evidence to be available to show the individual contribution of each member of a group and your teacher will be expected to identify your individual role in the group work, it will be far easier for you to justify your work if you have planned, worked and evaluated from a specific perspective from the very beginning. However, it is important that everyone in the group contributes at all stages, so do not have someone sitting around insisting that they are not going to participate until the editing phase begins.

Having a clear media institutional context

All media texts are produced by individual media institutions and the institution that creates a text is usually a defining factor in the end result. A celebrity interview programme to be shown on prime time BBC1 is likely to be a very different type of programme to a celebrity interview programme shown late at night on cable or satellite. You must define the type of institution for your artefact early on and allow this to have some bearing on the resulting text to show that you understand how much influence the institutional context has.

Having an identifiable audience

As with the institutional context, no text is made in isolation. The audience should be an integral part of the decision making at all stages. One of the most common mistakes in media production exercises is that groups become so wrapped up in the artistic integrity of their piece that they forget that the primary objective is to appeal to an audience. As mentioned earlier, audiences are usually segmented – even highly popular television programmes such as *EastEnders* tend to have defined target audiences, even if they are very large in numbers, and most films define a very tight audience to target from the very beginning.

Creative opportunities

It is worth remembering when you are thinking about your project that you have a great deal of freedom of choice, even though your main brief is prescribed. Although you are working in an assumed institutional context, you are not constrained by these factors. Your constraints are probably the technology to which you have access and the range of experience within your group.

You can be creative and original with your approaches and solutions to the problems that you face, but beware of the temptation to allow the technology to dominate your choices. While an extensive use of filters, intricate transitions and other special effects may seem an effective way of demonstrating technical expertise, they may not be appropriate for your product. It is a difficult balance to strike – on the one hand you want to demonstrate your skills and your control of your medium, on the other hand material that is too 'creative' and uses superfluous trickery can fall into the trap of being self-indulgent and thus lose its supposed audience appeal. Only you or your group can make the final decision about what is appropriate for your product, but remember that originality for originality's sake is rarely successful. True creativity is tempered with restraint and the most difficult skill to learn is to be creative while tweaking the edges of commercial culture, not straying so far away from the designated context that your artefact loses its plausibility as a media text rather than a piece of fine art.

Is it viable as a project?

You must be practical with your intended content. If you plan a project that is too long or too challenging you will inevitably be disappointed with the result and the outcome will probably be less successful than a piece which is tightly constructed.

The key constraints to bear in mind here are:

- **time/length** – if there is a length of time recommended in your particular brief it is because it is unlikely that you will produce something of high enough quality if you create something longer. If the brief states 2–3 minutes, stick with it. Two minutes of well shot, tightly edited thriller is far more convincing and appropriate than a five-minute extended opening that is repetitive and loosely edited. If you are creating a new webzine, by all means indicate on a navigation bar what other areas might be available, but if six pages are specified you will not get as much credit for fifteen mundane pages as you will for six high-quality pages reflecting industry codes and conventions and creating an exciting and innovative artefact;

- **technical facilities** – if you have access to a single camera and limited access to an editing suite, deciding to create an effects laden sequence to match *Star Wars* may be over-ambitious. Excellent work can be achieved with a single camera and simple facilities – after all, when you are planning your 'shoot', you will probably not be taking your shots in narrative order anyway so you have the opportunity to retake the same shot from different angles, so that you can choose the best one for your completed narrative. Indeed if you have the patience, excellent results can be achieved by creating an animated piece (although be prepared for the amount of time this requires). One simple way is to use a digital camera and upload each shot on the camera to become a 'frame' in your narrative – or you could use an ordinary camera or even drawings and scan them into the computer, then edit them using your editing software just as you might do with conventional analogue or digital video material;

- **experience** – it may be that members of your group have a great deal of experience in the use of your chosen technology. If, however, you decide to add a multi-layered exploding title as the opener to your movie without having the experience to produce this particular sequence, the process of learning the skills for this may detract from the project itself and thus you might ask yourselves whether a similar, more straightforward effect might suffice;

- **institutional context** – if you have decided to produce a music programme for a local radio station with a youth oriented target audience, a programme featuring in-depth analysis of Mendelssohn's orchestral works may not be appropriate. If you decide to create a 'spoof docusoap' (and remember that spoofs are especially difficult to create effectively), this will have substantial implications for the form and structure of your piece. Creating a piece which did not fit your specified institutional context would clearly be viewed as less successful than a piece which did fit the specified context;

- **audience** – this is closely related to the institutional context you define for your project. If your audience is defined as 'under 5s' for example this impacts on the discourse used, *mise-en-scène* and length of project or segments of the project. If you are creating a webzine targeted at high-income, middle aged professionals, the design, discourse and content will be very different to a webzine devoted to the exploits of the Tweenies for example.

Planning a production

Organisation of time, people and equipment

By now you have got a pretty good idea of what you want to create. Now you need to think about the practicalities. Start by drawing up a plan to show how much time you can give to the project. Map out on this plan deadlines for the completion of the **pre-production**,

production and **post-production** phases, remembering to allow time for evaluating and keeping your production log.

You will then need to decide what equipment you will need and map this on to the plan, making note of exactly when you will require particular pieces of equipment. It may be a good idea to book all the equipment you will require for particular sessions at this stage. That way you can be sure that you will have access to the necessary equipment when you need it. In the real world, of course, not only do we book the equipment a long time in advance but we also have to pay for the equipment even if we don't use it, so planning when we will need access to a recording studio to complete the radio broadcast, or the high-quality printers to print off our final adverts is essential. **You** need to make sure you can get the equipment when you need it – you cannot be credited for your project if you have not completed it on time because someone else was using the editing studio!

If you are using people as actors, for example as the studio host or as interviewees for a radio documentary or actors in a film, they also need to know well in advance when they will be required, for how long and what clothes or other props they might need to bring with them. It is no good filming some shots one day and then catching your main actor in the corridor another morning and asking if they can find the same clothes so you can carry on filming that afternoon. **Performers in your film do not count towards the total number of people permitted for group work.** Choose the best performers available to you. They do not have to be part of your Media Studies group.

Designing the product

The methods you employ to plan your original designs will depend upon your chosen medium. Time-based media such as film sequences/trailers and television adverts are usually planned using a storyboard. New media work can be planned with a storyboard, but hierarchical or 'mesh' diagrams may be more appropriate to show interactivity. Radio work is usually planned using an annotated script and schedule, and print work with flat-plans and mock-ups. Not only does the specification require that you include evidence that you have planned your artefact efficiently, but it is essential to plan the artefact properly if you are to be able to engage fully with the requirements and opportunities.

The production process

Once you have decided on your roles in the project, you need to start keeping a production log and to be researching/producing/reflecting at all times. This log is your evidence of your contribution to the project. Use it to demonstrate the aspects of your work that might not be immediately obvious to an outsider. For example, evidence of detailed research might be annotated print adverts for similar products, showing how you have deconstructed the products. Evidence for audio work might include transcripts of programmes and analysis of structure of similar programmes. Make a note of the decisions you make as you go along, and the reasons for them. All this will help you when you come to write up your production log.

Audience research

There is a balance to be struck here. While there is no substitute for first-hand research about your artefact it would not be appropriate to conduct a full-scale research exercise, for example collecting information from 150 questionnaires in the time available for your project. The most important aspects of audience research to bear in mind are:

- asking at least a sample audience about similar products;
- product testing on a sample, post-production.

In both cases a small sample – perhaps five to ten people from the designated target audience – would probably suffice as long as you remember that this is just a sample and not guaranteed to be fully representative.

Existing products and practice

No real producer would dream of establishing a new product in isolation. At times our world is described as being 'media-saturated' and one aspect of this is that all new products relate in some way to current and previous products. There is a vast range of media texts across all the media and it would be considered short-sighted of a producer to create a text without exploring the marketplace and assessing the competition. You need to be prepared to analyse at least two existing products that are relevant for your chosen artefact. You might wish to include this analysis as an appendix to your evaluation so you can easily make reference to these texts as comparison in your evaluation. This will also count as supporting evidence of your researches.

Whilst it is necessary to offer evidence of planning as required by the specifications, it is not necessary to include everything you have done in the material presented for external moderation. Your teacher must, however, see the stages of planning and research in order to give you an assessment.

Construction – general

There is a range of 'competencies' defined in the specification that are really the basic skills which we expect you to be able to use when working in your chosen medium. Your ability with these skills, thinking and planning, understanding what you can do, what is effective and – above all else – why you think that **your** way is the best way to communicate to your audience, will be deciding factors in assessing the quality of your final artefact. Successful work will use these techniques and skills to good effect; less successful work will show an insecure grasp of these competencies and how they affect communication. It is worth writing out the list and keeping it with you, while you are planning, particularly to ensure you have demonstrated your mastery of these areas.

There are also established forms and conventions assumed in each of the briefs given. For example, we conventionally expect to be told the name of the film in an opening sequence. It is assumed that material broadcast on radio is audible! We would not expect to hear a presenter say 'look at this', for example, unless it was immediately followed by an audio description. All this may seem very obvious, but it is surprising to examiners and moderators the extent to which these basic points are ignored. Institutional determinants, globalisation, media saturation and skilled marketing and advertising mean that the audience for any contemporary media product is explicit and clearly identified at the planning stage of development.

Evaluation – general

Lastly, you should bear in mind that you have to provide an evaluation for your artefact and that this is assessed. We will look at the evaluation itself in more detail at the end of this section, but your planning stages are part of the production log – you are required to attach copies of your storyboards, flat-plans and so on to the production log to provide evidence of planning and process.

The production log is not a diary of events or a record of progress. Rather it is a summative and reflective document reflecting your working practice as a group and your individual contribution. As a record of your individual contribution to the group work the production log can be vital as it should show how you overcame hurdles, skills you have learnt, successes and failures during the pre-production and production stages, and how your artefact is meeting the criteria you have defined for yourselves.

❶ PART ONE

Approaches to Practical Skills
Film and Television

Formal brief for OCR AS specification

The opening sequence of a new thriller, including the titles (at least two-minutes duration).

Preparatory Exercises

- Create a ten-second video in which one of your group appears to play a musical instrument exceptionally well.
- Recreate a clichéd comedy scene by shooting a sequence in which a ridiculous number of people seem to emerge (comfortably) from a small car or from behind a tree.
- Record a 'chase' scene working in groups of three so you can organise a pursuer, victim and camera operator. If you have more people in your group, you have more opportunities to experiment with sound and lighting. Plan a storyboard and try to use the minimum number of shots, but also try to vary angles, framing and pacing. A good preparation for this exercise is to ask each group member to prepare a storyboard and reach a consensus regarding final storyboard before shooting. With a review afterwards, once the material has been edited, this can be a valuable 'trial run' for the actual project.

Making the moving image

'*I've always tried to be aware of what I say in my films, because all of us who make motion pictures are teachers, teachers with very loud voices.*' George Lucas

ACTIVITIES

Additional or alternative exercises

- Create a 30-second 'day in the life of' video of an individual, using as many brand names and close-ups of various products used by the person as possible.
- Create an opening sequence or title sequence for a new consumer affairs programme.
- Recreate an early soap powder advertisement in the style of advertisements from the 1950s, as a lead-in to an episode of a soap opera.

Defining your project (Film and Television)

Start by examining a range of relevant film openings or adverts for similar products. For example, try to do a detailed analysis of three openings or six adverts, ideally for six different products. For each text:
- analyse how the shots are organised and chosen;
- identify the target audience and consider how the text addresses them.

This should give you a good basis on which to draw up a set of conclusions about the form, style and content of your piece. On this basis you should be able to decide on the content of your text or texts and begin to plan your work.

Preparation (Film and Television)

Part of your planning is the general logistics of creating a media text that was covered earlier in this chapter. Now you need to be specifically thinking about the content of your text and planning how, what, where and when it will be created.

Remember that adverts are sales devices, intended to appeal directly to a specified target audience and to interest them in the product. You might want to remember relevant advertising principles at this point, such as **AIDA** = get the audience's attention, spark their interest, establish a desire for the product and then tell them the action necessary to acquire the product. Remember that the opening of the film will be crucial to the audience's understanding and expectations. Careful thought must go into the setting up of characters, themes, setting and atmosphere.

Storyboards

Once the idea has been formulated it must be defined in detail, and this is done using a storyboard. Storyboarding is, in essence, drawing a cartoon of the video that you will make. Each shot in the movie is drawn and then labelled with movement notes, dialogue, sound effects and any other important information. It also gives you the opportunity to look at your text in detail and see if it is really going to work. In recent years, storyboarding has become even more advanced as directors look for even better ways to plan their stories. Two examples of this are *The Return of the Jedi* and *Jurassic Park*. For both movies, complex sequences were pre-filmed using models and representative figures. In *Return of the Jedi*, the planning team used moveable figures and dioramas (painted scenes in which models are used and lit to create illusions of action) to plan and time complex sequences such as the speeder bikes. The team of *Jurassic Park* however, took it further, filming the entire film first using claymation (like *Wallace and Gromit*) to watch every shot in the movie before investing in the kind of technology they needed to film it properly.

There is no getting away from storyboards – they are an essential part of planning a moving image piece and, properly used, will help you reflect critically on your artefact before you begin actual filming. This will mean that you are confident about why you are using your chosen *mise-en-scène*, framing, camera angle and shot length to create the required effect, and you will be clear about how you want to edit it together to make it successful.

There are many different ways of creating a storyboard and varying degrees of detail possible. Some film producers like to produce full colour illustrations for each shot, with annotations about camera angle, editing, and so on to produce almost a paper version of the film before they start. Others prefer to keep a functional storyboard where the drawings are more basic but there is far more technical information regarding camera angle, shot length, editing, framing, lighting and *mise-en-scène*. See the example below.

Once you have completed the storyboard you can create the shooting script. This is another essential document, which defines all the technical aspects of each shot, lists equipment needed for each shot, and probably also lists the required personnel, props and so on.

The shooting script is usually broken up into shooting days. Filming is not done in chronological order – if you are shooting a series of television adverts for a product, you may decide to shoot all the close-ups of the product for the different adverts on one day, so you can control lighting, use the same prop and so forth. Equally, you may have to shoot particular scenes on one day, as that is the only day one of your actors can manage.

As part of the shooting script you can therefore list all the equipment you will need to ensure you don't forget anything vital, you can make a note of continuity issues, such as clothes and hairstyles, and list all the props needed for a particular shot – in this way you will achieve more as you will be better prepared.

Holding a shot steady

The basic way of making sure that you hold a shot steady is to use a tripod. Whatever size camera you are using your shots will be far more professional if they are steady. Aim to use a majority of shots where the camera is static.

Try to use the 'zoom' function as little as possible. While it is common in amateur work, we rarely use zooms in professional shooting unless it is for a particular effect. If you want to zoom in on a face to show a reaction to a piece of news, for example, that can be very effective. However, for most other shots, it is far better to shoot a sequence of short shots and avoid a zoom effect.

There may also be occasions where you don't want a steady shot, of course, such as when the camera is following someone running through some woods. If you choose to have a shaky shot, to establish a particular mood in your sequence for example, then that is a valid decision – providing your audience can see the difference between these shaky shots and the fixed shots and can understand your reasons behind it.

Framing a shot

Only include what is necessary in the shot. There is a difference here between film and television: film tends to use a wider frame, even when not working in wide-screen; television tends to work more with close-ups. Close-ups are important in film as well, but are used more sparingly. A full-screen close-up of Julia Roberts on the screen at the multiplex can be very effective, sometimes. Television uses more close-ups to create a greater sense of intimacy and communication between the audience and the programme.

The range of shot lengths that you can use is fairly extensive. There is a main set of five frame types that we refer to, and subsets of these that can be specified for particular effect. These are listed below, and some examples are given to show the effect of each (see page 90 for colour plates).

Extreme Long Shot	*Establishing shot – showing figure in its full context*
Long Shot	*Focus on figure*
Mid-Shot (medium shot)	*Common shot to link sections*
Close-up	*Important shot for actor – often used to show strong feelings*
Extreme close-up (big close-up)	*Used for a particular effect*

The convention when framing shots is the use of the **rule of thirds**, whereby you imagine two lines on the camera lens, dissecting the frame into nine sections (i.e. two vertical lines and two horizontal lines) – the resulting intersections are the points to which the human eye is naturally drawn. Thus you can bring greater attention to a character's face or an important object by placing it slightly off-center. (This is why newsreaders, for example, are often placed slightly to the side of the screen with a logo or a blue screen to show images behind them.) An image that is centered in the frame is very stable, yet visually it is very inactive. You want your audience to actively watch and scan the image. By placing the images around the frame you encourage this concentration.

Extreme close up from The Blair Witch Project. *See page 90, figure 4.*

Midshot from Lawrence of Arabia.

Using a variety of shot distances and camera angles

Variety is the spice of film as well as life. Once you have formed your basic plan and decided what shots might be appropriate, it is worth taking a step back and checking that you have made use of a range of shots – conventionally we start a sequence with an **ELS (Extreme Long Shot)** as an **establishing shot** for the action to follow, and use a variety of **CUs (Close-up)** and **ECUs (Extreme Close-up)** to focus on characters' faces during a conversation. You may want to use **POV (point-of-view)** shots to communicate a character's feelings or perspective, for example if they are being chased, or an 'over-the-shoulder shot' to show reactions during a conversation while keeping both characters in focus.

Longshot from I Know What You Did Last Summer. *See page 90, figure 5.*

It is easy, with a bit of planning, to make the same classroom seem welcoming, suitable for children or adults, threatening, evil, depressing or romantic. By controlling the *mise-en-scène* in this way the audience will usually accept your film more readily. It is difficult for the audience when you make little effort with the *mise-en-scène*. If nothing else, you can use lights to create long shadows – maybe even with a green or red filter – for a horror effect, or use a filter over a light to create a soft romantic light. You do need to produce a sequence that is clearly readable as the opening of a film in the thriller genre, or produce at least three adverts that meet the brief set.

Camera angles are also extremely important. The two most important angles are **high-angle** and low angle. A high angle shot means that the camera looks up at the character, often implying a sense of power. A **low-angle** looks down on characters, reversing the effect of the high angle and making them seem small or weak. To see mastery of the use of camera angles study Orson Welles' *Citizen Kane*. Less commonly, you may want to use a '**Dutch angle**' (also referred to as a canted angle). This is achieved by tilting the camera slightly, and can convey a sense of urgency or fear to a scene, especially when it illustrates a character's reaction or shows the point-of-view of someone who is drunk.

There are a number of other ways to draw attention to key points in a frame. Among these are colour, light and movement. It is always important to make sure the main elements contrast slightly. In many early Westerns, filmed in black and white, the heroes frequently wore white hats to distinguish them on the screen and when fighting with a group of villains who would be wearing black hats. Think also of situations in films where a particular colour may have special significance – an obvious example would be the colour red in horror films.

A figure standing still while many other figures rush around them is a clear focal point. A slow pace of movement can enhance a mood of peace or romance or even menace. A whole style of film known as **film noir** developed from careful use of light and dark to communicate emotion and atmosphere, with shadows across faces and scenes shot in low light conditions to establish mood and danger. Equally, you can use light and dark to indicate characters' feelings and situations – a wood is far more frightening in the dark, for example, than on a bright sunny day. If you don't have the facilities to film at night, try filming at dusk or manipulating the film during editing to make it darker for the same effect. Filming on a dull day and using a deep-blue filter can also give the impression of a night scene (this is called shooting 'day for night').

Whenever people are in your shot it is important to frame them properly. Your characters must have headroom, meaning that you can't have the top of their hair on or above the top edge of the frame as it makes them look cramped. You also need to think about what is behind them so they don't appear to have plants growing out of their heads! Similarly, you don't want too much room between the top edge and the character's head or it makes them look out of place and tiny. When a character moves within a frame it is always important to give them what we call 'lead room'. For example, if you're filming a character as he runs, frightened, down a wooded path, as you track alongside him you should give him enough room in front so that he looks as if he is running in the frame, not constantly on the verge of running out of it. If you don't your audience may become more aware of the framing than the content and lose the impact of the piece.

When filming dialogue, or any other scene where you change between character perspectives, it is important to remember the **180° rule**. According to this rule, there is a line in any given scene that splits it into two halves. When shooting a scene that switches back and forth between points of view, all shots must be made from the same side of the line otherwise the scene will look mismatched.

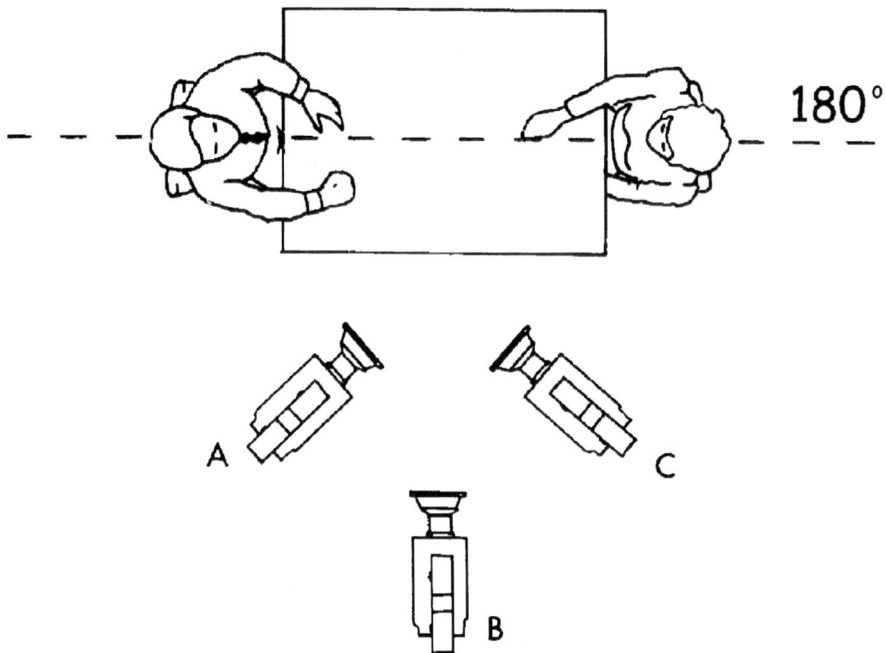

The 180° rule

You must maintain the same arrangement that was in your establishing shot. If you suddenly 'cross the line', the character who was initially facing right is now facing left from the new perspective, and since the other character is still facing in the old direction you have two characters facing left, and if they try to talk to each other that could very confusing for the audience.

Shooting material appropriate to the task set

Although this might seem obvious, there are certain tricks which can be useful, for example, probably not all your shots will need to be on location – a close-up on a hand going into a bag, for example, can be shot almost anywhere and slotted in. Equally, you may be lucky and be shooting outside at a time when the light is particularly effective or something happens that you can use. If in doubt, aim to shoot three times as much material as your final piece will last, without allowing for retakes. That way you will allow enough material to reject some (possibly two-thirds or more) during editing and also give options to develop your material in various ways during editing.

As a part of this, it is worth remembering to think about continuity. If you are shooting a chase sequence in the woods over two days and your heroine appears in a different floaty dress on day two, it may not do much for the credibility of your final piece if her dress changes colour mid-chase! The same comments apply to lighting, outside and in, and any other elements of the *mise-en-scène* that might be affected. This is why, on real shoots, a continuity person is employed to check things like whether Mel Gibson's hair is curling the same way on each day of shooting a particular scene. In reality a series of Polaroids are taken for every scene so continuity can be sure of repeating the same costumes, hair, and so on if a scene is shot over several days; you should be able to rely on memory and notes!

Editing so that meaning is apparent to the viewer

There are various methods of editing material together and all may have their uses. A few are explored here with examples. Part of the craft which you will be learning is to decide how to edit your material together as well as possible and how to use effects, control, cuts and other techniques to appropriate effect.

The most common type of **transition** used in film and television work is the **cut** between shots. Shots are usually between three and eight seconds long (depending on the tempo you are establishing) and the cut simply changes between shots. A **fade** can be useful to suggest a passing of time or change of place/action, and a **dissolve** is most commonly found at the beginning or end of a dream sequence, for example. A fade is where the image appears from or fades out to (usually) a black screen. A dissolve is where one image fades to be replaced by an emerging second image. Wipes and other 'transitions' available on most non-linear editing systems are rarely used in film and television unless a particular effect is intended, such as implying an alien transport or a character descending into a nightmare. With all effects the simple rule is 'don't use them without a very good reason'.

When shots are being linked together there are various ways of suggesting continuity. Common structures can involve patterns such as establishing shot, action shot, bridging shot, reaction shot to create a sense of action – shot of woods, shot of victim running, close-up on knife, shot of pursuer, or the typical shot/reverse shot to show two people having a conversation. Editors sometimes refer to 'matching' shots – for example, they will make sure the eye line between shots is matched, or will match on movement (a popular convention is to match on walking), or will use an angle change on the same scene to give a different perspective, or a bridging shot, such as a close-up or a neutral shot, to give variety or add fresh information for the viewer or to cover problems such as crossing the line. In this situation we usually refer to the different shot in the middle as a **cutaway**, which can also be a valuable device either to change or build atmosphere or to disguise problems such as crossing the line or slightly different framing.

A good way of keeping the action continuous is to keep the soundtrack running underneath all the changes – for example a conversation continuing as the shot/reverse shot happens, or a voice-over continuing over a close-up of a key prop.

Even simple actions take up a great deal of time on film. Imagine a sequence of a person getting dressed. In real life this process can take two or three minutes or more, but this would not make exciting footage to watch. Everything is edited, including 'fly-on-the-wall documentaries', to keep the action moving and keep it interesting. If that same person pulled clothes out of a wardrobe and in the next shot walked into the kitchen, the obvious conclusion the audience will make is that the person got dressed.

Editing can serve to create atmosphere. The human eye, when viewing a scene does not remain stationary. If you were watching two people having a conversation you would automatically switch your focus from one to the other. Good editing mimics this, but controls your perspective and hence your opinion about the action. If you see Person 1 getting aggressive and Person 2 getting upset, your sympathies may lie with Person 2. If the editor shows you the letter that Person 1 is holding revealing that Person 2 has been convicted of murdering Person 1's parents, your sympathies may well be different.

Editing can also control atmosphere by use of rhythm and pacing. An example of this would be a fight sequence. As the two enemies approach each other the shots are long, keeping the pace slow. As tension builds, the shots become shorter, building energy. When the fight begins the shots become short and fast, giving the scene energy that the audience feels. Finally, one fighter falls to the ground and the shots lengthen again. The energy of the scene drops and the audience relaxes. The editing of shots has created a rhythm that heightens the power of the scene.

Alfred Hitchcock used the example of a scene where a group of people sitting around a dinner table was blown up by a time bomb. In a real-time version of the scene the people sit down at the table and the bomb goes off: end of scene, end of people. But no real suspense would be generated by this approach. In his second version the people gather, talk, and casually sit down at the dinner table. A shot of the bomb ticking away under the table is shown revealing to the audience what is about to happen. Unaware of the bomb, the people continue their banal conversations. Close-up shots of the bomb are then inter-cut with the guests laughing and enjoying dinner. The inter-cutting continues (and speeds up) until the bomb finally blows the dinner party to bits. The latter version understandably creates far more tension and emotional impact.

Often, a function of editing is to suggest or explain cause. We may see a dead body on the living room floor during the opening sequence of a film, but who killed the person and why is not revealed until the very end. It makes a more interesting story – one that would be more likely to hold an audience – if we present the result first and reveal the cause gradually over time.

Careful editing can also imply cause, speeding up narratives. If we are shown a shot of someone with all the signs of being drunk (effect), we can probably safely assume they have been drinking (cause).

Example: a woman drives up to a house in a car. She gets out. She enters the house and goes upstairs. She walks towards a door. She hears noises coming from within. She pushes the door open.

If this sequence of actions were shown in 'real time' it would take about five minutes and viewers would get bored. Editing allows the sequence to be cut down so that the focus is clearer and the tension built more quickly. A shooting sequence for the same 'event' is given in the example below. The time in seconds for each shot is given in brackets.

Example: woman drives up to house (5), gets out and walks to door, looking for key (5), ELS of her walking up drive from perspective of neighbour mowing lawn (5), MS (Medium Shot) following gaze of neighbour to drawn curtains at bedroom window (3), MS of woman walking up stairs (3), ECU on door handle as woman reaches for it and pauses (2), MS of room from perspective of woman as she walks in (5).

This makes a total of seven shots and 28 seconds in screen time instead up to five minutes in real time. Our imagination fills in the missing parts – the walk into the house, the history implied as known by the neighbour, her thoughts as she hears the noises, and so on.

Editing is the final control of meaning for your artefact. Imagine the visual effect of arranging the shots described below in these sequences: 1–2–3, 3–2–1, 2–3–1, 2–1–3.

1. MS: a man jumps from an exploding house.

2. MS: a fire breaks out in the living room of the house.

3. LS: the house explodes.

1–2–3: man jumps from a house seconds before it explodes.
3–2–1: a house explodes forcing a man to jump away from the fire.
2–3–1: a man jumps from a house after a fire causes an explosion.
2–1–3: because of a fire, a man jumps away just in time to escape.

PART TWO
Print

Formal brief for OCR AS Specification

You are asked to create one of the following:

- The front cover of the colour supplement for a new Sunday newspaper and at least one main double page spread article. The work must feature at least three original images (**minimum** four pages in total).
- A series of advertisement using at least three original images, from a campaign for health education or charity to include advertisements for magazines and/or newspapers, billboards and flyers/brochures (**at least six advertisements in total**).

Preparatory exercises

You should try to undertake at least one of these tasks and ideally at least four of them in the weeks preceding your work for the project or as part of your ongoing practical skills development during the terms leading up to the exam. As we have said before, you cannot expect to write copy and take pictures for the first time when undertaking this project or learn how to use a DTP package as you go, without there being an impact on your final artefact.

ACTIVITIES

- Use an interview piece from a film or men's magazine and try rewriting it for a different audience and/or editing it down. This gives you a chance to develop copy-writing skills and to learn to identify both the most important sections of an article and also to analyse how a particular voice is constructed for a particular magazine. Example: a *Marie Claire* piece rewritten for *The Face* or a 1000 word article in *GQ* reworked as a 400 word piece in *Loaded*.
- Find a selection of adverts for different chocolate bars and see how far you can swap the text and the images before the identity of the chocolate bars is changed? Are any of these so readily recognised that this limits the changes? What can this tell us about the branding of these bars?
- Choose a well-known national charity and deconstruct a selection of recent adverts

taken from different places (e.g. leaflets, billboards, magazines, newspapers). Can you identify the elements which remain constant throughout the different media? Which elements change? Why is this? How far do the images and text reflect your assumptions about the charity? Is there a reason for this? Can you apply the AIDA (Attention, Interest, Desire, Action) principle to these adverts? What can you say about the way they are constructed?

- Try deconstructing the layout of a newspaper article to identify house style and approach and then remodel this to suit a different newspaper or magazine so that you can see how the layout of a particular magazine affects the content decisions.
- Take a range of photos of someone to use as the key image for an article to be published in *Cosmopolitan* and identify which shots would be most suitable for different themes, such as holidays or date rape or disability. Be prepared to justify your decisions to the rest of the group.
- Analyse a range of Sunday supplement front covers:
  - target audience – who and how targeted
  - media institutions – what is revealed about the institution? What level of institutional knowledge is expected?
  - reading the media – how is the magazine constructed visually to meet these aims? What language is employed to suit its context?
  - How does this impact? What representations are used? How might the ideology of this institution be perceived?

Planning your artefact

- Know your market – define what your artefact will be and be prepared to justify why you think it is credible and viable. If you decide you want to produce a gardening supplement for a new Sunday newspaper similar to the *Independent on Sunday* for example, you need to be able to justify why you think this is a viable publication and how it will fit the audience profile and publication style of the *Independent on Sunday*.
- Once you have defined the general outline of your product you need to prioritise the content – what will the lead story be or the key image? If you are creating a series of adverts for a national charity for example, what is the central piece of information or main theme that you want to get across in your campaign?
- A newspaper supplement will probably not have a logo as such although it will usually have a masthead that works the same way. By defining the logo or masthead early on in planning a project you start to define the newspaper's identity which helps keep your focus.
- You should also list the images which you will need to create and decide on which is the central image to be used.
- Most publications have a limited style of photographs used and a

limited colour palette (which may even be black and white for some Sunday supplements) and you need to define what your palette and image style is at this point so you know what images you will be constructing. Following on from this you need to decide on appropriate fonts and heading/sub-heading/pull-quote to reflect the theme and style of your artefact.

Use of IT to create an artefact

- If you are going to use DTP to produce your artefact you would need a level of competence with a DTP programme – which might be as sophisticated as Quark Xpress or might be a simple programme such as GreenStreet Publisher. Both will allow you to produce good quality artefacts. DTP programmes allow you to put stories and pictures into boxes, which can be edited on the page, moved around and stacked at will, frames and backgrounds can easily be added and a pasteboard facility allows for continued modifications. If you construct your artefact in a word-processing programme you will find it difficult to manipulate your layout as easily since word-processing programmes do not like working with a large number of columns, pictures or boxes.
- You will need a degree of confidence with a picture-editing programme which will allow you to manipulate the graphics necessary for your artefact. Again, you may not have access to a high end product such as Photoshop but a programme such as Paint Shop Pro would be more than adequate for the picture manipulation required and a lot simpler for a novice to learn.
- You will need a basic understanding of the design principles behind DTP work and will need to develop an understanding of the conventions of layout, graphics, colour and page design and learn how to work to a grid or template for every page. If you are using Quark or a similar programme, you can make use of the master page layout to ensure your pages are the same and to avoid the necessity of pasting common elements onto each page in turn.

General print design principles

- make bottom margins wider than the top as the eye is more comfortable with this;
- keep pictures and text aligned – use guidelines to keep everything neat
- show awareness of the need for variety in fonts and text size;
- don't use more than two fonts in a publication. Conventionally one

serif is used for the body text and one sans serif for titles etc. Make sure that is a clear contrast between the two fonts. If in doubt make the contrast greater, not smaller;

- group components on your page to keep it neater and more professional. Use a box to demarcate the central story on the page, for example, or to explicitly link a caption with a picture;
- use WOB (white on black) for greater contrast – use shades of grey for the box if black is too harsh. This can be useful for black and white work in particular – it is a favourite device on the front cover of tabloid newspapers for example.

Appropriate images and text

If you are writing a story about snowboarding you would not use a photo of a gerbil for example (unless the gerbil was snowboarding). While this level of integration of text and image might be taken for granted it is also worth remembering that this extends further. If you have created a set of pages for inclusion in a broadsheet Sunday newspaper, the use of cartoon clipart such as that given away free with computer magazines would probably be totally inappropriate – however appealing it might seem as an initial filler. If you are taking a picture of a 'film star' (friends and family are usually only too pleased to become 'stars' for a day!) to include with the article, the style of photo will also be dictated by the publication. The photo selected by *The News of the World* would probably be different to that selected by *The Independent*.

'Found' images

Pre-existing images from other media sources should be avoided, but if you *do* need to use them, you must be prepared to make significant alterations to them so that they become 'your own work'. You should also acknowledge their source in your written evaluation. In general, taking your own photos is a much better option: getting friends and family to dress up as 'characters' or 'celebrities' for your Sunday supplement or adverts gives you the opportunity to show your skill with the camera and subject matter.

Register and tone

It is also important that the tone of your articles is relevant. The vocabulary used in *The Times* is deliberately different from that used in

The Sun. If you were to create a supplement for a new newspaper in the style of either of those newspapers that did not reflect the language of the parent publication, it would be inappropriate.

The **register** of a particular publication is also significant. The register of *Loaded* is different to that of *GQ* and again, artefacts that did not use an appropriate register would probably be largely unsuccessful.

The **register** refers to the style of language employed by a publication. The register you use when talking to your friends or when talking to a little baby is very different. We use this different register or style of language all the time, adapting and adjusting as we go. Print publications must decide on appropriate register and this becomes one of the defining features of the publication.

Construct still images using technical and symbolic codes effectively

Using technical codes effectively simply means that you know how to frame shots and take shots that can be used in publication. The symbolic codes are mixed up in this but can be summarised as 'intention'. If you want the photograph of a politician to seem a positive portrayal you would frame it, catch an expression, construct the *mise-en-scène* and so on to present a positive impression. It is just as easy to use a photograph to create a negative impression.

Technical effects such as filters or effects which are available in most photo editing software can also be used to good effect – especially for advertising campaigns. However, you need to ensure that the focal product is not obscured in any way, unless that is intentional as part of the campaign message. For example, if you were advertising a brand of trainer which you were implying will make you a faster runner you might want to use a motion blur effect to give an impression of speed. The blurring effect called a Gaussian blur can be used to soften an image and create a drop shadow or halo effect.
To see the effect of the Gaussian blur and how to create it, access the web site:

http://www.manifold.net/products/r5/5manual/mfd50Image_Gaussian_Blur.htm

Other soft focus effects can add glamour to a portrait that has a hard edge to the image e.g. a 'vignette' filter.

It may be worthwhile accessing websites dedicated to your own photo editing software as these can give useful additional help and advice.

Some images are best presented separately, others may be most effective with text wrapped around them or used in a creative way. You need to be able to crop images, resize them, flip them or use a clipping path if you are to be able to manipulate them appropriately well for your artefact. In particular you should usually try to crop images tightly – a tight focus on a face is far more effective than a long or mid-shot, usually as readers can then identify with the image much quicker. If you are creating an advertising campaign for a product, your images of the product would probably need to be tightly cropped close-ups for example, not out of focus long shots.

Clipping paths – these are used so that you can isolate an image from its background. Advice on how to use this technique effectively, using either Adobe Photoshop or Adobe Illustrator can be seen on the following web sites:

http://www.ruku.com/clipath1.html

http://www.adobe.com/print/tips/illclippath/main.html

Alternatively, using a search engine simply type in 'clipping path' and see what you come up with.

What is your purpose?

The function of your supplement or adverts is the essence of your communication. If your supplement is intended as a beginners guide to home decorating, then that is your function. A precise and well-defined function is essential. If you do not define your function properly before you start, your artefact will be unfocused.

Define your target audience

Who is your message intended for? If you are targeting young children, your register and information level will have to be understandable to them. On the other hand, if you are targeting high income earners, then you register will be more sophisticated. So define who your target audience is, because that will decide how your message is presented.

Make the 'flat-plan'

How many pages or adverts are you going to make? What size will they be? Where will they be placed? How will these factors affect your designs? What will the balance be on these pages? For example, with the supplement, how much space on the pages will be taken up with advertising? Are you creating a broadsheet or a tabloid? What proportion of text to image is appropriate for your publication? What is the average story length for your publication?

Develop your concept

The concept of 'theme' is the underlying creative idea of your artefact. Even in a big advertising campaign, the theme will remain the same from one advertisement to another, and also across mediums. This is central to an ad campaign – the audience needs to be able to identify the theme quickly and easily so that it can begin to establish a brand loyalty. For a Sunday supplement, there may well be a 'theme' for the whole supplement and this will be reflected not only in the copy but also in the images, titles, layout, choice of adverts and general 'look' of the supplement.

The visual

Research indicates that 70% of people will only glance at an ad, and only 30% will pause long enough to read the copy. It is not dissimilar when people are flicking through a newspaper. They will glance at the pictures and may glance at an effective title but will not read the copy unless they have been attracted by either the visual or the headline. Also it is better to use a photograph unless you have decided to use a graphic for a particular reason. The image should be the key focus of any page and should be effective and striking if it is to catch the attention of your target audience.

The 'hook'

Your main headline should act as a 'hook'. The aim is to affect the reader emotionally, either by making them laugh, making them angry, making them curious or making them think.

Think of the AIDA principle again – **attract** the target audience, create **interest**, establish **desire** and then explain what **action** will fulfil the desire you have now created.

Keep the headline short and snappy but strong. It can take time to think of a good line but it is usually worth it.

The copy

Keep the copy near your title where possible and try to create a visual continuity which will draw more people to the important information or action you want them to read. Use a serif typeface for your copy whenever possible. Use sub-heads or pull quotes to break up the columns of text and create interest and signposts through a long article if this is appropriate for your chosen publication. (Some of the broadsheets do not use subheadings and may only use a single pull-quote as a hook, for example.) However the by-line and image of the writer is usually very prominent in these publications as that can be a key hook for the reader.

Finally

The single most common mistake is visual clutter. Don't be afraid of white space on your page – especially in advertising where the white space can help to focus the eye very quickly. Less is always better than more. So if you're not certain whether something is worth including, then leave it out. If your ad or page layout is chaotic, people will simply turn the page, and your message will never be read.

It is always valuable to test your publication as well. For example, make a draft copy of your adverts and check that your target audience understands them and relates to them. Once you have a mock-up of one of the pages for your supplement you might want to lay them next to pages from the parent publication or similar supplements to compare layout, approach and structure. You should also test market these drafts on your target audience once you have done all this.

Remember that the feedback from these tests can be very valuable for your evaluation.

3 PART THREE
Audio

Formal brief for OCR Specification

You are asked to create the following:
An extract from a documentary series, or current affairs programme, to include studio presentation, interviews and a theme tune/jingle (approx. five minutes duration).

Preparatory exercises

You should try to undertake at least one of these tasks and ideally all three of them in the weeks preceding your work for the project, or as part of your ongoing practical skills development during the terms leading up to the exam. As we have said before, you cannot expect to record a documentary piece, interview and jingle for the first time when undertaking this project or learn how to use recording equipment as you go, without there being a knock-on effect on your final artefact.

ACTIVITIES

- Record an audio version of a simple song or poem, using music and sound effects in the background – *Old McDonald's Farm* can work well.
- Record a 'day in my life' with audio notes about your day recorded as you go through the day and edited into a five minute summary of your day with appropriate music or sound effects to create interest.
- Compose and record a 20 second jingle for your Media lessons.

Planning

Design your project

First you need to decide if you are going to be working on a documentary or a current affairs programme for this project. Study at least two examples of your chosen genre and make detailed notes about the structure of the programmes:

- station identity, scheduling and audience profile – how do these affect the form and style of the programme?
- typical length;
- integration and employment of presenters;
- length of segments, number of adverts, jingles and 'non-studio elements' such as traffic news;
- use of language and register and balance of four codes of radio – talk, silence, music and sound effects. Impact of this arrangement?

Drafting your programme

Before planning the programme you need to decide exactly what sort of programme you are going to create, on which station it might be broadcast, and the format, style and content of the programme.

You should define the target audience and identify three key ways in which your programme will explicitly target them (for example, a jingle based on a song which they would be likely to know very well, or celebrity guests who would appeal to a particular audience).

Once you have decided on the structure, form and content of your piece you are ready to plan the construction. Start by identifying which elements you can produce as 'stand-alones' to be re-recorded during the final programme. For example, you can produce a jingle as a stand-alone or the title sequence/music for your programme.

It is usually a good idea to write a complete script for a radio programme so the presenter(s) know what they need to say. Drying (that is, forgetting what you have to say next) on air is very obvious on radio and not as easily covered as it can be on television, so a script will be a valuable resource for those presenting. You may want to script specific elements such as interviews separately and you may find that a list of questions is more effective than a script for an interview for example.

Once you have recorded these sections they can be added into the running order if you are working in a recording suite, or simply played from a different tape recorder as part of the recording process if you are having to use a very low-tech approach. If you are working low tech in this way, please remember that your teachers and moderators will mark the quality of your work, not the quality of your equipment. As long as you have tried to work professionally, the quality of the recording tone for example, will not be a factor when your work is being assessed. However, it must be audible!

When the script has been written, you should write a detailed cue sheet for the programme with accurate timings, so you know when the stand-alones, such as jingles are going to be placed. It may be that you wish to leave some of the studio-based sections less precisely scripted to allow your presenters a degree of freedom. This is fine if they are happy to work this way but at least one or two rehearsals and trial runs to get things running smoothly are recommended.

Technical issues

Always wear headphones when recording

You need to monitor the sound quality and stop recording if things are not right. You don't want to spend all day recording and then discover that the time has been wasted.

Microphones

You are unlikely to have access to professional quality microphones but you can do a lot to ensure the best possible sound quality. Put microphones about 10–15 cms away from the mouth of the person talking. Be careful about getting too close as you may pick up some of their sounds, such as the 'p' sound or 's' sounds too clearly and this distracts from your material as well as sounding unprofessional. If you are find it hard to get rid of these sounds, move the microphone slightly to the side of the speaker's mouth and see if that helps.

Preparation

- always bring at least one extra set of batteries;
- always have more than enough tapes on hand;
- always write-protect your tapes after you finish an interview;
- label and number your tapes. If you are recording several 'takes' of a show and you don't label them carefully or are not careful with the file names you choose, you will not be able to remember which is the final version and may end up submitting an early version which is not as good.

Tips and Tricks

Always record two minutes of 'room noise' after finishing an interview or any part of a programme not recorded in the studio. When you start editing your documentary or current affairs programme, you can use this sound to make smooth transitions in and out of the scene and between the narrator's voice and the subject's voice. You can also record and use other material as backing material to add atmosphere or mood.

Interviewing Tips

Conduct interviews in the quietest place possible. It is far easier to add sound tracks or additional sound played on a second cassette recorder during an interview or part of the studio presentation than it is to try and hear speech with noise such as a television in the background. In addition, you cannot easily edit out the noise you do not want and may end up having to re-record to get better sound.

Start interviews or segments of the programme by asking questions and letting the answers serve as introduction. 'Who are you? How old are you? What do you do and how long have you been doing it?' or whatever introductory question is appropriate for the particular story.

Help interviewees to be more descriptive. For visually descriptive information, ask your subject to 'paint a picture with words' of whatever you need them to describe. In addition, emotional content works very well on radio. Questions like 'How does this make you feel?' tend to yield good tape.

Finally

- Remember that you can keep re-recording your material until you get it right.
- Remember your audience all the time and keep asking yourself 'will they want to listen to this?'
- Test your programme on a sample audience before submission to see if it works. Can they identify the branding of the programme/the style/ the content and so on? Do they feel they are part of the target audience?
- Make sure that the listener's attention is held throughout the programme. This can be done with frequent changes of activity (narrator, interview, jingle, traffic, adverts, jingle, news summary, narrator again) and the use of familiar items (jingles for example) coupled with fresh elements such as interview pieces.
- Keep to your time plan. Not only is radio always a pacy medium but your original plan ensures frequent changes of noise and balance of elements to keep the audience's attention.

- Be aware that the project is defined as an extract from a longer programme; so you may choose to record only one part of the programme that may be the beginning, middle or end. We would normally expect a piece of this sort to be no longer than ten minutes. The Specifications suggest approximately five minutes. We have specifically excluded music programmes to help you avoid the 12 minutes of music and one minute of links approach that does not demonstrate much skill in the medium.
- Remember that this programme is designed to appeal to a target audience. What is the USP (Unique Selling Point)? Why should they tune in to this programme? Are you directly appealing to your target audience?

4 PART FOUR
New media – ICT

Formal brief for OCR AS Specification

Produce a homepage and at least six linked supplementary pages (incorporating at least three original images) from a new entertainment webzine.

Preparatory exercises

- Analyse a range of 'branded' sites to see how the branding affects the experience.
- Do a detailed deconstruction of some very successful sites such as *BBC Online* or *The Onion* and some less successful sites. Visit www.websitesthatsuck.com for examples of bad design and be prepared to explain why these sites are effective or not effective.
- Compare and contrast the online presence of key entertainment players such as Time Warner with their other advertising and promotional methods. How central would you say their web presence is to their branding. Why is this?
- Design a basic homepage for yourself with certain elements – title, image of self, centred, saved as a JPEG, some text in a table, anchors to scroll up and down the page and links to at least two external sites as a practice run.
- Design a basic site map layout for a local company, and set out the basic pages with links to show how the site would work as a mesh, a hierarchy or a linear site.

- Create an animated gif that might be suitable as a logo on the entry page of a site trailing a new horror film. Present your animation to the rest of the group and explain how it reflects the chosen film. Note: If you have never created an animated gif before, you may want to use a simple software package such as 'gif Animator' to help you. This can be downloaded from www.ulead.com/ga/runme.htm
- Design three to four pages giving information about your Media course and post it up on the web to test it properly – use images, text and maybe sounds and video extracts.
- Study at least three current webzines, of which at least one should be entertainment based, and write a short report about the form and function of each one.

Defining your project

Planning

- Plan in detail and ensure your site is 'sticky'. A sticky site is one where there is enough interesting material on every page to make visitors want to stay with the site;
- Use a mesh or hierarchy to link the pages. Make sure you include links back to the home page on every page and think about links to other sites as well;
- You may need to consider using frames to make your site look professional – for example a navigation frame.

Basic planning

- Can the end user immediately understand what the site is for? Are the titles easy to understand and readily visible?
- Can they follow the links between the different sections and understand the structure of the site? 'Hidden' links may seem clever but can be really irritating. If the list is complicated, why not use a picture or a series of pictures to set the links up?
- Is it easy to find the way back to the home page or opening page? (It's a good idea to use a 'home' icon or a suitable piece of text on each page to aid this.)
- Does each entire page fit inside the user's computer window so they do not miss anything or need to scroll the page? There are occasions when a scrolling page is appropriate, such as a more text-based page but it should never require more than four clicks to jump up or down the page. If you have more information it is generally better to create more pages and link them.

- Is the page too cluttered with too many links? Or too many graphics? Or too many moving parts that don't stop? (Remember – that cute animated gif which you have dropped into the top corner of the page may be very distracting to the viewer. Only use it if it is *directly* relevant to your page).
- What is the USP (Unique Selling Point) of this site? In other words what is unique enough about this site to make it 'sticky'?

Layout and Design

- Is the text easy to read? Are the graphics easy to understand? Your site may reach an audience for whom English is not their first language. Make sure the language and structure are accessible.
- Think about the fonts you use – 'sans serif' fonts such as Arial, Verdana, or Comic Sans are much more appropriate than serif fonts (such as Times New Roman) which are hard to read on the screen. We usually teach designers that they should restrict themselves to only two fonts on a page – one for the 'body text' and another for the titles.
- Be careful about the fonts you choose to use. It is all very well using the 'perfect' font for something but if that font is not installed on the viewer's computer, their machine will just guess a font, destroying all your hard work and intentions. Designers usually create these 'fancy' fonts by actually making the word or phrase as a picture and importing it into the page as an image. That way the formatting of the font is not affected.
- Do the graphics support the site by establishing an appropriate theme to reflect the intentions of the site? It's good design practice to think about the size and position of each graphic and keep a similarity. In addition we like to keep the colour palettes restricted. Try not to use too many colours as it gets hard to read.
- Does the product look professional? It can be worth learning how to make rollovers or downloading some good quality buttons for example to make your site look more professional. In the world of web design, where the 'catch' for customers is measured in seconds – looks really do matter.

Poor design elements –

or what to avoid?

Backgrounds

- grey default background colour;
- colour combinations of text and background that make the text hard to read (No lime green backgrounds with yellow text!);
- busy, distracting backgrounds that make the text hard to read – for example a busy graphic with large dark areas such as shadows behind black text.

Text

- no margins;
- centred paragraph text;
- paragraphs of type in all caps;
- paragraphs of type in bold;
- paragraphs of type in italic.

Links

- links that are not clear about where they will take you to;
- links in body copy that distract readers and lead them off to remote, useless pages (while links to valuable remote sites such as a reference to support a point being made may be very valuable);
- text links that are not underlined so you don't know it's a link;
- dead links – always check!

Graphics

- large graphic files that take forever to download;
- graphics with 'halos' around them where they have been poorly manipulated;
- missing graphics (because the creator did not copy the files from their hard drive!);
- anything that blinks, especially text;
- animations that never stop.

Navigation

- having to scroll sideways;
- unclear navigation, overly complex navigation.

General design

- entry page or home page that does not fit within standard window (640 × 460 pixels);
- no focal point on the page or too many focal points on a page;
- navigation buttons as the only visual interest, especially when they're large;
- lack of contrast, for example the use of two fonts from the same family;
- non-contrast background and text.

Good Design Elements

Text

- background does not interrupt the text;
- text is big enough to read but not too big;
- the hierarchy of information is perfectly clear;
- columns of text are narrower than in a book to make reading easier on the screen.

Navigation

- navigation buttons and bars are easy to understand and use;
- a large product has a clear map page.

Links

- link colours coordinate with page colours;
- links are underlined so they are instantly clear to the visitor;
- the links give the visitor a clue as to where they are.

Graphics

- buttons are not big and overpowering;
- every graphic link has a matching text link;
- graphics and backgrounds use browser-safe colours;
- animated graphics turn off by themselves.

General design

- good use of graphic elements (photos, subheads, pull quotes) to

break up large areas of text and the style of the page reflects the content;
- every page in the site looks as if it belongs to the same site: there are repetitive elements that carry throughout the pages (this is 'consistency of design' and usually means the same background, layout, colour scheme and navigation structure appear on each page).

Using Images

JPEG

Photographs, as well as other images that are similar to photographs should usually be saved in JPEG format.

Save as:
- 72ppi (pixels per inch) – used when referring to the resolution on the screen;
- lowest quality level (although you may need to use higher levels to achieve a reasonable image), experiment with the slider;
- formal options – choose Baseline optimised for the best colour quality or choose Progressive to enable the file to load progressively from low resolution to high resolution as the page downloads;
- RGB colour mode (changed via Image>Mode>RGB colour from the top menu bar but you should find you are working in RGB colour most of the time anyway).

NOTE: JPEG compression throws away information in order to reduce file sizes. If you resave a JPEG file, it will throw away even more information as it compresses the file again. The amount of information lost will depend on the image so always keep your original, uncompressed file in case you need to start again with your JPEG!

GIF

Diagrams, cartoons and simple drawings are best saved in the GIF format. GIFs are 8-bit, not 24-bit so you don't need to worry so much about the colour depth.

Save as:
- 72ppi;
- indexed colour mode (changed via Image>Mode>Indexed Colour from the top menu bar);
- reduce the colour palette to the minimum necessary to maintain the image;
- to save a GIF in a graphics programme you need to complete your work on the graphic and then choose File>Export>GIF89a Export from the top menu bar;
- choose the 'adaptive palette' in the export dialog box and set colours to the smallest number available. Click the Preview button to see what the file will look like. If it doesn't look good enough, close the Preview window and try a higher number of colours. Keep adding colours until your image becomes acceptable and then click OK;
- click the 'interlace' checkbox and click OK to interlace your image.

Technical skills to develop

Use images, text, sound and video for the task set

Web based material depends on a combination of text and image to create meaning. In some cases sound and video are also vital. For example a site to promote a new film would be a poorer site if it did not include at least one trailer for the movie. However, video and sound need to be used sparingly on a website as there can be difficulties with downloading sound and video material as it takes so long.

Use appropriate software for developing your site

While it is perfectly possible – indeed common for web programmers to create web sites by hard coding HTML, it is unlikely that media students will want to spend the time and effort required to learn this skill. There is a wide range of software available to do the work for you and allow you to concentrate on the design aspects of your site. These range from free software through to professional products. If you have access to excellent software such as Macromedia *Dreamweaver* all well and good, but there are plenty of cheaper products which will do the job such as *First Page 2000*. The most important thing is to ensure that you can use the programme.

Key design pointers

Think about using a background colour. Do not use a background image unless it is for a very good reason. They make it very hard to read a page. As with print documents, use contrasting font sizes and styles in your formatting e.g. using bold and headings. Do not use serif fonts on a web page – they are very hard to read. It is best to use a sans-serif font and to use a standard one such as Arial or Courier. If you use a complicated font and the 'reader' does not have a copy of it on their system, their computer will substitute a different font and all your formatting will come to nothing. Many web editing packages will only let you use the common sans serif fonts, for this reason.

If you do want to use a particular font for a particular effect, the best way is to create an image of the text on a suitable background by using an illustration package or your photo-editing package and putting it into your page as an image. That way the formatting cannot be altered whatever fonts are installed on the viewer's computer.

Identify your target audience

Identify the target audience for your site quickly as this will define your approach. A site aimed at four to six year olds will probably use different fonts, colours, images, layout and content to one targeting 25–30-year-olds. A site appealing to high-income earners will be very different to a webzine presence for a magazine such as *Loaded*. You will probably need to carry out some research, once you have started to plan your site and defined your target audience to identify how best to appeal to this audience on the web. This research can prove a valuable part of your evaluation.

Appeal to your audience

It is also important to ensure that your site is easy to navigate and interesting, and that the images set an appropriate context for the site, just as with print based work. In other words, you need to make sure that as the site comes up it is communicating with the reader. Just as a magazine front cover or the opening sequence of a television programme set the context of the programme to follow, so a site's opening page should establish its position quickly – background colour, layout, use of images etc. should all add to the effect.

Following on from this, the opposite is also true. It is easy to get carried away with a website and include too many effects. Endless animations, over clever menus, too many flashing lights, a background sound to every page and text scrolling across the page can detract from the site itself and can even put people off going there. If you keep visiting the best sites, you will notice that there are clear thematic links between pages, navigation is 'transparent' (that is, easy to grasp), the pages are uncluttered and straightforward and they load quickly.

Link your pages effectively

This means that you have to create 'hyperlinks' to the different pages in your site, possibly within the pages themselves if they are too big to fit in a browser window and probably to other sites. We would expect to see a 'menu bar' or some navigation system somewhere on every page. Link text is normally identified in some way by being in a different colour and underlined. If your pages are long enough that the viewer would need to scroll down the page, it is better to create a 'table of contents' at the top of the page with links to the different sections on the page and 'back to the top' links at the end of each section to make it easier for the viewer to 'jump' around the page.

It is also a good idea to use images as links when you can, either by creating little 'icons' which can be used as links e.g. a picture of a house to represent the home page of your site or by using larger images or parts of images. For example, if you were creating a site with information about various stars from a particular film, you might want to use a still from the film showing all the characters but with a link for each star from their face to 'their' page.

Using the conventions of web publishing appropriately

Most of the essential points have been made here and you must now see that you cannot make an appropriate web page without some degree of research regarding similar pages to see what conventions are used in that type of site. Secondly you cannot make an appropriate web page without making some investment in learning the software and what it can do. Some effects such as 'rollover buttons' and 'drop down menus' can really add to the effect of your page, others merely detract and should be avoided.

An example of a typical web page layout follows:

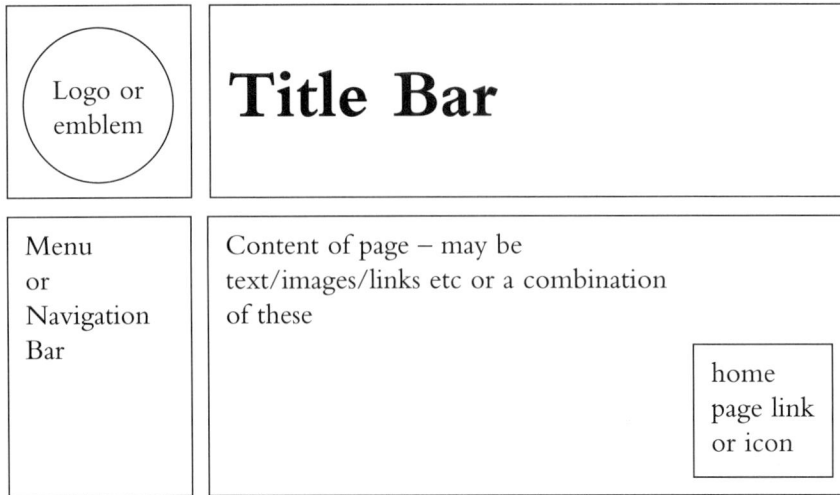

⬭ Logo or emblem	**Title Bar**

Menu or Navigation Bar	Content of page – may be text/images/links etc or a combination of these home page link or icon

Obviously there are many other ways of laying out a web page – look at examples for similar sites to get an idea. Look in particular at sites that are deliberately 'divergent' to create impact or where the production values are very high, such as film release sites. Try the *Gladiator* site or the *Crouching Tiger, Hidden Dragon* site to get ideas about how the production values of a film can override conventional design principles to create something powerful and effective which creates a clear branding and concept in the users mind.

⑤ PART FIVE
Production Log

There are four sections to the Production Log and they are all important. There is also a maximum length of 2000 words for the whole log so editing skills are important. The Log is not a description or diary but a reflective and analytical review of your work to be developed alongside the product to ensure that the theoretical aspects of practical production are foregrounded during the production process as well as the practical points.

Section 1

The Log needs to start by clearly identifying the chosen brief. You then need to explain what research you have undertaken into contemporary products and services. Specific reference must be made to research into similar media texts and target audience.

Section 2

It is essential that you plan your work properly using appropriate documentation, such as the planning sheets that have been suggested in the earlier sections, to give evidence of the planning process.

Storyboards, scripts, original photographs before cropping or manipulation should be essential working documents during the planning and construction process, so immaculate records are not expected. A perfectly drawn storyboard for an advert that does not deviate in any way from the final product has usually been created after the advert was finished, as an artificial exercise to conform to exam regulations. Not only is it usually fairly easy to spot 'post-production planning' in this way, but also using this approach will not enable you to score as highly. Battered sheets with evidence of redrafting are sometimes more credible as genuine working documents and if the production log indicates that they were indeed essential planning tools, you will probably score well despite their poor condition.

You are also required to show evidence that you have carried out audience research – which might be quantitative or qualitative or a mixture of both, but it must be relevant and the conclusions clearly taken on board while creating your artefact.

Section 3

The next section of the Log is the evaluation of the construction process. You need to give an analysis of how you approached the production process, the decision making which was undertaken, working practices, successful and unsuccessful ideas and approaches and analysis of how the artefact was formed. This is perhaps the most difficult section of the Log, since it is very easy to allow this section to become a 'production diary' that will gain very little credit because it is simply a description of the production process and not, as it should be, a reflective analysis. As a rule of thumb, when writing this section you should beware of writing sentences which begin 'Then' and be especially wary of falling into the recording habit, making statements such as 'we then needed to put the clips in order on the timeline' rather than the more reflexive 'when ordering the clips on the timeline we wanted a balance of length of shot as well as a thematic structure and development. We lost some clips due to clumsy lighting and so had to 'cover' these gaps with a cut-away to a close up to ensure a smooth sequence.' The latter example has not only justified decisions made without simply documenting them, it has also shown an understanding of an appropriate technical vocabulary and the opportunities and difficulties inherent in the editing process.

Section 4

The final section of the Log is an evaluation of your production. You should deconstruct the product in some detail and give comparative analysis against a range of equivalent productions and within the context of the designated target audience. It is quite appropriate to reflect that the production is not fully successful at this point, as long as you can indicate how you might have made it more successful. The limiting factors here will be the word limit. You may use annotated pictures here. You must also ensure that the analysis does not become a repetition of the production process but remains a deconstruction of the final production.

It's not easy to get all that into 2000 words. However, remember that this limit was set intentionally to require you to think carefully about what you include in the Log. If there were no limit, there would be a danger of rewarding length of analysis more than quality of analysis and this would be unfair. The quality of thought and intention in your production and the technical ability and creative skills that you have employed in creating this production will be rewarded, not endless notes.

Effective use of an appendix

The specifications state clearly that *"pre/post production paperwork should be provided in an appendix to the log, as evidence of planning."*

You should include details of research you have undertaken into similar products. Photocopying an A4 advert onto a piece of A3 paper, deconstructing it in terms of form, style and function as well as content, to provide evidence for your design approach can give far more information than a mundane essay type approach about a series of advertisements.

As suggested above, planning sheets such as storyboards, scripts, original art work and layout plans may also be included in the appendix. If you have used questionnaires as part of audience research, then a chart showing the results might be included together with a copy of the original questionnaire.

All of this is regarded as evidence of research but it is not included in the formal word count of 2000 words.

Important note

However, there is a difference between **teacher assessment** and **moderation**. Your work will initially be assessed by your teacher and then (depending upon the number of candidates in your centre) the candidates' work will be sent to be externally moderated.

It is essential that your teacher sees **all** the documentation that offers evidence of research and planning. It is on this that your mark for planning and research will be assessed. However, when it comes to submitting your work for moderation to an external moderator, you do **not** have to include every single item. Moderators do not expect to receive every response to your questionnaire, or every annotated analysis of half a dozen colour supplement front covers. At most select the items that you and your teacher think best represent your research and planning work and present these as your appendix.

Preparing for moderation

Although the assessment procedures are primarily the responsibility of
your teacher or lecturer, there are some very important things that you
can do to help yourself and your work.

Firstly, you should ensure that your work is neatly presented. If you have
made produced work on videotape, finding the time to put it into a case
with a title inlay will help. You may not have time for a proper video front
cover but the tape box **and** the tape itself must be labelled with your name
and candidate number, and your centre number as well as the name of your
film.

If you are presenting a print artefact, try to get a laminated colour copy
to send off if you can. (Any local printing shop can do this if there are no
facilities at your school or college.) Again, do not forget the sticky label
on the back telling us who made it with your centre name and number.
The same advice goes for all the mediums – make sure you have labelled
your work carefully and taken time to present it as well as possible. Every
loose item must be separately labelled.

Whenever possible, valuations should be word-processed and you should
use a header or footer, ensure that your name, candidate number and the
number of the page appear on every page of your analysis so that pages
do not go missing.

Finally, it is worth making sure that you have a copy of the project
yourself before your centre sends it off for moderation. You will then
have a backup copy if anything should happen to go missing.

Section 4 Part 1
Textual analysis

PART ONE
Moving image

Introduction

As part of your study of media texts, OCR's AS Unit 2731 (Textual Analysis) gives you the opportunity to develop your analysis skills and assist you in learning how media texts are constructed. The texts for Section A (Technical Aspects of Moving Image Language and Conventions) for 2002 are from studio-based television programmes (game shows, quiz shows and discussion/chat programmes) and for 2003 and 2004 the texts will be from action/adventure films. The skills learned here are perfectly transferable if you are studying for examinations with another examination board.

Section A of the Textual Analysis paper focuses on technical analysis. This means that you need to study the techniques used to construct the given texts, rather than simply studying the text in depth. This is intentionally a detailed focus, to ensure that you can research the forms and conventions of the specified genre in detail.

Remember that the examination is 'unseen'. This means that you will not know in advance what the text is that you will watch in the examination. This is done so you can study a range of texts in the specified genre and look at how the forms and conventions are used, rather than simply studying a single text and then being tested on how well you can remember your notes about that text. The questions you will have to answer will assume that you have never seen the text before, and thus will ask about the technical codes used in the text without any assumption of knowledge of the text outside this extract.

It is *not* a unit where you need to study the history of the genre in depth or know details or facts about a particular programme. This is because we want you to learn about how texts are constructed and to learn to use technical vocabulary and approaches while analysing texts. These are essential skills for both understanding how media texts are constructed and for constructing your own texts for practical production units. Your understanding of media debates and ideologies is tested in other units.

Form of the assessment

The extract given will be between three and five minutes long and there will be 30 minutes allowed for four viewings in total, with time allowed to take notes after the first viewing. However, you will be able to read the questions before any viewings so that you know what you need to be watching for. We assume that it will take you 45 minutes to plan and write your response to these questions. The text may or may not be familiar to you. The intention is that it is unseen so it does not matter whether you have seen the programme before. You will be thinking about the technical codes employed in the text, not the content of the text, so you won't need to know any background about it.

Genre

You will need to show evidence that you have studied the conventions of the relevant genre. The codes employed in a text are defined by the genre and thus the conventions associated with that genre. It is a generic convention of news programmes to provide a summary of that day's stories at the beginning of the edition. It would make for a less effective game show, however, if the host announced the winner and the final score as part of the opener to the programme.

Equally, there are technical codes associated with a genre. When a guest on a talk show appears we expect to hear applause from the audience and the signature music of the programme, or a piece of music that represents the guest. When we are watching *EastEnders*, for example, we do not expect a round of applause or the theme tune to be played each time a character enters an episode.

ACTIVITIES

- In groups, make a list of ten conventions that you associate with the genre of game/quiz/talk shows or action/adventure films
- Identify at least four texts within your chosen genre and qualify their use for each of these conventions in terms of 'very strong', 'moderate' and 'does not really conform'.
- Swap lists with another group and attempt to order their conventions from 1 to 10 in terms of their importance.
- Swap lists with a third group and create a short definition of the genre using the first three or four conventions on their list.
- Feed back these definitions to the rest of the group and discuss how they might be improved. Are there any that might be interchangeable between genres? Can you adjust your definitions so they are exclusive to your chosen genre? Once you feel each one is fairly representative of a genre you might like to put them up on the wall to keep you focused.

Overview on textual codes

The codes, used in film and/or television programmes can be categorized into technical, character/presenter and representational codes. All are important when analysing a text, but you should remember that the key focus of your unseen analysis is technical codes. Social and representational codes are important in your analysis, but are identified via the technical codes used to establish them, rather than in their own right.

Technical codes

Technical codes, such as the camera, the lighting, the editing or the use of sound and music, create expectations, control the audience's perceptions and signify the genre of a programme. These codes are very different for different genres, such as soap operas or game shows. They are intended to engage the audience with the text. It is the use of technical codes to create tension during the last moments of a game show, for example, which helps us to respond emotionally. One key code can be the lighting of characters, for example whether a character's face is lit from top or below, giving him/her a soft or a harsh expression. Another example would be the camera angle: while a high-angle shot makes the character seem small and vulnerable, a low-angle shot can make them seem powerful and strong. This is one reason why actors who are short may need to stand on a box in certain shots, to ensure the right effect.

Character/presenter codes

Character/presenter codes include the costume, make-up, gestures and language of a character. Presenters in chat shows or quiz shows can be considered almost in the same way as characters in works of fiction. These codes signify much about the character to the viewer, such as their social grouping, job or their character. Stereotypes are often used because they build on the viewers' previous experience in terms of television/film observation and in their own world. They are therefore predictable and can be either maintained and used almost as a 'shorthand', or broken for dramatic effect.

Representational codes

There are representational codes such as the dialogue and the narrative employed in a text. They establish whether it is a current affairs programme, a comedy, or another genre. We are constantly confronted with genre in this way through television and film, and we are able to respond appropriately as they fit with our own experience, ideology and knowledge of the world. Even if we do not understand a foreign programme we can still 'read' the signs and codes and understand that type of programme it might be.

ACTIVITIES

- If you have the Internet, satellite or cable television find examples of a game or talk show and an action adventure movie made in a foreign language.
- Identify at least five conventions of the genre that is the same as those for English language programmes. How do you know what genre it belongs to? (Narrative, setting, props, characters, dress codes, verbal codes?)
- Are there any conventions that are different?
- What expectations did knowing the genre lead you to have of the programme?
- Why is this?

Moving on – Specific Analysis

Now that you have explored the genre conventions and basic codes, you need to study specific texts in detail to look at how the technical codes are employed to establish the genre. In the unseen examination you will be given a short extract of a text to watch and you must comment upon how the text communicates with/manipulates/engages the audience through the use of the technical codes. As a conclusion for each question about the technical codes you will be asked to comment upon the rationale behind this approach and reflect on its success. This is intended to ensure that you do not simply describe the technical codes employed without considering their function. You must go beyond describing *what* you see and hear and explain *why* and *how* the texts are constructed in the way that they are.

We will look at how you might approach an answer to a particular text later, but first we need to clarify the form of the technical codes you need to be able to analyse, and consider their likely function in the text.

It will not be relevant or feasible to discuss all of these codes for every text in 45 minutes, but you cannot make an informed decision about which are the most significant codes unless you can select from a wide range of possible codes upon which to reflect.

The list of codes that follows, although comprehensive, is not in any way intended as a definitive list. Some of these codes may be irrelevant to the text you are given; there may be other codes, which are not mentioned here but are useful for considering the unseen text. By researching a range of relevant texts and considering as many of the possible codes as possible, you should gain an understanding of the likely codes and conventions to be employed in the unseen text and be confident that you can deconstruct it appropriately.

Six technical areas:
- Camera techniques framing and angle
- Camera techniques – movement
- Editing
- Manipulating time
- Sound
- Graphics/special effects

FOCUS

- Collect video clips of four examples of game/quiz/chat shows or action/adventure movies from other cultures, as above, and show them to an audience outside your media class (children can be a good audience). Can they identify the genre of the programmes even if they don't understand what is happening?

- What genre elements do they observe? Why do you think this is?

- Are these the same genre elements that you observed? Why is this?

Camera work/Cinematography

The camera is **subjective** when the audience is engaged as a participant (e.g. when the camera is addressed directly or when it imitates the viewpoint or movement of a character). The hand-held cameras on stage during the altercations on the *Jerry Springer* show can be used to show the view of the action being seen by one of the participants.

The **objective** view involves positioning the audience as an observer. For example, the 'privileged point of view' involves watching from omniscient vantage points such as being able to see both the picker and the candidates during a round of *Blind Date*. Keeping the camera still whilst the subject moves towards or away from it is an objective camera effect since the camera seems higher status as it does not move.

Blind Date

The person looking and talking **direct to camera** establishes their authority or 'expert' status with the audience. Only certain people are normally allowed to do this, such as announcers, presenters, newsreaders, weather forecasters and interviewers. Contestants in a game or quiz show, or guests on a chat show are mediated by the host or question master much of the time, and indeed the framing is usually such that they need to look off camera or to the side to address the host or question master. In *Blind Date* for example, Cilla addresses the camera directly at various times, yet the contestants do not. If they are seen addressing the audience it is usually in long shot to maintain that contrast in role. Interestingly, in *The Weakest Link* Anne Robinson is frequently framed with her back to the camera while she is speaking, which helps to sustain the coldness and tension of the text. It is the *mise-en-scène* and editing that maintains her position of authority. Address to camera in this way is rarely seen in film since it breaks the 'fourth wall' convention and controls the tone of the text.

The Weakest Link

85

Camera techniques:

Framing and camera angle

Long shot (LS) – a shot that shows all of a fairly large subject (e.g. a person) and usually much of the surroundings. This is useful to give a perspective and context for a scene, for example a long shot of a robot framed in a laboratory would give a different interpretation of events to a shot of the same robot framed in an old people's home.

Extreme long shot (ELS) – sometimes used as an establishing shot. In this type of shot the camera is at its furthest distance from the subject, emphasising the background and reducing the importance of the subject. For example, the use of an ELS at the beginning of a round in *The Weakest Link* acts as a marker to differentiate the new round and to start the build-up of tension to the end of that round, while also indicating how many contestants are left, how dependent they are on Anne Robinson, who is centre frame and raised above contestants (back to audience), reduces size and thus importance of individuals against the set, and so forth.

Establishing shot (ES) – used at the beginning of a sequence to define the location and to give the audience a perspective on the action to come. At the beginning of *The Weakest Link* we see a shot of the studio, fully lit, with the contestants waiting; this sets the context for the show to follow.

Master shot (MS) – used at the beginning of a sequence as a reference point for the rest of the sequence to follow. It shows the composition and the key relationships between the subjects and enables the audience to contextualise the action before it happens.

Medium long shot (MLS) – in the case of a standing actor, the lower frame line cuts off his feet and ankles.

Mid-shot (MS) – in such a shot the subject and its setting occupy roughly equal areas in the frame. In the case of the standing actor, the lower frame passes through the waist. More body language can be seen as the face, chest and hands are in frame.

Close-up (CU) – a picture that shows a fairly small part of the scene, such as a character's face and neck, in great detail so that it fills the screen. It abstracts the subject from the context. There are also: MCU (medium close-up) – head and shoulders; BCU (big close-up, sometimes referred to as extreme close-up, ECU – forehead to chin.

Close-ups focus on emotions or reactions, and are sometimes used in chat shows to show people in a state of emotional excitement, grief or joy. BCUs are rarely used in quiz or chat shows; MCUs are less intense, the camera maintaining a sense of distance and thus maintaining a sense of dignity for the guest.

Angle of shot – conventionally, in 'factual' programmes, the subjects should be framed at eye-level only. In a high angle the camera looks down, making the viewer feel more powerful than those on screen, or suggesting an air of detachment. A low-angle shot places the camera below the subject, exaggerating his or her importance.

Point-of-view shot (POV) – a shot made from a camera position close to the line of sight of a subject, to imply that the camera is 'looking with their eyes'. This is a very rare device for quiz/game/chat shows, but it can be effective, such as the POV used to imply the viewer is a member of the audience at the beginning of the *Jerry Springer* show, or the POV that shows us Jen's 'defenceless position' as she watches the slaughter of her bodyguards by Dark Cloud in *Crouching Tiger, Hidden Dragon*.

Movement

Zoom – when zooming in the camera does not move; the lens is focused down from a long shot to a close-up whilst recording. The subject grows in the frame, and attention is concentrated on details previously invisible as the shot tightens. It may be used to surprise the viewer. Reverse zoom reveals more of the scene (perhaps where a character is, or to whom he or she is speaking) as the shot widens. Zooming is unusual because of the possible disorientating effects.

Tracking (dollying) – when tracking, the camera itself moves (smoothly) towards or away from the subject while the focus remains constant. Tracking in (like zooming) draws the audience into a closer relationship with the subject; moving away tends to create emotional distance. Tracking back tends to divert attention to the edges of the screen. The speed of tracking may affect the viewer's mood. Fast tracking (especially when tracking in) is exciting; tracking back eases tension. Tracking in can force the audience to focus on something such as the expression of a contestant. During chase sequences the camera will often 'track' with the action to emphasise the sense of speed.

Pan – the camera moves from right to left or left to right to follow a moving subject. A space is left in front of the subject to ensure that the pan 'leads' rather than 'trails'. A pan usually begins and ends with a few seconds of still picture to give greater impact. The speed of a pan across a subject creates a particular mood as well as establishing the viewer's relationship with the subject.

Hand-held camera – a hand-held camera can produce a jerky, bouncy, unsteady image, which may create a sense of immediacy or chaos. The hand-held cameras on the stage during confrontations on the *Jerry Springer* show add to the tension being built with their unsteady images.

Steadicam – the steadicam is a hand-held camera worn as a kind of harness by the (highly skilled) cameraman. It uses a gyroscope system to ensure the camera remains perfectly level and smooth as the cameraman moves. For example, a steadicam was used at the beginning of *Gladiator* to film the battle scenes, so the camera could be within the action to engage the audience more directly.

Editing techniques

Cut – a change of shot from one viewpoint or location to another. This may be done to change the scene, vary the point of view, elide time or lead the audience's thoughts, for example at the opening of *Gladiator* where the CU on a hand trailing through grass in the sunshine cuts to a MCU of Maximus waiting to begin the battle. The audience immediately makes the assumption that the hand and the character are connected.

There is always a justification for a cut, even if it is as obvious as switching between a shot of Cilla Black and a contestant during the introductions on *Blind Date*. Where the 'transition' itself is important it can be highlighted, for example, by using a fade to black to suggest a passing of time or a change of scene.

Reaction shot – any shot (often also a cutaway), in which a subject reacts to a previous shot.

Invisible editing – the vast majority of narrative films are now edited in this way. The cuts are intended to be unobtrusive except for special dramatic shots. It supports rather than dominates the narrative: the plot and the characters are the focus. The technique gives the impression that the edits are motivated by the events in the 'reality' on screen.

Colour Plates

Figure 1

Figure 2

Figure 3

Figure 4

Figure 5

Figure 6

Figure 7

Figure 8

Figure 9

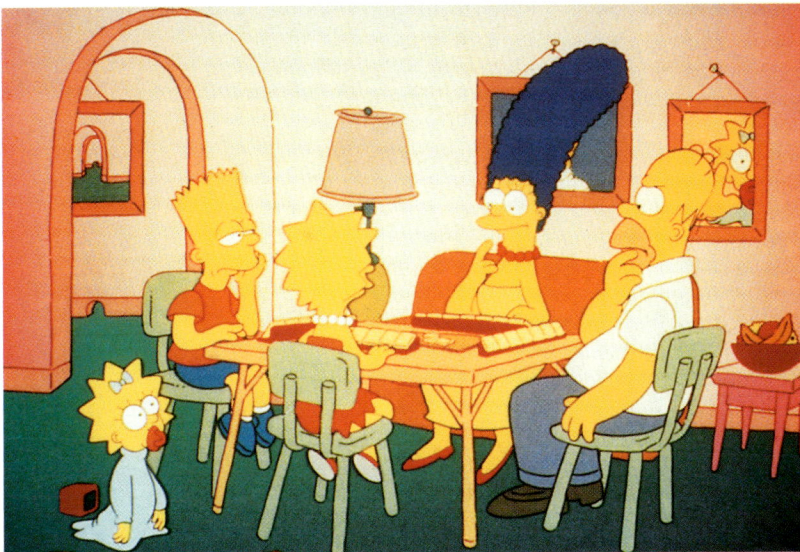

Figure 10

Figure 11

Figure 12

Figure 13

Figure 14

Figure 15

Figure 16

Figure 17

Figure 18

Figure 19

Figure 20

Figure 21

Mise-en-scène – meaning is communicated through the relationship of things visible within a single shot. Composition is therefore extremely important. All features of the background, costume, proxemics, lighting, style of production and framing are significant. For example, it is the *mise-en-scène* of *The Weakest Link* that establishes the aggressive, dark, serious tone of the piece and creates tension. The use of the raised central stage area with rotating podium, dark lighting with backlighting for the contestants, limited colour palette, harsh tones, dull costume and vulnerable positioning of the contestants are all significant.

Setting – can be location or studio, realistic or stylised. Aspects of the setting or props in the text may take on symbolic meanings, such as the red and blue pill in *the Matrix*.

Costume and make-up – these follow on from and develop these concepts. Toward the beginning of *Crouching Tiger, Hidden Dragon*, the elaborate costumes into which Jen is forced serve both to emphasize the importance other family and position (indicating the reason why she should not misbehave), but also to reveal the restrictions and limitations of her world (showing why she feels stifled and longs to break free).

Costumes in *The Matrix* are futuristic and aggressive, with frequent use of sunglasses for effect and impact. This heightens the atmosphere of the film and imparts depth to the characters.

Sound

Music or sound, that belongs 'within the frame' or can be considered to be a natural part of the narrative, is called **diegetic** music. The source of the sound is often, but not always visible on screen. When the sound (usually music) is used without being part of the action (such as the use of a music track behind Graham's comments on *Blind Date* or the music played whenever Neo is pushed between the matrix and reality in *The Matrix*, it is defined as **non-diegetic**.

Music is a key sound code. The type of music used in a text can convey a great deal of information about the mood and tone of the text. Tension can be established, emotions communicated and the music can be used as a comment on the action, to set the context for the next sequence or to provide closure, such as at the beginning and end of a round in a quiz show or the entry of a new guest on a chat show. The music can be very powerful in shaping in the form of the text. The rhythm of music can dictate the rhythm of the cuts, such as the way the drum controls the cuts in the fight sequences in *Crouching Tiger, Hidden Dragon*, or can be used to establish tension in *The Weakest Link*.

Silence can also be used to create tension in the audience. It is almost used in *The Weakest Link* (there is only the faintest hint of a soundtrack while Anne Robinson waits for contestants to answer questions and indeed the text does not use buzzers, bleepers, klaxons or any of the other assorted noises which are frequently used in quiz shows to control the game and indicate correct or incorrect answers, relying on the contrast between Robinson's voice and the pauses and then short answers from the contestants to build up atmosphere (interestingly, there is no visual 'scoreboard' either to sustain this air of mystery).

Voice-Over/Narration where used is important. Graham, on *Blind Date*, who provides the voice-overs during the 'refresher' before the picker makes their choice, has become a iconic figure himself and a signifier for the programme itself, with the way he defines and controls the tone and the action at this point. The commentary can be used to mediate the audience's interpretation of the visuals, particularly if the tone is moderate, assured and reasoned. In films, it may be the voice of one of the characters, unheard by the others providing a counterpoint to the action.

Sound can be used as a **bridge**, to maintain continuity in a sequence by running a soundtrack under a series of images to link them. This can be useful in chase sequences for example to both create tension and to link the parallel stories of chaser and victim. The music in *The Matrix* acts as an underscore in this way on several occasions.

Special Effects and graphics

Titles are central to the opening of a text and may be interspersed at different points during the text to act as information (such as an overlay giving information about time and place) or as markers to define the action (the context information at the beginning of a film – such as at the beginning of *Gladiator*) or to provide visual interest and reflection (such as the revision section in *Blind Date*) or as vital information such as the use of subtitles in *Crouching Tiger, Hidden Dragon*.

The style of text on screen can be deconstructed just as with a print text and choice of font, colour, size and so forth will all be directly related to the text.

Graphics can be used in many ways. Where used, they can be analysed as part of the *mise-en-scene* of a piece and should not detract from the text. Still images can be **superimposed** on each other on screen to create an effect – superimposed images are merged to some degree as opposed to **overlaid** images, which hide whatever is behind them on the screen. **Insets** are a particular type of overlay, used to show the waiting partner backstage who is unaware of events, during the opening of a sequence on the *Jerry Springer* show for example. Dramatic irony can be established this way as the audience is in possession of knowledge, which the guest in the inlay does not have, and thus the audience judges the guest in the light of this information.

CGI (Computer Generated Imagery) is becoming increasingly common in film and television and yet increasingly hard to identify. Whereas with older texts it is easy to identify that two characters in a car apparently driving down a motorway are in fact in a static car in front of a **back projection** of a road it is not so straightforward with more sophisticated techniques and equipment.

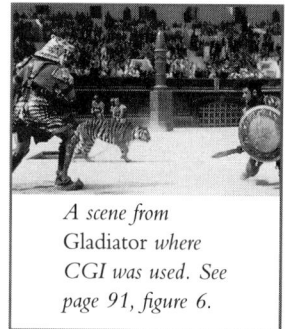

A scene from Gladiator *where CGI was used. See page 91, figure 6.*

Most action/adventure movies make great use of special effects in this way now. Some of Oliver Reed's final scenes in *Gladiator* had to be constructed using CGI, since he died part way through shooting the movie. The Coliseum and the vast vistas of Rome, which comprise much of the impact of the film, are almost all created using CGI.

Action is frequently shot against a '**blue screen**' or a '**green screen**' so that the appropriate background can be constructed using CGI and the two merged to make the scene. The use of the blue screen or green screen means that this simple colour is easy to identify and '**key out**' of the scene using a computer. It is, however, important that actors or presenters do not wear clothes of the same or similar colours or they can seem to disappear off screen.

Talk and Chat shows

Talk and Chat shows have become very popular. They are cheap to make, because the guests come free. In Britain Sky TV runs Oprah Winfrey [who also appears on Channel 5], Geraldo, Jenny Jones and Sally Jessy Raphael; Channel 5 runs Ricki Lake and Gloria Hunniford; Channel 4 has Montel Williams [who also appears on Granada Breeze] and Jerry Springer and Trisha both appear on ITV. The BBC boasts Kilroy and Esther.

Chat shows, for our purposes, range from the gentle celebrity interviews of Parkinson through the more rebellious but still respectful approach of Frank Skinner. Graham Norton remains respectful with guests but can be outrageously controversial with the audience.

ACTIVITIES

Make a list of all contemporary talk and chat shows and identify the audience groupings for the various programmes. Once similar audiences have been identified, the points of similarity between different texts could be identified.

ACTIVITIES

You have been asked to create a new show, to be shown on E4. You should:
- investigate the target audience for this channel
- define the show – format, type of guest, style, set and content
- select a celebrity who could host the show and explain why they would be suitable
- storyboard the title sequence for the show
- present your ideas to the rest of the group and justify your choices.

Game/quiz shows

It is not always easy to differentiate between game shows and quiz shows. Traditionally, the quiz show was seen to be academic with a 'question master' and contestants. Some may be seen to have a severely formal style such as *Mastermind* and *University Challenge* whereas others may be less formal but nonetheless just as combative: shows such as *Fifteen to One*, *The Weakest Link* and *Who Wants to be a Millionaire*. The quiz show is based upon factual knowledge. There are questions to be asked and answers to be given, whether as an individual or as part of a team.

The game show was seen to be a different form of entertainment. Rather than a question and answer, game shows were not 'knowledge based' much was left to chance and the prizes were usually earned by being 'game for a laugh' such as in *The Generation Game*. Initially the 'game' show was indeed that – a game for adults. Yet Japanese game shows for example have not really caught on in Britain, given that the torture and ritual humiliation experienced by the competitors (not contestants) is very different.

There are also celebrity quiz shows whose principal aim is to provide (usually comic) entertainment in which right or wrong answers are mostly irrelevant. They are, however, very popular. This sub-genre seems to be almost the exclusive domain of the BBC with *Never Mind the Buzzcocks* and *Have I Got News For You* on BBC 2; and *A Question of Sport* and *It's Only TV . . . But I Like It* on BBC 1.

ACTIVITIES

1. Record episodes of different game shows from different countries and see if you can identify elements that are culturally dependent and thus unappealing to viewers from other cultures. Is this a form of target audience?
2. Research and explore how a game show is repackaged for different countries. For example, in mainland Europe, *Blind Date* is seen as a more serious game show and contestants are more concerned to develop relationships rather than simply enjoy the dates. However in Australia the emphasis is far more on enjoyment and this affects many aspects of the show.

Once you have found some examples of the show, view one segment from each show and see if you can identify how the show has been mediated by the culture of viewing. Do you find these alternative versions interesting or do you prefer the British version? Why is this?

The premise of a game show is that the focus is on the contestants who are there to win prizes. Yet in fact many game shows are really focused on the host. The contestants are there to provide a structure. A good example of this was *Blankety Blank*, where the 'real life' contestants were clearly less important than the celebrities who were doing the guessing and far less important than the host, whether that was Terry Wogan or Lily Savage. In many game shows, the contestants are shepherded on and off the set by an assistant to the host (usually young, female and glamorous to act as a foil for the usually male host), and always directed through the stages of the game. The host remains centre stage and can move, the contestant is often hidden behind a 'desk' or forced to stand to the side while activity takes place in the centre.

Blind Date is one of the most successful game shows and again, it is the host, Cilla Black who provides the identity and link for the programme in Britain and thus defines the programme. It is seen as bright, brash, cheerful and a little cheeky and this is reflected in the answers given by contestants and the details revealed in the individual holiday reports.

The Generation Game however is more of a conventional game show in that the objective is to win prizes being prepared to suffer a degree of humiliation in the name of entertainment. The true star of the show is Jim Davison and like other hosts of the show he has created his own style and repetitive elements to define the show. There is a far greater reliance on special effects, such as time-lapse skits that are vehicles to display Jim Davison rather than focus on the contestants. The 'experts' who appear on the show are ushered on and off the set quickly and do not get a chance to intervene in the proceedings.

The newest breed of game show exemplified by some (non-studio based) game shows such as *Big Brother* and *Chained* show that the audience is becoming more aggressive in the desire to watch the suffering of others and to expose them on every level.

DISCUSSION

Do you feel that game shows make for good television? Do you like the shows? Why are the two questions different?

One commentator has said, 'Television's glory is the belittlement of people and trivialisation of data, and the game shows are one of the medium's most playfully vicious institutions'. Do you agree?

ACTIVITIES

Make a list of all the quiz and game shows you have seen. Next to each one, write the name of the host. Each host has an image to keep up.

Write down some words to describe each host's image. You may be able to name their distinctive features such as catchphrases, appearance or their brand of humour. These are their trademarks and an important part of their television personality.

How important is this image for the show? Why is this?

However, there is not one archetypal quiz show; the range of types of show varies immensely – from a show such as *Family Fortunes*, seen as downmarket and 'low culture' to an intellectually based show on the other such as *Mastermind* or *University Challenge*. There are no means of generalizing these game-quiz shows and thus categorization of style within the genre is necessary. Shows such as *The Weakest Link*, *Going for Gold*, *Fifteen to One*, *Blockbusters*, *University Challenge* and *Mastermind* submit to far less criticism because the value of prizes is substantially smaller than in blockbuster quizzes such as *Who Wants to be a Millionaire*. However, the treatment is similar – they aim to entertain the audience and maybe educate them. In short, all quiz shows must aspire to combine knowledge and entertainment, this knowledge or skill may subsequently be traded for prizes – whether these prizes are consumer, status, sexual and intellectual reward, they are still the motive force.

DISCUSSION

Given such a wide selection of quiz shows available on the television, discuss the following questions:

Why is there such a demand for this type of entertainment?

Is it the audience's natural quest for knowledge?

Is it their desire to be continually enlightened or is it merely a route of escapism?

Is it competitiveness?

Game and quiz shows frequently trap and trip contestants purely for entertainment. Ridicule can be achieved through many means; probing of sexual habits on *Blind Date* for example; sarcasm by the host on the *Generation Game*; or amusement from the 'losing factor' whereby the viewers indulge in a perverse sense of humour activated by the failings of the contestant as in *The Weakest Link*.

The premise for most quiz shows however is that they are perceived as educational. Whether it is trivial knowledge or specific, high intellectual information, the process is fundamentally linked to the schooling process. Some shows emphasize the relationship more than others, for example, on *The Weakest Link* a Victorian classroom scenario is apparent. Host Anne Robinson (teacher) fires questions at the nine contestants (pupils). Elimination results with failure until the one winner remains. Even the cruel way that she dismisses the losers and the use of the 'post-mortem' are part of the 'school' image presented. The tone of the early editions of *The Weakest Link* has become exaggerated into situation whereby the 'cruelty' is not taken seriously and the contestants play up to Anne Robinson as part of the 'game'.

ACTIVITIES

Watch an episode of a game show and a quiz show and identify at least five key moments in each show where your sympathies change. See if you can analyse how and why you are manipulated by the text at these points.

Identify the pivot point in each section of the text and use 'thought bubbles' to identify the thoughts of the contestants and host at this point. What insights does this give you into the way the text has been filmed?

You have been asked to prepare a proposal for a new studio-based game show, which will be a combination of *Chained* and *The Weakest Link*.

List the factors from each text, which you would borrow. Be prepared to justify your choices

Design the set for the new show and be prepared to justify your choices.

Define (or cast) the host for the new show and be prepared to justify your choices.

Choose a title for this new show, which will reflect its content and scheduling.

Case Study

The Weakest Link

David Young, Head of BBC Light Entertainment pioneered *The Weakest Link*. Its creators, Dr Finton Coyle and Cathy Dunning, sold the BBC the show, which was originally brought in to add more substance to what was seen as a 'soft' daytime schedule. No one guessed that it would become such a gigantic hit for the BBC.

It has a simple format – eight contestants try to bank up to £2500 a round by answering consecutive questions correctly in a series of against-the-clock rounds. Thus, there is a grand (theoretical) total of £10 000 available to the winner. The theory is that the nine contestants must work as a team to bank as much money as possible yet only one will take away anything at the end of the show. At the end of each round, the contestants vote out the player who they believe, rightly or wrongly, contributed the least in money and/or correct answers to that round. This is followed by some very aggressive questioning from Anne Robinson designed to intimidate the contestants and then the loser must make the 'Walk of Shame' into the camera, accompanied by the terse 'You are the weakest link – goodbye'. They are then required to present a post-mortem to camera, in close up, explaining their feelings at this moment and extracting perhaps a moment of revenge by nominating who they hope will be evicted next.

At the end of every round each person votes out which of the other contestants they think is the Weakest Link by writing the names of another contestant on the ovals of metal in front of them. Whilst this is going on, a male voiceover (the voice of authority) tells the audience that 'the statistics show that the strongest link for this round was Simon who got all his questions correct and banked £600. The weakest link was Nigel who not only got all his questions wrong but is beginning to hesitate. Of course only the contestants can decide.'

When the contestants hold up their nominations, Anne Robinson will ask why they picked that person. The answer to this is usually 'because they answered their questions wrongly' so seems an attempt to intimidate rather than a serious question. She will sometimes respond with cutting comments before dismissing the 'weakest link' in a style intended to reflect that of the most sarcastic and bad tempered of teachers.

The set is dark and intimidating and strong lights create texture and harsh and unusual shadows. The blue light behind the contestants much of the time maintains the coldness from Anne Robinson's tone and even the music is harsh and staccato to reinforce the tension. The delivery of the questions to the contestants is aggressive in itself, the use of the central podium for Anne Robinson forces all the contestants to focus on her and makes any friendships between them difficult since they cannot interact with each other very well. Anne Robinson delivers with her back to the camera a lot of the time, which further sustains this coldness, and her costume for the show is black and unstyled to maintain this serious image. With the use of the close up feedback sections and the strain of the walk to camera on dismissal, many aspects of the mise-en-scene add to the tension and power of the show.

The show has been described in terms of a combination of *Fifteen to One* crossed with *Big Brother*. Certainly it would not have been so successful five years ago and yet now the phrase 'You are the weakest link, goodbye' has become a national catch phrase.

Case Study

Blind Date

Each episode of *Blind Date* involves two events. A screen divides three contestants of one gender from a single questioner of the other. In each case, it is the questioner's task to decide which contestant he or she would like to share a date with. After making the decision the questioner first meets the losers and then the winner, as 'the screen goes back.' A week later viewers will see the edited highlights of the date the two have won as they take turns in reporting on its success or otherwise. Sometimes friendships blossom, very rarely marriages, and more often just general dislikes – which is usually the most popular with the audience.

There are many comments, which can be made about the text as it is deconstructed. For example, Cilla frequently patronizes the females but not the men, unless they have 'posh' accents. There is a heavy emphasis on good looks when the questioners cannot see the contestants. To what extent do those appearing on the programme do so to find a date or is their motivation different?

The construct is simple. Cilla Black plays matchmaker to three girls and one guy (and later, three guys and one girl). After introducing us to each of the three girls, each looking for love, we are introduced with the 'lucky fella' who will be going on a date with one of the said three females. These terms are used almost every week to define their roles. Once the questions have been asked, the quick reminder given by 'our Graham', the contestant must choose their date. Having done so, they how see the 'two that you turned down.' Cilla rubs this in, 'and how could you turn down number two, the lovely Claire from Bradford?' But then it is the moment of truth, the screen is taken away and the two get to see each other for the first time. The winning couple get to go on a trip together. The location of the blind date is chosen by one of the people drawing an envelope from those offered to them. There is always a debate about who will 'pick'. Although the show pretends that each of the envelopes offered a different holiday, the choice of dates is pre-selected or effectively rigged, but for good reason – an entire film crew has to go on the dates with the couple, and this takes some significant advance planning.

The other half of the show is finding out how the dates from last week went. This is the funny bit of the show because more often than not it's not so much *Blind Date* but Blind Hate. The documentary tends to show the date as positive (while ensuring plenty of advertising opportunities for companies involved), but it is the section afterwards that is the high spot. The people are filmed talking about their partner retrospectively. This is viewed on the sofa in the studio and whilst one person is talking, the other person's reactions are show in an insert in the corner of the screen. More often than not, this is followed by a disagreement, which is always given closure by Cilla 'Will you be seeing each other again?'

The show is formulaic (as shown by the number of lines which can be quoted every week), bright, brash, loud, simple and very effective. Given that the shows producers take care to construct a text, which appeals directly to the relevant national attitudes to game shows and relationships, is it inevitable that it is so successful? Would it change if Cilla were to change?

ACTIVITIES

Select two sections of no more than four minutes each from *Blind Date* and *The Weakest Link*. Using the skills that you have studied on textual analysis earlier in this chapter, compare and contrast the techniques used in the two shows. Concentrate on what atmosphere the two shows create and how they might have different ways of appealing to their audiences.

Action/Adventure Films

A substantial number of Hollywood films are action/adventure films. The term is often used to define a single genre, since it can often be difficult to differentiate between the two. Films that might be included within this genre include *Raiders of the Lost Ark* and *Romancing the Stone* as well as the James Bond films.

ACTIVITIES

- You are the casting director for a new action/adventure movie that will be similar to *The Terminator*. Draw up a character description for your lead character assuming he will be a conventional hero. Decide who you feel should play this role. Now draw up a character description for the villain and decide who should play this role. Present your decisions to the rest of the group.
- Define at least five conventions for this role (such as 'tall, dark and handsome, wearing sunglasses').
- Justify this choice of conventions to the rest of the group.
- Now describe and cast a non-conventional hero and villain for this movie.
- What are the implications of these changes?
- Is this an easy task?
- Why do you think this is?

Remember that Action/Adventure Films replace Talk/Chat/Game/Quiz shows for the unseen textual analysis for examination in 2003 and 2004

Action/Adventure Films are exciting stories in exotic locations. The plot will be action driven with danger and excitement throughout. The audience may experience conquests, explorations, battles, discovery, creation of empires, and situations that threaten to destroy the main characters. Adventure films historically were intended to appeal mainly to men, creating major heroic stars through the years, such as Arnold Schwarzenegger and Sylvester Stallone. These courageous, patriotic, or altruistic heroes often fought for their beliefs, struggled for freedom or overcame injustice. More modern films have been more balanced with female stars as well. From this came movies such as *Speed* and now *Crouching Tiger, Hidden Dragon* continues the trend. Within the genre can be included the traditional 'swashbucklers' and epics, disaster films, or searches for the unknown. This genre may include stories of historical heroes, kings, battles, rebellion, or piracy.

The action/adventure film first became popular with weekly Saturday *serials*, running in instalments that often had 'cliff-hanging' endings to entice viewers to return for the next show. Heroine Pearl White in *The Perils of Pauline* (1914) was the first major super-star of the serials. Some of these successful B movies, such as Flash Gordon, Buck Rogers and Captain Marvel are still popular today and these early cartoon celluloid transformations defined the early genre.

Steven Spielberg's *Raiders of the Lost Ark* (1981), the first of a very successful trilogy, was a tribute to these early Saturday morning matinees with comic-book archaeology hero Indiana Jones (Harrison Ford) battling the Nazis while searching for the sacred Ark of the Covenant. The adventure-action-romance-comedies *Romancing the Stone* (1984) and its sequel *The Jewel of the Nile* (1985) starring Michael Douglas as the American soldier-of-fortune, and Kathleen Turner as a romance novelist were similarly successful.

The first full-length adventure films were the early swashbucklers from the Hollywood studio machines. These included many 'stock elements' such as lavish sets, costumes and weapons of the past. They were often built upon action scenes of sea battles, castle duels, sword and cutlass fighting, and the rescuing of the female lead. One of the Hollywood's most famous 'swashbucklers' was Errol Flynn who appeared in such films as *Captain Blood* (1935), *The Adventures of Robin Hood* (1938) and *Sea Hawk* (1940). Burt Lancaster, who had been a circus performer, established his reputation by alternating his serious and sensitive dramas with high action acrobatic roles in films such as *The Crimson Pirate* (1952).

Action/adventure Films have tremendous impact, continuous high energy, lots of stunts, possibly extended chase scenes, rescues, battles, fights, escapes, non-stop motion, spectacular rhythm and pacing, and adventurous heroes – all designed for pure audience escapism with the action/adventure sequences at the centre of the film. The cinematography and sound is directly structured to sustain this level of activity throughout. Within the genre these days, there can be said to be many genre-hybrids: sci-fi, thrillers, crime-drama, kung-fu, westerns and war. Always, however, they have a resourceful hero(ine) struggling against incredible odds or an evil villain, and/or trapped in various modes of transportation (bus, ship, train, plane, etc.), with resolution achieved at the end of the movie, after two crisis points along the way. Action/adventure films have traditionally been aimed at male audiences, aged 13 to mid-30s, although modern action/adventure films have featured strong female characters to attract a wider audience.

Among the most well-known and well-defined modern day action/adventure-hero is James Bond. Beginning in the 60s, the slick Bond 'formula' appealed to large audiences with their exotic locations, tongue-in-cheek dialogue, high-tech gadgets, fast-action suspense, impossible stunts and stunning women. The action hero battled unlikely and incredible criminals, usually without even staining his dinner suit.

The action/adventure-film genre has been among the most successful genre in recent years. Raw, indestructible, powerful and muscular heroes of modern, ultra-violent action/adventure films are often very unlike the swashbuckling heroes of the past. Each decade has tended to define its own heroes for the genre and this has defined the style of action/adventure film. Arnold Schwarzenegger made a career out of starring in action films in the 80s and 90s, most notably in the action/adventure films *Conan the Barbarian* (1982), *Commando* (1986), *Raw Deal* (1986), *Predator* (1987), *Red Heat* (1988), and *True Lies* (1994), and also in the hybrid sci-fi/action/adventure films. His more recent films have been less successful – perhaps because he has attempted to move beyond the action/adventure genre?

To analyse the technical codes for the action/adventure genre is essentially the same as to analyse the technical codes for most mainstream Hollywood output. There are stock conventions used in action/adventure films but these should be familiar to you from many films that you have seen. The process of analysing will be more straightforward since you will have a more secure frame of reference than if you were researching a less populist genre.

ACTIVITIES

Select two short sequences of not more than five minutes long. Using the skills that you have studied on textual analysis earlier in this chapter explain how the sequences reflect the codes and conventions of action/adventure movies.

Section 4 Part 2
Comparative Textual Analysis

Aim

The aim of this section is to understand the concepts of **representation, messages and values** using two texts for comparison and in response to one of four set topics. You will be assessed in the form of a written essay and you will compare two selected texts. The specifications state that, 'Candidates need to be prepared to analyse the representation of social groups (including self-representation as appropriate) and messages and be able to describe the relevant kinds of social significance for the chosen topic.'

By now you will have studied the various technical terms and techniques that determine the languages **and conventions** of television chat/talk/quiz/shows.

In this section, the topics we are studying are those set for examination through to 2004. The following three topics are set for 2002–2004

- Consumerism and Lifestyle magazines
- Celebrity and the Tabloid Press
- Minority Interests and Radio.

The fourth topic set for 2002 is
- Social Class and American Cinema

For 2003–2004 this fourth topic changes to:
- Gender and Television Situation Comedy

Getting started

On page 120 are two examples of typical questions that will be set for each topic. But remember that you will not have a choice of questions for each topic in the examination. There will only be one question for each topic.

Consumerism and Lifestyle magazines

- Compare the ways in which the two magazines you have studied reinforce or produce readers' aspirations in their representations of a lifestyle.
- Compare how you two chosen magazines represent a vision of the values and possessions of an ideal lifestyle, in relation to the target audience for the magazines.

The case study below compares the society gossip magazine, *Hello!* and the magazine sold by licensed street-sellers, *The Big Issue*.

Celebrity and the Tabloid Press

- Compare the representation of celebrity in the two tabloids that you have studied.
- Compare the ways in which the visual and written elements of your two chosen newspapers define and represent celebrity.

The case study below compares the *The Mirror*'s coverage of the sacking of Chris Evans and the use of Big Brother with *The Express*' coverage of an interview with Prince Charles.

Minority Interests and Radio

- In a comparison of the two radio programmes you have studied, discuss how they represent the interests of a particular minority and how that minority is defined.
- Compare two examples of the representation of minority interests on radio.

The case study below compares Woman's Hour (Radio 4) and AIROS (American Indian Radio on Satellite).

Social class and American Cinema

- Compare how representations of social class/status are reflected in the themes and subject matter of your two chosen films.
- With detailed reference to two characters, compare the ways in which social class/status is represented in your two chosen films.

Gender in Television Situation Comedy

- Compare how gender is represented in the two sitcoms you have studied.
- With detailed reference to two characters, compare the ways in which gender is represented in your two chosen situation comedies.

This case study below compares *The Flintstones* and *The Simpsons*.

Messages and Values

How do we interpret the **meaning, messages and values** of texts, for example, film images and sounds?

- **Meaning**
  We can do this, firstly, by analysing our own responses, thoughts and emotions to the material in the texts.
  Do we feel sad, angry, exalted, indifferent, excited or happy? Do we want to watch it again?
  How far do we feel convinced that the texts are 'truthful', relevant to us, or meaningful? Are there elements to celebrate and enjoy?
  Do we think that these texts were made for another person, or social group and their interests and values? Do we have a need to reject these texts and disagree with the way they have represented certain elements? Is there a problem with the wrong subject matter or is it more the treatment, the tone or the style of representation?

- **Messages and values**
  Secondly, we may look at the texts' **intended** meaning and analyse how they are constructed to produce **explicit** and **implicit** meanings.

  Explicit: the producer's viewpoint
  We may not know what the author actually thought about the meaning of their texts, although we can often find out from interviews. The point is we can usually tell if we are *meant* to be shocked or amused. For example, in the film *Erin Brockovich* (2000) the main character swears at her boss and the words are meant to shock us for their forthrightness. Later, we are meant to laugh at a joke we know is going to be played on her by the boss winding her up. We can tell that we are *meant* to laugh or cry at certain points of a film by the treatment of elements of the screenplay such as the dialogue, the actors' mannerisms and the music, for example.

Explicit message

Explicitly, a film such as *Erin Brockovich* is about the misuse of power by a large corporation and one individual's campaign to expose the greed behind a large-scale pollution cover-up. The tale of the underdog and the individual against the state is a strong American theme.

Implicit message

The implicit message in the film is that the way women get what they want is to exploit their sexuality. The film overtly emphasises the physical features of Julia Roberts, the actress playing the real life heroine. There is even an explicit acknowledgement of this to the audience when she admits that she gained access to the water board's files by flaunting her 'boobs'. The film is based on a real life person but the Hollywood star is a woman whose commercial selling point has partly been her sexuality. The director had made this screen persona dominate the real personality of the real Erin Brockovich. However, the film's ultimate message is fairly open-ended about the role of independent women in society who have to work and bring up a family at the same time.

Subtext

Does the text have a message about life, morality, society or social groups? Is there any attempt to smuggle in ideas that might be considered taboo or provocative in another culture or period of history? Does the film have anything to say about the attitudes, **messages and values** of contemporary society?

Consider, for instance, the fantasy film *Big* (1988) in which Tom Hanks plays a little boy in a grown up man's body. He is a toy manufacturer and is able to persuade business colleagues to particular courses of action through his practical and boyish enthusiasm. When he invites a women back to his room to play on his bed he really means play as a child's activity, whereas the woman interprets this as meaning something sexual. This tension between innocence and experience is the subtext. The viewer reads this but the characters in the film cannot.

Summary

While we have so far used the example of film as a way of talking about messages and values, the idea of the social context is true for the press, magazines, radio and sitcoms. In analysing the texts you should consider social themes in terms of:

- Gender
- Sexuality
- Race
- Age
- Class
- Disability
- Belief system

Preparation

Once you have selected which topic/medium you are going to study you should be provided with two specific examples of texts and then you will compare them in terms of similarity and/or difference. This entails you having a full and detailed knowledge of these texts, and being able to provide a close detailed analysis of key elements and contexts, audiences and production.

TOPIC ONE

Consumer and Lifestyle magazines

Aims

In this section you will be studying the phenomenon of consumer and lifestyle magazines, what they tend to portray, and how they relate to the real aspirations and concerns of their readership. You will be **comparing** the advertisements in the magazines, *Hello!* and *OK!* and contrasting the treatment of the style and content of *Hello!* with *The Big Issue*.

Through **content, textual and contextual analysis** you will begin to understand the role of commercial audience profiling, research and targeting for demographic and advertising purposes. At the same time, you will develop the analytical skills to interpret the typical forms and conventions, representational meanings and the editorial values of the case studies selected.

Objectives

As with the other topics in Unit 2732 the main objective is **to develop the textual analysis skills to compare two texts in terms of what they represent**. It is advisable, therefore, to select two texts that offer the richest areas of **contrast** and **difference** for comparison.

You will need to consider what the magazine assumes about its reader's tastes and consumption patterns, lifestyle aspirations, idealised and actual attainments and material wealth. You may wish to select two titles from different categories such as one women's and one man's lifestyle magazine or you may wish to take two magazines that are separated, for instance, by class. For example, you could compare the high society fashion magazine *Harpers and Queen* with *Prima*, targeted at the lower end, 'tea-break' market, age 25 and over. *Prima* mixes 'home help, true life stories and exclusive celebrity interviews'. Both *Harpers and Queen* and *Prima* are owned by National Magazines that took over Gruner and Jahr (G+J) in July 2000.

Youth Audience

Research the layout of the magazine racks and the position of magazines in a large newsagents like WH Smiths, or a supermarket:

1. How many different types of magazine are available for the 14–18-year-olds?
2. How does the figure for this age group break down into male and female numbers?
3. Are any magazines unisex?
4. From observing the layout and display of all the shop's magazines identify which type of magazines take up the most space? Draw a plan to explain where the different groupings of magazine are placed e.g. are all the in-house WH Smith titles nearest the queue for the tills? Which magazines are the most prominent and accessible?

Mode of address

The mode of address is the manner, tone and attitude of speaking to the reader. Usually in teenagers' magazines the voice is meant to be friendly, in a big sister or brotherly way. This is very different from the authority tone as if they were a news presenter. In the case of *Hello!* the mode of address is created by the captions and the visual voyeurism – here you are, a privileged glimpse of the stars showing off at their house or their parties. You are the outsider, if you are not rich and famous, or you are the centre of attention, forever smiling, if you are one of the subjects.

'baby glossies'

New arrivals on the scene are the 'baby glossies': *ElleGirl* (EMAP) and *CosmoGirl* (Natmags) prove that the market believes there is more disposable income to be spent. The National Magazines Company's research shows that 94% of teenagers buy a magazine every month. More spare cash is available according to Datamonitor because of three trends: the average age of parenthood has gone up, there are more dual-income families, and parents have less time on their hands – and therefore more guilt. The average teenage girl spends £64 a month on fashion and beauty (according to NatMags).

In the context of a decline in sales of women's magazine the teenage pound is a new possible earner. But success depends on whether the advertisers think it is worth supporting as well as the potential purchasers of the product.

In terms of advertising fashion *Elle* would be favourable with respect to fashion designers such as Ralph Lauren and the cross over from teen to adult is blurred at the moment.

Advertising

Unlike newspapers, magazines aim to make a profit through a mixture of cover price and advertising. 66% of business magazines are given free to people who match the publisher's criteria. In this case, revenue comes mostly through advertising. Approximately 78% of revenue comes from display advertising. Magazines have a ready-made pre-defined target audience, so they provide an effective point of contact for advertisers and their target audiences. This usually means that advertisers will attempt to research, identify or simply 'guess' the type of lifestyles associated with that magazine's profile which is outlined in press packs and in data directories such as BRAD (British Rate and Data).

If the audience is aged 13–17 and are fun-living pop music lovers and buy *Smash Hits* it might be assumed they would buy a CD or a poster of a famous band. However, only market research would confirm if they had the disposable income to buy any more music or pop culture related goods. For example, the opening edition of *Hotdog*, the recently started (2000) film magazine, was littered with advertisements for DVD players. However, there is likely to be a good percentage of that readership who are not high income earners i.e. under twenty so will not be buying expensive consumer goods. Sometimes, advertisers use a splatter gun approach in order to catch everyone but some of those reached may be unable to immediately purchase the goods.

Audience profiles

When *Red* came on the market in November 1997 it described itself almost entirely as a lifestyle magazine, for women who had 'grown out of *Elle* and *Marie Claire* but are not quite ready for *Good Housekeeping*'. *Red* is meant to be 'exciting, slightly dangerous and its attitude, challenging and of this age. Red Woman is confident, self-assured. She may be a career woman, she may be married, she may have children – but they don't define her'. Ian Monk EMAP public relations, (cited in *Media Guardian*, Monday November 3rd 1997). 'She is from 'middle youth'. If you are the kind of woman who wants the best rather than the latest, who knows that diets don't work, who rents *Toy Story* as well as *Trainspotting* who will only go to the pub when she knows there will be a seat ... then *Red* is for you.'

'Middle youth' is supposed to define those women in the age group 25-35. They 'read cookery books in bed, realise diets don't work and fancy Ewan McGregor (star of *Trainspotting* and *The Phantom Menace*) and Jeremy Paxman (Current Affairs news journalist) at the same time.' The magazine contains the usual features on fashion, shopping, health, beauty and stars, and the fashion models are slightly older than most of the women in many of the glossies. Other magazines in, or overlapping with, this bracket might include *Cosmopolitan* and *Marie Claire*.

'Defining Moments of a Red woman' (according to press pack, 1997):

- You buy pressed olive oil instead of Mazola.
- What suits you is more important than what's in.
- You own more than four sets of bedlinen.
- You only go down to the pub if you can sit down alone.
- You know diets don't work.
- You spend so much money on a haircut you have to lie to your partner.
- You celebrate your birthday on a holiday with a weekend in the country rather than a night out.
- You spend money on a holiday where you don't get a tan.
- You know polenta isn't a make of car.
- Your are fussy about the coffee you drink.
- You video *Home Front* (diy programme).
- You rent *Toy Story* and *Trainspotting*.

ACTIVITIES

Identify products and advertising brand names you think suit the Red woman profile for the following items. Discuss with partner and share your ideas with the rest of the class.
a) A video
b) Coffee
c) Holiday
d) Cooking/food

A C T I V I T I E S

Content analysis

Select two different magazines from within one category, preferably ones you have never looked at yourself before:

Gender eg women's (eg *Bella*, *Vogue*), men's (any computer/console magazine),

Age eg *Saga* (over 50s*), Red* (mid 20s to mid-30s), *J-17* (14–17),

BBC Children's *Toybox* (2–5)

Specialist eg Music, Film, Gardening etc

Lifestyle eg *Homes and Gardens*, *The Lady*, *Country Life*, *The Oldie*, *Motor*, *Caravan Monthly*, *Woman's Realm*

1. How many advertisements are there, in each of the publications?
   - Make notes on each advertisement and specify the fraction of page taken up. ¼ page, ½ page or full page.
   - How many pages does the product advertising take up?
   - How many pages do features take up?
   - How many pages do the listings inserts for TV and Radio etc take up?
   - How many pages do the Small ads take up?
2. What types of advertisements are there, eg perfume, charity appeal, computer game, furniture etc? How many of each type are there?
3. Create a block or pie chart to illustrate proportions of advertisements to other content.
4. How much space (pages) is devoted to:
- the editorial
- letters pages
- full page articles?

Aspirations

An aspiration is a desire for something better. In the service-led western world this is very much focused on material goods – better clothes, houses, cars etc. In other cultures where spiritual betterment is prioritised, how much you have is less important than how you can achieve spiritual purity such as in a Buddhist belief system. In a market economy culture like the UK's it is considered part of society's shared values to produce and to consume more material goods and wealth.

The recent growth in television make-over programmes such as *Changing Rooms* and *Home Front*, is substantial. So much so that there are now presenters who are celebrities in their own right with books and TV spin offs built around their popularity. There is an increase in the number of television programmes about looking after the body, with whole digital channels dedicated to diet and general health.

Consumerism

Critics of consumerism argue that we live in a world where some people have no basic health, house or education. Therefore, it is argued, to accumulate more wealth and material possession than is necessary is excessive and morally unfair when so many people within our own society are homeless. If we compare the glamorous looks and appearances of men and women in glossy magazines with the look and appearance of starving children and adults in our newspapers and news bulletins, what can we say about the values of our society? Or is this simply a question of accepting the *status quo*?

Consumerism might be viewed as an excessive value when buying becomes more of a compulsion than a necessity, a question of vanity rather than sanity. If you have enough shoes why do you need a second or third pair of trainers? Magazines, with their extensive use of advertisements to support their financing are one of the main places where goods and services are promoted. Not only are you introduced to the perfume or the DVD itself but there are images associated with the products to entice you into the idea of potential ownership and enviable social status: for example, more wealthy-looking, sexier, more cool. The commonest value in advertisement messages is 'If you have one of these you will be in with the in-crowd, or, you will feel much better with it.'

Audience Definitions

It may seem an obvious statement to make, but a definition of an audience depends on who is defining it. It may be reliant upon:

- industry: circulation and readership figures and target readership; constructed audience
- government: demographics
- advertisers: segmentations – lifestyle and aspirations
- social scientists: values; passive/active; uses and gratifications; identity; effects

Market researchers love to find new categories to entice advertisers and magazines to target. Does an individual who has no partner and is over

40 have spare cash? If so, what type of interests do they have? What would they spend their money on if they were offered the right product or service? Do they go abroad more than once a year? Do they always use the same airline? etc.

Segmentation

Advertisers use their own categories of people in addition to the categories of demographic groups. These groupings can vary enormously but one model is the one that divides people into seven segments:

1 succeeders 2 aspirers 3 carers 4 achievers 5 radicals 6 traditionals 7 underachievers

These descriptions are meant to provide information about people's attitudes and psychological character. By splitting people into these groups advertisers attempt to estimate whether their audiences are likely to spend money on their products or not. For example, if it is known that a family spends a great deal on holidays every year it will be worth a company trying to target them to sell them holidays. One way they can do this is to research which type of magazine they are likely to buy.

Social values

Another way of defining the audience has come from social scientists who want to provide information to their clients, who are usually commercial clients wanting to target their products in media entertainment to sell. As well as the class labels, there are also attitudes to consider. Five attitudes are:

1. Traditionalist – keep things the way they are
2. Materialist – have something now, pay later
3. Hedonist – to play, or enjoy life now
4. Post materialist – to be something later
5. Post modernist – to have, to be, and to play.

Current trends

Mintel, an industrial business and market research agency, has recently identified some trends:

- The highest number of circulation magazines tend to be entertainment, women and teenager's magazines.
- There has been a slight decline in the newly buoyant men's and computer magazine markets, though they are still performing strongly in some cases.
- Massive growth in the customer magazine market is now up to 10% of the market ie the house magazines produced for companies such as Sainsbury, Waitrose, Marks & Spencer.
- There is a growth in aspirational in-house lifestyle magazines, for example, for WH Smith – *Buying a New Home, Fit and Healthy, Improving Your Career and Getting Married* BBC – *BBC Top Gear, BBC Good Food, BBC Gardener's World.*
- Customer magazines have now risen to a target audience of a billion consumers: in 1999 they earned £197 million and by 2000 they had brought in £227 million.
- The dramatic drop in advertising revenue during the period January 2001 and June 2001 has been, in part, due to the decline in confidence about new technologies and e-commerce. Many new technology related advertisements have been withdrawn and several magazines, some long-established like Melody Maker, have also been closed due to lack of advertising money to support them.

Source: MINTEL – *www.sinatra2.mintel/reports* June 10th 2001

This information is itself a product and while summaries are free, for more detail they would need to be bought (for several hundred pounds).

ACTIVITIES

Consider the unique selling point of the magazines you have selected. Analyse
- the images and words on the cover and
- the editorial
- letters page.

Make sure you cover the following concepts:
- messages and values
- forms and conventions
- layout and design

A typical cover of a glossy mainstream leisure, lifestyle magazine shows what is inside and doesn't tend to include any articles on the front. It includes

- Pugs
- Issue number
- Masthead
- Cover price
- Main cover line
- Straplines
- Feature article photographs
- Main cover lines – 'sell-lines'
- Puffs
- Typeface
- Point sizes
- Bar code

Forms and conventions: typical elements

All magazines have some elements in common, even if they are a listings magazine or a simple advertising vehicle. Common elements are:

- Advertising
- Advice columns
- Book adaptations
- Campaigns
- Competitions
- Contents page
- Covers
- Diaries
- Do it yourself features
- Fiction
- Horoscopes
- In our next issue
- Letters page
- Make-overs
- Merchandising
- Opinion columns
- Quizzes
- Reviews
- Strips (comic)
- Supplements
- Surveys

ACTIVITIES

Select two magazines and check how many of the above list there are in the magazines. Are there any different elements? What reasons do you think there are for these differences?

■ ■

A C T I V I T I E S

Compare the covers and content list of two consumer or lifestyle magazines:
What are the main elements of the cover lines?
How do they define the age of their audience?
Denotate and connote the images and printed text on the front cover.
What is the difference between the two magazines?

Case Study

Case Study denotation and connotation

Activity   Compare the front covers of Hello! and The Big Issue.

1. What images of masculinity are presented on each?
2. What are the messages and values of the two magazines?

Hello! April 24th 2001

The cover of *Hello!* (edition Number 269 April 24, 2001), is a good example of a general lifestyle magazine. It is a European-wide concept which fills many of the pages with pictures of the rich and famous at parties and gatherings, as well as organising photo-shoots of famous people in their homes with their families, with a change of clothing for different settings, offering a chance to show off a variety of costumes and furnishings.

It is unusual in not having an editorial or a letters' page. The messages and values of the magazine are loaded in the images and the weaving of star photographs between advertisements and features.

It has simple and clear cover lines telling the consumer exactly what the main feature articles and inside contents are. The main cover puff is 'World exclusive pictures' situated in the middle of the banner head where the magazine's name is. 'Brooke Shields Weds in Secret' is the second puff and this emphasises the exclusivity of the scoop.

In the main picture that occupies two thirds of the front cover is Hugh Grant with no shirt and leather trousers, smiling and looking directly at the camera more or less on the level with the camera. He is kneeling and leaning across the picture as though about to lie down on his brown skin jacket. He is actually adopting a common female model pose which is partly feline and partly come hither. The background is white and bare of any connotative objects or colours. He is evenly lit and the skin colours are warm in contrast with the shiny black trousers. His hair is typically stylishly tousled and his hairless chest makes him youthful and boyish, combined with his impish grin. The headline HUGH GRANT (in black capital letters) OPENS HIS HEART ABOUT THE BREAK UP WITH LIZ HURLEY is placed behind him to the top right.

The masthead is in white lettering on a red block. The two other pictures on the front left are of the famous American actress and activist, Jane Fonda and on the bottom right are Prince Charles and Camilla Parker-Bowles.

Both these pictures are in close up. The name of the magazine is imprinted at the base line of the page under the two cover lines about Prince Charles, Camilla Parker-Bowles and Jane Fonda. All three celebrities share the history of traumatic break ups with their partners. All appear to be happier now despite their break ups.

Formally, the graphic letter design and the art work layout is very plain – there is little attempt to layer the images or the graphics so that there is a one dimensional effect to the layout. Everything is parcelled into boxes with the central panel containing the 'star'. The message of this effect seems to be that you get what you see – in more documentary mode more than fictional. But the clothes and furnishings are clearly fanciful and out of context.

The outline of the lettering and their names are in white on red background. The contents list on page 35 is the only clue to what else is in the magazine. It is deliberately designed to make you look through the whole magazine, and there is unconventionally no editorial page or reader's letters.

Inside cover contents list

The 'Seven Days' TV & Radio guide 54 page insert, TV Film Guide, includes: various features on television programmes, interviews with TV stars; film previews, events and book reviews, travel, music and theatre reviews, spring fever accessories property, interior home style, health page, TV and soap roundup pages.

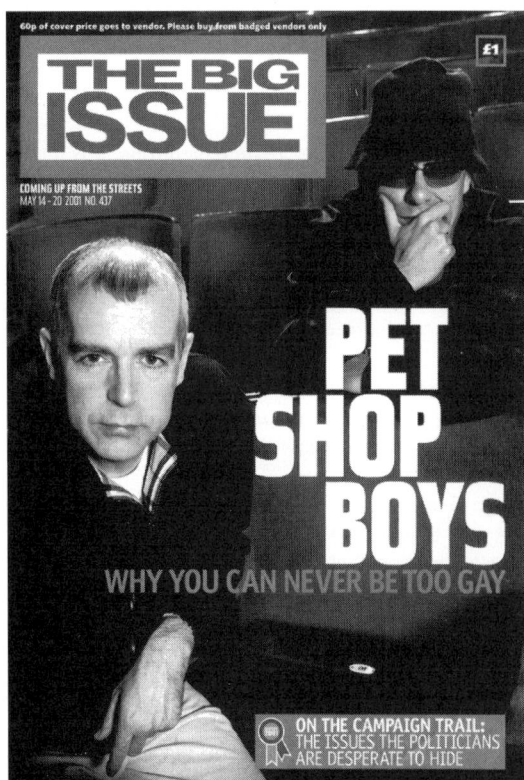

Front cover of The Big Issue *May 14–20, 2001.*

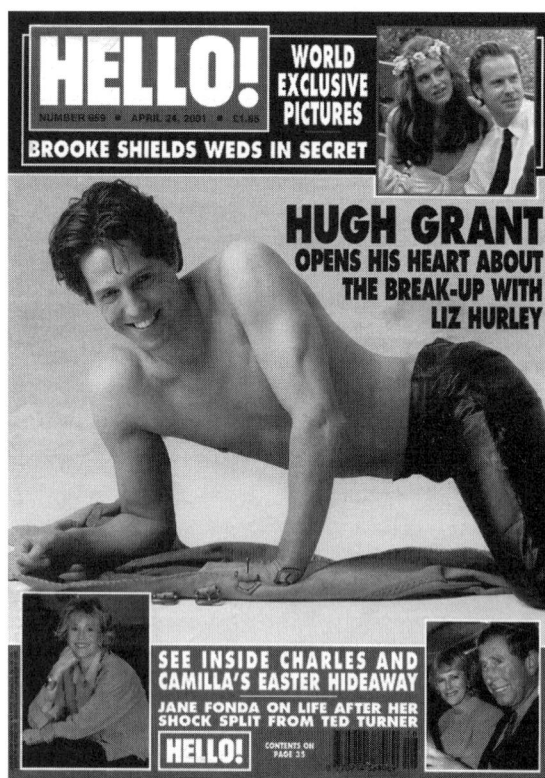

Front cover of Hello! *edition Number 269 April 24, 2001.*

Case Study

The Big Issue May 14th–20th 2001

The front cover of *The Big Issue* does have famous people on it, although it is just as likely to feature ordinary people. The puff is 'coming up from the streets' and the political nature of the magazine is made even more obvious by the statement above the masthead '60p of cover price goes to vendor. Please buy from badged vendors only.' In this sense the image of the magazine has been preceded by its position as the street as the point of purchase, thus giving it a uniqueness akin to *Metro,* a London newspaper available on the Underground. The masthead of the *Big Issue* is carefully weighted to emphasise the ISSUE and the sans serif font is unfussy and clear. The sell lines are kept to a minimum, presumably because its readership knows more or less what types of story are in it.

On this cover, two men sit facing the camera, they are sitting in the aisles of a cinema or stage auditorium, one is wearing a rain hat and sunglasses and is holding one hand near to his mouth in a pensive anonymous mood. The other man has an open necked shirt with vest – he is balding and is smiling his hand is hanging casually down – we see him from the knee up. The lighting is minimal and there is no attempt to glamourise them through overbright lights or lavish fashion statements. In fact, they are almost too understated but the ordinariness of the image they convey allows them the anonymity they prefer and talk about in the feature inside.

The headline is: PET SHOP BOYS: Why you can never be too gay. The effect is to confirm a widely known fact that the duo who are famous for their music are in fact gay. This gives the *Big Issue* a sense of an exclusive, as they wish to talk more fully about being gay to this newspaper for which there will be a more sympathetic audience.

There is one more sell line which is 'On the Campaign Trail', so there is no big extravagant sensation picture or story to illustrate the drama of an election.

A C T I V I T I E S

Which magazines do you or your family purchase?

Are there any magazines which everybody reads? Are there magazines which only one person reads? Construct a survey of ten people in a particular group, for example: Girls or boys aged 11–14 or girls or boys aged 14–19

Find out what magazines they like and why.

Is there a common response? Are there any big differences of response?

ACTIVITIES

Study a range of magazines targeted at teenagers 11–19 and young adults 15–24.

Discuss the range and variety of interest in the contents for the audience of each magazine:
- front cover (images, headings, puffs, straplines, and price)
- the contents page
- the advertisements.

Eg: Female: *More, Sugar, 19, Looks, Clothes Show, Mizz, J17, Smash Hits, TV Hits, Big. TOTP, Live and Kicking, Marie Claire, Cosmopolitan, Red, Black Woman, Woman's Journal.* Male: *WWF, Hip-Hop, Jockey Slut, Select, NME, Melody Maker, Face,* Loaded, *Maxim, FHM, Men's Health, Playstation titles.*

Most leading magazine titles are owned by a small number of companies. In the consumer sector IPC Magazines is the largest publisher. Reed Business publishing is the leading Business publisher. Both companies are owned by Reed-Elsevier. Other major companies include BBC Magazines, Conde Nast, D.C. Thompson, EMAP, G&J of the UK, H. Bauer, The National Magazine Company and Reader's Digest. HarperCollins is owned by News Corp which is the same company that owns the film company, 20th Century Fox, as well as the newspapers, *The Times* and *The Sun*.

TOPIC TWO

Celebrity and the Tabloid Press

Aims

In this section, you will be focusing on the representation of celebrities in the tabloid press.

Through content, textual and contextual analysis you will explore news values and the ideological construction of the individual as hero/heroine or villain in our society. Through analysis of the representation of celebrity in the press you will study how personality and commercialisation are valued over social issues and informed democratic debate and public accountability.

Objective

The main objective is to develop the textual and contextual skills to compare two texts in terms of what they represent about celebrity.

ACTIVITIES

Name two famous females and two males who are often in the news.
Identify what profession or background they have:
e.g. sports, television, film, music, royal family/gentry, government/MP.
Look at the ways that they have been represented in the press, both positively and negatively.

Who is a celebrity?

Three separate stages have been identified in the 'life-cycle of a celebrity'. Firstly, there is the climb to fame. Then, often a negative personal event occurs, for example, divorce or alcoholism, and the fame turns to notoriety. This can enhance their reputation, or ruin them. Finally, if they do return to the limelight they have to renew their image. Vanessa Feltz had to resign from her television show talk show when it was discovered that some of the audience participating were actually actors.

She made a comeback by losing a great deal of weight and became a TV presenter and commentator on various shows.

In recent years, three factors have emerged in relation to celebrities since the 1950s. First, there are far more Public Relations companies, agents and spin doctors who manage a celebrity's profile, find them work and present their image to the media. Max Clifford is a famous agent in his own right and he has made a name for himself defending the underdog and the publicly rejected. Several extra-marital lovers of various government ministers have benefited from his 'help'. In search of exclusive scandals some newspapers 'trap' celebrities into revealing their weakness for money, drugs, sex, gambling etc. They are recorded with bugging devices admitting, in private, their crime, vice or misdemeanour.

Secondly, there are many more media outlets for celebrities to create a cross-over campaign of product branding (star image) that expands media awareness. Television, poster, film, magazine, billboards and radio offer different opportunities for saturation of publicity outlets.

Thirdly, the old elite, the Royal family and the aristocracy have been replaced by sporting, music and television celebrities; so much so that since the death of Princess Diana, David and Victoria Beckham have been dubbed the new 'royals': stories about them cover their every movement and action: including driving offences, tattoos, haircuts, their son's £10,000 first birthday party, exclusive *OK!* wedding photos, Posh's diet and clothes, Beckham's sarong, his contract with Police sunglasses etc.

In addition, there is now the possibility that everyone can achieve what Andy Warhol, the 60s pop artist, prophesised, 'everyone will have their fifteen minutes of fame'. The 'characters' who entered the Channel 4 Big Brother House and lived together became national celebrities. The ordinary person who becomes famous through documentaries, endlessly failing their driving test, or dealing smartly with airport customers are often given national coverage in the tabloid press. This is usually for the mutual benefit of the newspapers and the programme makers circulation and audience figures.

Ironically, *The Sun* wrote a sharp criticism of the first *Big Brother* contestants after the show had ended because it was felt that they had all been grasping for media attention in order to make a living:

SADA, ANNA, MEL, TOM, ANDY, NICHOLA, NICK, CRAIG, CAROLINE, DARREN AND CLAIRE … please leave our lives immediately. Your fifteen minutes of fame are well and truly up.

You are not celebrities, you just happened to be part of a TV freak show that is now over. You are spoiling the memory of *Big Brother*. Go home and go back to your jobs. We don't care about you anymore.

Editorial, *The Sun*, October 8, 2000

Myths

The presence of a real princess in the UK is part of what sustained the fascination with Princess Diana, at home and abroad. When the relationship with Prince Charles was breaking down media attention intensified and the fairytale turned into a soap opera. The archetypal stories about princes and princesses which all children grow up with are also relevant to the creation of the public sharing of the royal family's 'story'. When, effectively, the fairytale story was tragically ended, many public emotions were focused on the funeral. It was a massive national media event. In the months that followed print and broadcast media were criticised for creating a sense of national hysteria.

Public figureheads such as the royal family or the prime minister are seen to represent moral standards of behaviour. Whereas, musicians, actors, sporting and television celebrities tend to represent models of attractiveness, beauty or aspects of professional skill. They are identified with, admired, reviled, worshipped or attacked for their good or bad looks, age or attitudes.

Ordinary people can become celebrated for sporting achievements or in some cases for total failure. Eddie the Eagle, Great Britain's failed Olympic ski-jumper had several months notoriety for being so hopeless.

1. Look through any edition of a tabloid newspaper. How many celebrities/elite persons can you identify?
2. How many pages are devoted to stories about celebrities? What percentage is this of the total number of pages?
3. Categorise the celebrities into groups: sports, television, film, royal family, motor racing, government/MP, other.

Which group has the greatest proportion of stories?

Contextual analysis

Newspaper competition

The decline in newspaper readership since the 1970s has been matched by a rise in television viewing, increased interest in magazines and the recent arrival of new technologies such as Walkmans, mobile phones computer games and the Internet. With changing leisure patterns and more diverse forms of entertainment newspapers have fought a very competitive battle with each other and with other media to hold onto their readerships. This has led to changes in newspaper format, content and style, audience and ownership. It has also led to the increased reliance on celebrities and the audience's love of the characters in soaps, or musicians. Thus a famous person more often than not adorns the front of newspapers, so they can draw people in. The rise and fall and re-emergence of Princess Diana before she died, some argue, effectively sustained the newspaper industry throughout the 80s and 90s.

Format

Most tabloids are A3 size. *The Sun*, *The Star* and *The Mirror* have large mastheads that use red as the dominant colour. This is the reason that they are sometimes referred to as 'red tops'. They use large typeface for their headings and straplines. A photograph usually dominates the space and copy is kept to a minimum on the front page.

Content

The content of tabloid newspapers usually contains most of the following:
Special offers
In-depth features
Supplements
Pages of letters
Gossip columns
Sports
Television and radio listings
Crosswords, horoscopes and cartoons

Sales Boosting Tactics

In the last twenty years all newspapers have tried to increase sales of newspapers. Many strategies have been employed, including savage price cutting wars, but one of the more successful has been by extending coverage of the lives of celebrities. The broadsheets have also been accused of 'dumbing down' their content and both tabloid and broadsheet have tried to mix news about politics with more lifestyle and human interest features.

Ethics

Press Complaints Commission

There has been a great deal of debate as to whether the media focus on the lives of public people has been unhealthy, especially in prying into the private aspects of their relationships.

Is it simply that news editors are satisfying the public's basic instinct to gossip about the lives of the rich and famous? Should there be rules governing press intrusion and harassment of individuals going about their private business? What rights should be given to people who make their money and status from being famous, to restrict journalists from reporting their activities, especially in public spaces such as restaurants and beaches?

The Press Complaints Commission is a self-regulating body that is designed to advise on whether the industry is conducting itself fairly. There is a code of conduct that is not legally binding. Recent cases concerning the names of children under 16 (not permitted) and the use of long lens photography (intrusion) has highlighted how newspapers are keen to provide any extra images of celebrities private to sustain a story about them.

All members of the press have a duty to maintain the highest professional and ethical standards. This Code sets the benchmarks for those standards. It both protects the rights of the individual and upholds the public's right to know.

The Code is the cornerstone of the system of self-regulation to which the industry has made a binding commitment. Editors and publishers must ensure that the Code is observed rigorously not only by their staff but also by anyone who contributes to their publications.

1. Accuracy

(i) Newspapers and periodicals must take care not to publish inaccurate, misleading or distorted material including pictures.

(ii) Whenever it is recognised that a significant inaccuracy, misleading statement or distorted report has been published, it must be corrected promptly and with due prominence.

(iii) An apology must be published whenever appropriate.

(iv) Newspapers, whilst free to be partisan, must distinguish clearly between comment, conjecture and fact.

(v) A newspaper or periodical must report fairly and accurately the outcome of an action for defamation to which it has been a party.

2. Opportunity to reply

A fair opportunity to reply to in-accuracies must be given to individuals or organisations when reasonably called for.

★3. Privacy

(i) Everyone is entitled to respect for his or her private and family life, home, health and correspondence. A publication will be expected to justify intrusions into any individual's private life without consent.

(ii) The use of longlens photography to take pictures of people in private places without their consent is unacceptable.

Note – Private places are public or private property where there is a reasonable expectation of privacy.

★4. Harassment

(i) Journalists and photographers must neither obtain nor seek to obtain information or pictures through intimidation, harassment or persistent pursuit.

(ii) They must not photograph individuals in private places (as defined in the note to Clause 3) without their consent; must not persist in telephoning, questioning, pursuing or photographing individuals after having been asked to desist; must not remain on their property after having been asked to leave and must not follow them.

(iii) Editors must ensure that those working for them comply with these requirements and must not publish material from other sources which does not meet these requirements.

5. Intrusion into grief or shock

In cases involving grief or shock, enquiries must be carried out and approaches made with sympathy and discretion. Publication must be handled sensitively at such times, but this should not be interpreted as restricting the right to report judicial proceedings.

★6. Children

(i) Young people should be free to complete their time at school without unnecessary intrusion.

(ii) Journalists must not interview or photograph children under the age of 16 on subjects involving the welfare of the child or of any other child, in the absence of or without the consent of a parent or other adult who is responsible for the children.

(iii) Pupils must not be approached or photographed while at school without the permission of the school authorities.

(iv) There must be no payment to minors for material involving the welfare of children nor payment to parents or guardians for material about their children or wards unless it is demonstrably in the child's interest.

(v) Where material about the private life of a child is published, there must be justification for publication other than the fame, notoriety or position of his or her parents or guardian.

7. Children in sex cases

1. The press must not, even where the law does not prohibit it, identify children under the age of 16 who are involved in cases concerning sexual offences, whether as victims, or as witnesses.

2. In any press report of a case involving a sexual offence against a child –

(i) The child must not be identified.

(ii) The adult may be identified.

(iii) The word "incest" must not be used where a child victim might be identified.

(iv) Care must be taken that nothing in the report implies the relationship between the accused and the child.

★8. Listening devices

Journalists must not obtain or publish material obtained by using clandestine listening devices or by intercepting private telephone conversations.

★9. Hospitals

(i) Journalists or photographers making enquiries at hospitals or similar institutions must identify themselves to a responsible executive and obtain permission before entering non-public areas.

(ii) The restrictions on intruding into privacy are particularly relevant to enquiries about individuals in hospitals or similar institutions.

★10. Innocent relatives and friends

The press must avoid identifying relatives or friends of persons convicted or accused of crime without their consent.

★11. Misrepresentation

(i) Journalists must not generally obtain or seek to obtain information or pictures through misrepresentation or subterfuge.

THE PUBLIC INTEREST

There may be exceptions to the clauses marked ★ where they can be demonstrated to be in the public interest.

1. The public interest includes:

(i) Detecting or exposing crime or a serious misdemeanour.

(ii) Protecting public health and safety.

(iii) Preventing the public from being misled by some statement or action of an individual or organisation.

2. In any case where the public interest is invoked, the Press Complaints Commission will require a full explanation by the editor demonstrating how the public interest was served.

3. In cases involving children editors must demonstrate an exceptional public interest to over-ride the normally paramount interests of the child.

It is essential to the workings of an agreed code that it be honoured not only to the letter but in the full spirit. The Code should not be interpreted so narrowly as to compromise its commitment to respect the rights of the individual, nor so broadly that it prevents publication in the public interest. It is the responsibility of editors to co-operate with the P.C.C. as swiftly as possible in the resolution of complaints.

Any publication which is criticised by the P.C.C. under one of the following clauses must print the adjudication which follows in full and with due prominence.

(ii) Documents or photographs should be removed only with the consent of the owner.

(iii) Subterfuge can be justified only in the public interest and only when material cannot be obtained by any other means.

12. Victims of sexual assault

The press must not identify victims of sexual assault or publish material likely to contribute to such identification unless there is adequate justification and, by law, they are free to do so.

13. Discrimination

(i) The press must avoid prejudicial or pejorative reference to a person's race, colour, religion, sex or sexual orientation or to any physical or mental illness or disability.

(ii) It must avoid publishing details of a person's race, colour, religion, sexual orientation, physical or mental illness or disability unless these are directly relevant to the story.

14. Financial journalism

(i) Even where the law does not prohibit it, journalists must not use for their own profit financial information they receive in advance of its general publication, nor should they pass such information to others.

(ii) They must not write about shares or securities in whose performance they know that they or their close families have a significant financial interest, without disclosing the interest to the editor or financial editor.

(iii) They must not buy or sell, either directly or through nominees or agents, shares or securities about which they have written recently or about which they intend to write in the near future.

15. Confidential sources

Journalists have a moral obligation to protect confidential sources of information.

★16. Payment for articles

(i) Payment or offers of payment for stories or information must not be made directly or through agents to witnesses or potential witnesses in current criminal proceedings except where the material concerned ought to be published in the public interest and there is an overriding need to make or promise to make a payment for this to be done. Journalists must take every possible step to ensure that no financial dealings have influence on the evidence that those witnesses may give. (An editor authorising such a payment must be prepared to demonstrate that there is a legitimate public interest at stake involving matters that the public has a right to know. The payment or, where accepted, the offer of payment to any witness who is actually cited to give evidence must be disclosed to the prosecution and the defence and the witness should be advised of this.)

(ii) Payment or offers of payment for stories, pictures or information, must not be made directly or through agents to convicted or confessed criminals or to their associates – who may include family, friends and colleagues – except where the material concerned ought to be published in the public interest and payment is necessary for this to be done.

Published by The Press Standards Board of Finance Ltd., 30 George Square, Glasgow G2 1EG. Registered in England & Wales No. 2554323.

Newspaper and Magazine, code of practice
Source: The Press Standards Board of Finance Ltd.

Read paragraphs 1 to 6 inclusive of the Code of Practice. You are the editor of the local newspaper and you also have children who attend school in the area. You are also a school governor and are keen to maintain the favourable reputation of the school in the community. You have a duty to inform the public of matters of 'public interest'.

ACTIVITIES

1. Read the PCC adjudication on Carol Smilie's case set out below.
2. What do you think is right or wrong with the judgement?
3. What sort of story would justify using long lens photography ie in the public interest?

Carol Smilie is a TV presenter often on *The National Lottery*, holiday and home makeover programmes.

PRESS COMPLAINTS COMMISSION : ARCHIVE REPORT

Complainant name: Messrs Dibb Lupton Alsop, on behalf of Ms Carol Smilie
Complaint Date: 16/01/00
Clauses noted: 5
Publication: Sunday Mail
Complaint:

Messrs Dibb Lupton Alsop, Solicitors of Manchester, complained on behalf of Ms Carol Smilie that an article published in the Sunday Mail on January 16 2000 headlined 'TV star Carol's grief over mum' was an intrusion into her grief in breach of Clause 5 (Intrusion into grief and shock) of the Code of Practice.

The complaint was upheld.

The article, on the front page and two inside pages, reported the funeral of Ms Smilie's mother and was accompanied by pictures taken outside the crematorium. The complainant's solicitors said that the piece was an unjustified intrusion into Ms Smilie's grief which had been compounded by its prominence. Photographers at the church had earlier been asked to leave but the mourners had not seen the ones at the crematorium, who were clearly some way away using long lens photography. The newspaper said that the funeral had been announced publicly in a newspaper and that it was not uncommon for newspapers to report on the funerals of prominent individuals or their families. At such times the prominence of the article was a matter for the editor. The paper's own photographer left when asked to do so and did not take any photographs, although a freelance photographer subsequently offered the photographs that were published. There would have been no sense of intrusion at the time as the presence of the photographer had not been detected. They published a short statement in a subsequent issue which said that it was not their intention to cause further distress to Ms Smilie or her family.

Decision: Upheld
Reasons:

In considering this complaint, the Commission considered a number of factors. Firstly, the editor would have been aware – by the fact that his own photographer had been asked to leave – that the family did not appreciate the presence of photographers. This should clearly have indicated not only that their physical presence was objectionable but also that published pictures of the occasion would not have been welcome. Secondly, the Commission considered the point that, because the funeral involved a celebrity and had been announced in a newspaper, it could in some way be taken to be a public event. It was not persuaded by this argument. The funeral was not of a celebrity but of the relative of one – and Ms Smilie had not sought to exploit it for publicity and had indicated strongly that it should remain private. Indeed, the article itself noted that it was a 'private service'. Thirdly, the Commission considered the newspaper's contention that the question of prominence is a matter for editorial discretion. In normal circumstances the Commission would agree with this viewpoint. However, the article itself acknowledged that this was a time of grief and as such should have been 'handled with sensitivity' in accordance with the Code. In this case the prominence of the article had a direct impact on the sensitivity with which the matter was reported and the result was a breach of the Code. The publication of a short statement in a subsequent edition was not in the Commission's view a sufficient remedy to the complaint and the complaint was upheld.

ACTIVITIES

Textual analysis

In preparation for examination question:

Select two different tabloid newspapers: one 'red top' and one 'mid-range'. Study the front covers and at least two articles from each newspaper and discuss the similarities and/or differences in the ways that they represent celebrities.

To help you with this activity, here are samples of textual analysis of the front covers and articles of *The Mirror* and the *Daily Express* of July 7th 2001, although only the front covers have been reproduced.

Where appropriate, you should refer to aspects of analysis using the correct technical terms. Several of which are included here:

Pug – 'ears' at top left and right of page: price, logo promotion.

Masthead – title block at centre top: 'red top' tabloids have black or white title imprinted on a red block of ink. **The Express** is simply black on plain background.

Exclusive – a newspaper has the sole right to publish the story.

Headline – the main featured article; a bannered headline describes the TV title.

Splash – the main news item signalled by largest and dramatic headline.

Caption – words placed under picture to explain its content.

Kicker – a story designed to stand out from the rest of the page by its different typeface and layout.

Strap line – introductory headline just below the main headline.

Standfirst – introductory paragraph before the start of the feature.

Byline – the name of the reporter who authored the article.

Example textual analysis

Case Study

Daily Express

It is immediately evident that a large amount of the space of the front cover of the *Daily Express* is taken up with images of famous people. The gallery-like shots of celebrities illustrate the top banner under the masthead promoting FREE TICKETS TO MADAME TUSSAUDS. The other noticeable face is of Prince Charles alongside the main headline splash and article: *Camilla and Me, By Sad Charles*. Tucked in between these two blocks in a one inch wide horizontal section is a head shot of Tim Henman, British tennis player, rained off in the middle of his 2001 semi-final duel with Goran Ivanisevic. The wordplay on his name 'Henmania' suggests he is adulated by women (Hens) and that his potential victory was clichéd 'history in the making'. He is called 'Britain's hero'. Messages about patriotism and star idolisation are rife.

The Express logo (in red) at the centre of the masthead carries the same connotations of heroism as the red inked image of a warrior knight. This has connotations of Saint George – patron saint of England or possibly Lancelot, Knight of King Arthur's round table. The paper has traditionally observed a pro-Royal family conservative stance.

This positive royal attitude is borne out by the uncritical account of Prince Charles's admission that he has not ruled out marriage to his girlfriend Camilla Parker-Bowles. The headline describes the Prince as 'sad' in a sympathetic way. As a 'continuity' story of the royal saga following on from his wife's death his 'unexpected' remark is deemed worthy of front-page prominence.

Inside there are stories involving the arrest of a 16-year-old suspected of killing a 15-year-old three days previously. This is not considered as 'meaningful' to the audience as the story around Prince Charles.

The strapline: 'Marriage isn't out of the question reveals Prince in his frankest interview yet' suggests that sincerity is a quality to admire, and that 'true romance' will result in marriage.

The story is a 'continuation' of the Prince Charles, Princess Diana and Camilla Parker-Bowles relationship, which Princess Diana spoke of in a TV interview with Martin Bashir – 'there was not enough room for three in this relationship'.

The format of the page is not dissimilar to many 'red top' tabloids in that there is little text and the amount of space dedicated to a special offer (i.e. to Madame Tussauds) is a third of the page. However, the font is a serif type that makes the headline CAMILLA AND ME, BY SAD CHARLES a more formal print. The newspaper's name is a distinctively serif style suggesting a slightly old fashioned literary style. This sense of an older, literate but middle-aged audience is further emphasised by the images of popular figures, heroes and heroines in the over 35-age group. Kylie Minogue, Tony Blair, Naomi Campbell, Chris Tarrant, Princess Diana, Mel B and Gary Lineker are important icons of Britishness for a generation who were young in the 80s. Kyle is Australian but by association she is part of the Commonwealth. By including these people in the line up the paper is targeting a particular popular choice for British people of a certain age.

The Mirror

Two thirds of the front page is taken up with a promotion for a competition to win £70,000. This promotion is arguably also the 'splash' article as the celebrity news story is much smaller and covers over a third of the page at the bottom. The face of the man holding the cash prize has an expression which could be interpreted as triumphant or aggressive, or both, as though he is a spectator spurring contestants on at a sporting event. He is instantly recognisable to thousands of television viewers as Stuart, one of the recently evicted participants from the *Big Brother* television show, for which there is also a £70,000 cash prize. Pages 20–1 include an extravagant splash repeating the details of the competition.

Intertextual references are a common feature of a newspaper editor's strategy to reach a larger audience. The intertextual references to television , radio and music industries are a pervasive element of this edition. Examples are:

● Robbie Williams and Kylie Minogue: 'I missed my chance to be Robbie's lover – whole of page 3.
● Brian from Big Brother (2) – whole of page 5. 'Under pressure favourite smashes plate'.
● Chris Evans: 'Virgin Sacked Chris after he played a Sheena Easton hit for Billie' – whole of page 9.
● Courtenay Cox – photo of *Friend's* star's bottom on beach – quarter page.
● Beckham wearing a cravat – half a page with a photo-parade of other illustrious actors wearing cravats – half of page 15.
● Jack Nicholson and Lara Flynn Boyle attending Wimbledon – quarter of page 17.
● Richard and Judy denied an on screen party on the last day before they leave *This Morning*, to go to Channel 4 – a third of page 27.

The Mirror is at pains to stress this is an 'official competition' by using a large point size serif typeface for 'The Official Game' under the headline Big Brother. This is done in the knowledge that *The Sun* on the same day was running its 'officially sanctioned' competition.

The image of *The Mirror's* interactive card contains the logs of Channel 4, the programme maker Endemol and BT as a sponsor. The game specifically appeals to the 4.8 million viewers who watch the television programme, *The Big Brother*. All these housemates are pictured in a montage on the gamecard. The age group of these individuals and it's prime target audience, is between 20 and 35, which matches the current demographic profile of *The Mirror's* readership.

The paper has a 'pug' (a small 'ear' at the top left and right), which states, 'Starting Today', and is shaped as an arrow pointing downwards. This lends a certain brightness and freshness to the layout.

There is alliteration in the 'secrets of my sacking', which is typical of tabloid language, keeping the tone light and bright.

Front page

The second item on the front page features the infamous radio jockey and ex-breakfast show presenter, Chris Evans, claiming he has been unfairly sacked. Underneath his image is the caption 'axed'. There are few words in the front page article and the remainder of the report is inside the paper.

3 TOPIC THREE
Minority Interests and Radio

- In a comparison of the two radio programmes you have studied, discuss how they represent the interests of a particular minority and how that minority is defined.
- Compare two examples of the representation of minority interests on radio.

The case study below compares a programme on a minority interest station with the approach taken on a national BBC station. This comparison might be appropriate material for a response to the second of these two questions.

Minority Radio

In dealing with the key issues of representation, messages and values, discussion on this topic can be divided in three areas:

- minority appeal
- broadcasting strategy
- radio as Institution.

These would include consideration of Presenters, Format, Scheduling, Finance and Audiences, Jingles, Advertising, Discourse, Key Moments (Textual Analysis) and Audience Responses.

Later in the section we will look at *Woman's Hour (Radio 4)* , and *AIROS* (American Indian Radio on Satellite), as specific Case Studies.

Representation of minority issues

For this case study area, the key word is **minority** and as a term it may seem obvious. We are all familiar with 'mainstream' radio such as Radio 1 or Capital Radio – but have you stopped to think about whether all audiences are catered for by these stations or indeed looked at the range of expressly 'minority interest' stations that broadcast now that the legislation has been relaxed?

The Codes of Radio

Radio is what is known as an 'intimate' medium because it addresses each listener as an individual. Radio is often used as 'background noise' while we are doing other things. We might be in the car, at work or school, studying or getting ready to go out but the key factor is that we are doing something else and our attention is not on the radio – we tune in and out of the show, depending on what we hear and use the radio as a secondary or even tertiary activity. [See definitions of consumption in the Introduction, pages 2–3.]

When we are searching for a station to listen to, we may not immediately be able to identify the name of the station we find; yet we will quickly be able to establish the genre of the station/programme and assess whether we are likely to be in the target audience. Indeed, when we find a station we are familiar with 'by accident' in this way we can almost always tell which station it is without needing to wait for the 'ident'

An ident is a jingle or phrase used as a 'signifier' to identify the programme or station

We quickly learn to interpret the use of codes and conventions to identify the type of station if not identify the actual station.

A significant advantage of radio advertising for potential advertisers is, therefore, that the audience can be seen as 'narrowcast' and thus advertisers can be sure of maximum exposure to the target audience, unlike most 'blanket' advertising which has a lower hit rate since it cannot be so explicitly targeted. The danger for the local commercial station is ensuring that they are broadcasting to a niche audience which is interested and also appeals to advertisers – and that there is a market for that particular brand of radio in that area. It also explains why we can be so explicit in our analysis of how radio stations cater for minority interests since the stations themselves are so often narrowcast in this way.

The four main codes of Radio

In *Understanding Radio* (London; Methuen 1986) Andrew Crisell defines the main codes of radio as being;

- Words
- Sounds
- Music
- Silence

He argues that all the signs in radio are sound based and thus the combination of these four signs and the manipulation/use of time is the way to deconstruct a radio programme. He suggests that each of these four codes can be treated as a 'sign' and deconstructed just as we do with visual signs. By listening to the combination of the use of these four codes over time during a programme we can deconstruct the programme effectively and draw conclusions not only about the style and format of what we are listening to but also its form and function – which means we can also draw conclusions about the target audience and the institutional factors which influence the chosen broadcast.

ACTIVITIES

Listen to the 'Breakfast show' on at least three different radio stations. Try to ensure that one of the stations is national, one local and that at least one of the programmes is one which you are not familiar with.

Using these factors and codes given above, try to deconstruct each of these programmes, looking at the way the programme establishes its identity, how it defines and categorises the target audience and how it defines and conforms to the identity of the station which presents the programme.

- How different are each of these 'Breakfast shows'?
- Does this surprise you?
- Why is this?
- Is this significant in how audiences are represented on radio?

Messages and Values

As you will have read in Section 2, the concept of **Representation** refers to the meanings in the media text that convey **messages** and **values** about people, places, events and ideas. All media texts contain ideas about society's values and belief systems. eg Media texts represent and reproduce ideas about a society's morals, cultures, religions, laws and social attitudes. Target audiences are the **primary** audience for a particular text. A target audience may be wide or narrow but every media text is targeted at a particular audience. A **minority** audience is a small audience – which may be a group in society which is/feels discriminated against or may simply be a 'small' audience rather than the 'mass' audiences at which many mainstream texts are targeted.

ACTIVITIES

Select a programme on Radio 4 to listen to, record it and answer these questions.
- How would you define the target audience of this programme?
- Is this a wide audience? Why is this?
- Now choose a programme from your local independent radio station and do the same.
- What differences do you notice in the target audience?
- Account for these differences.
- When you have done this, see if you can identify the ways in which each programme targets its audience – you might want to consider scheduling, use of music, presenters, vocabulary, use of background sound/other people, structure, content and presentation.

Radio and target audiences

Key criteria define minority groups and can be explicitly identified and exploited by radio institutions.

How do we know into what groups the audience are placed? In other words what techniques are used to establish, define and represent the audience on air?

The main issues in representation of minority groups on radio are reflected in the themes of community and identity.

ACTIVITIES

Study any radio programme.
Identify the language used in the programme:

1. How much implies that the audience are already members of a community?
2. How much is specific?

How can this identity be sustained? What methods are used to 'hook' the audience into returning?

Textual analysis and representation

With reference to your two programmes/stations, identify, where relevant, the different types of:

- Scheduling
- Presenters
- Music (eg theme tunes, jingles)
- Discourse (ie the language used on the programme and the style of speaking)
- Range of programmes
- Content
- Opinions stated/revealed/suggested by presenters
- Advertising placement

ACTIVITIES

Use the headings above to make a list of how the station/programme is represented. It is probably better to choose specific programmes to analyse here – analysing *Woman's Hour* for example. (Trying to address the whole of Radio 4 in an exam answer would probably be impossible.) Repeat this for your second chosen station or programme.

Carefully consider in your analysis how the two are similar or different.

DISCUSSION

In 1999 a Civil Rights Forum on Communications Policy in the United States found that stations that target minority listeners earn about 29% less in advertising revenue per listener than stations targeting mainstream audiences. 91% of representatives of minority-owned stations had encountered advertisers who were unwilling to buy ads on their stations. 61% of ads bought on minority stations were discounted an average 59%.

ACTIVITIES

Describe (denotate) a short sequence – maybe five minutes – of your chosen programme and analyse it in terms of the codes of radio discussed above.

What does this reveal about the station/programme?

How far does your analysis show how the station/programme creates and sustains a target audience?

How far does it allow you to define this target audience? Why is this?

ACTIVITIES

Write an analysis of the connotations of the following elements within your chosen programme:

- Music
- Voice
- Silence
- Non-diegetic sound
- Layering of sound
- Structure and timing of these elements
- Discourse
- Audience 'hooks'

Case Study

Woman's Hour

Woman's Hour was first broadcast on 7th October 1946 and was first presented by a man, Alan Ivimey. It was scheduled for an hour at 2pm as it was believed that women (all housewives) were able to listen to the radio at that time of day – probably while washing up after lunch. The content of this early programme was to focus on 'keeping house, health, children, beauty care and home furnishing' as those were deemed to be the primary interests of the target audience at that time.

The first programme contained an item on 'Mother's Midday Meal', followed by beauty tips about 'Putting your Best Face Forward'. Other early items included helpful items such as the best way to catch mice in the home or how to reuse blackout material after the war.

Soon *Woman's Hour* was receiving a thousand letters a week, asking for advice on many matters, such as children's eating habits, shyness and menstrual problems. It developed as a unifying forum for the voices of its listeners, gaining a reputation as a sisterhood of the airwaves and becoming a window on life for many housewives at the time.

The programme would develop to celebrate, educate, inform and entertain generations of women, and quickly became a national institution, familiar to each generation of women as it adapted to suit the generation it targeted.

When it was first devised, it was envisaged as a daily programme of music, advice and entertainment for the home. Early items ranged from the instructive and entertaining (including a guide to knitting your own stair carpet!), to increasingly controversial social and educational issues as the position of women in society changed and they demanded more intellectual content. The programme was the first to tackle subjects such as the menopause (in 1947), cancer (1950) and contraception (1962). The early broadcasts were live and early broadcasters still recount tales of the early interviewees, who used to arrive in time for lunch and were usually interviewed while still wearing their hats and gloves in the studio.

DISCUSSION

As a group listen to an edition of *Woman's Hour* (It is currently being broadcast at 10 a.m. every weekday morning.)

- How much has the content changed from that early brief?
- Is it relevant to the target audience today?
- How would you define the target audience?
- Does it address minorities within its target audience? Account for this.

ACTIVITIES

Record and analyse a series of at least four transmissions of *Woman's Hour*. What themes and issues can you see continued across these transmissions. Can you account for this?

What codes and conventions are used across all the transmissions? What does this tell you about the format of the programme?

See how much you can discover about the history of the programme. It has been running for many years, with many presenters. How has the programme changed over time? Why is this? Has the representation of women by and within the programme changed in that time? Try to collect a list of examples of these representations.

Case Study

AIROS

The American Indian Radio on Satellite (AIROS) network is a national distribution system for Native programming to Tribal communities and to general audiences through Native American and other public radio stations as well as the Internet. Although it does not broadcast directly to Europe, it can be listened to via its web page, at *http://www.nativetelecom.org/index.html*

Mission Statement

The mission of Native American Public Telecommunications (NAPT) is to inform, educate and encourage the awareness of tribal histories, cultures, languages, opportunities and aspirations through the fullest participation of American Indians and Alaska Natives in creating and employing all forms of educational and public telecommunications programmes and services, thereby supporting tribal sovereignty. We accomplish this mission through:

- Producing and developing educational telecommunication programs for all media including television and public radio.
- Distributing and encouraging the broadest use of such educational telecommunications programs.
- Providing training opportunities to encourage increasing numbers of American Indians and Alaska Natives to produce quality programs.
- Promoting increased control and use of information technologies by American Indians and Alaska Natives.
- Providing leadership in creating awareness of and developing telecommunications policies favourable to American Indians and Alaska Natives.

Building partnerships to develop and implement telecommunications projects with tribal nations, Indian organisations, and native communities.

The programme listing on AIROS lists the following programmes (among others):

- *AlterNative Voices* features Native music, interviews, and news reports relevant to Indian Country. *AlterNative Voices* is produced and hosted by Z. Susanne Aikman (Eastern Band Cherokee/Scot) and originates from KUVO-FM in Denver.
- *California Indian Radio Project* has the purpose-giving listeners an understanding of the rich mixture of old and new, beauty and sadness, contradiction and perseverance that characterises California Indian life. There are more than 300 tribes in California, and their cultures are ancient, spiritually complex and deeply woven into the land.
- *Native America Calling*, AIROS's flagship program, is a live one-hour call-in show, now distributed to 27 Native radio stations and the National Public Radio system, Monday-Friday at 1 p.m. ET.
- *Native Sounds-Native Voices* is a music service featuring traditional and contemporary Native American music. NS-NV is produced in two formats, the National Edition with host/producer John Gregg, Sr. (Hopi/Inupiat) and regional producers from across North America.
- *New Letters on the Air* began in 1977 as the radio companion to the distinguished literary quarterly *New Letters*. It is a weekly program that is one of the largest, and one of the best collections of recordings by contemporary authors, both from the United States and other countries. AIROS features New Letters on the Air programs about Native Authors.
- *Voices from the Circle* highlights Native news, music, issues, entertainment and storytelling from reservations and urban communities. The weekly program is produced and hosted by Barbara Jersey (Menominee/Potawatomi) and Jim DeNomie (Bad River Chippewa) at the Milwaukee Public Schools' WYMS and WLUW at Loyola University.

155

ACTIVITIES

Select one of the programmes available on the AIROS network, listen to it and then write a review of the programme in no more than 400 words, to go in the *Radio Times*. How can you represent the programme positively to a more mainstream audience?

Summary

You have been studying the concept of representation through case studies. To be able to compare both stations/transmissions effectively you will need to consider that:

- radio broadcasting offers lots of ways to address minority groups
- stations and programmes have particular identities which can be easily defined and representations explored
- as radio broadcasting has changed and progressed so has the representation of different groups
- new media are changing both access to radio stations and the way that stations operate.

TOPIC FOUR

Social Class and American Cinema

In dealing with the key issues of representation, messages and values discussion on this topic can be divided in three areas;

- Social class/status
- The American Dream/Nightmare
- American Cinema.

These would include consideration of Themes, Characters, Treatment, the Hollywood Film Industry and Audiences, Stars, Iconography, Hollywood Classic Narrative Structure and Elements, Key Moments (Textual Analysis), Audience Responses.

Representation as a process

In this section, the key word is **representation** and as a term it may come as a little strange at first. The idea of how we, as individuals, are presented is often most acutely felt. This may be in our first childhood photographs. The sense that these embarrassing photographs can bring about strong reactions – we do not feel the photograph captures our 'best side' or pose, and even worse the photographs do not reflect the 'real' person. On the other hand, the image is undeniably a picture of you and it is only one version of what you can look like. It is a likeness or a **representation** of you, whether you like it or not!

As another example, representations of places produced by house sellers in the estate agents or the tourist board or holiday brochures obviously wish to select the best images of the properties or places they are promoting. They do not show the worst aspects or the unpleasant aspects. The images are only partial views and therefore only provide a representation that is positive but selective.

Messages and Values

As you will have read in Section 2, the concept of **Representation** refers to the meanings in the media text that convey **messages** and **values** about people, places, events and ideas. All media texts contain ideas about society's values and belief systems. *Top Gun* (1986) celebrated the all-American fighter pilot and their patriotism, whereas *Fight Club* (1999) represented the working class American manual labourer as the unspoken, spiritually and materialistic poor, undervalued voice of America, literally an 'underclass'. Media texts represent and reproduce ideas about societies' morals, cultures, religions, laws, and social attitudes.

A scene from Fight Club. *See page 92, figure 7.*

ACTIVITIES

Carefully consider any film you have recently watched and enjoyed.
What do you think was the main focus of representation?
What was the minor focus of the film?
Consider defining the following as having minor or major significance:

- the **place** e.g. exotic locations are very important in James Bond films.
- the **social type of characters** e.g. lawyers, office workers, new technology computer specialists, cleaners
- the **events** e.g. the sinking of the *Titanic* in 1912 (*Titanic* 1997), racism in 1960 America (*Mississippi Burning* 1988), the Vietnam War (*Platoon* 1986)
- the **ideas** e.g. the **possible** conspiracy behind President John F Kennedy's death (*JFK* 1991) in 1963, or the delinquent working-class cleaner genius (*Goodwill Hunting* 1997).

Film and Representations of Social Class

In the film *Titanic* (1997), there is a representation of an upper class family, the DeWitt Bukaters, which we witness mainly through the viewpoint of the heroine, Rose, played by Kate Winslet. In contrast, the character of Jack Dawson, played by Leonardo DiCaprio, represents the poor, working class man. In a sense, these are traditional pre-first world war images of a three-tiered class society typified in the film. How do we know into what class the characters are placed? In other words what filmic techniques are used to represent the characters in terms of their class? In the film, we see that the upper classes are wealthy shown by their cars and their clothes. The poor have few clothes and they gamble in street cafés and fight each other. In the scene in which the passengers are boarding the ship, the upper class occupy a larger amount of space on the busy quayside with their cars, servants and possessions, and are seen to be snobbish, expensively clothed and very privileged – they are to sail in the ship's first class sections. The working class are seen to be dirty, uneducated and they have to mix together in third class, called steerage, areas. They are, however, depicted (patronisingly) as warm hearted and straightforward in their dealings with each other. Jack obtains a ticket to travel on the *Titanic* which he wins in a card gambling game at a quayside, working man's café just minutes before the tragic ship's departure.

How people travelled was frequently an indicator of class. Even the term 'posh' derived from the initials for 'Port Out, Starboard Home'. On cruise ships and on longer sea journeys to Africa and India the side of the ship for the best views and sunshine in the mornings and shade in the afternoon was to be on the port side on the way from England and the starboard side on the return journey.

Message

One **message** of the film is that love conquers all class barriers, when Rose and Jack fall in love. The hero may be poor but he is honourable and courageous.

Values

One value or moral assumed in *Titanic* is that it is a normal occurrence for boys and girls to fall in love. More than this, though, there is the Romeo and Juliet 'star crossed' belief that, whether alive or dead, pure love is eternal. Related to this idea is the belief that if you marry the right person you will ensure your continuing membership of that class. If you are lucky you will make a catch and marry above your income and therefore rise in status.

Treatment

In American cinema the Romeo and Juliet story has been dealt with in different ways, stylistically and within variations of plot. The idea of the mutual but fatal pact that is formed can be seen in the different variations of the star-crossed lovers theme where the two main characters are represented as not failing in *American Beauty* (2000), or fighting society in action-dramas such as *Badlands* (1973) and *Natural Born Killers* (1994), or being people of the same gender in the documentary drama *Get Fish* (1994), or different skin colours in social-dramas such as *Mississippi Masala* (1991), or in youth gangs from different ethnic in the musical *West Side Story* (1961) and the idealised romantic outlaws in *Bonny and Clyde* (1967).

Using these alternative treatments the American film industry can offer a variety of films that convey attitudes that will appeal to mass audiences.

Realism

'It's very realistic!' How many times have you said that about a film you have enjoyed. Much of a film spectator's pleasure comes from accepting the fictional world as presented to them. For many spectators realism is judged by its 'truthfulness' or its attention to historically accurate surface detail such as location, décor and costumes.

Although we know it is 'only a movie' we like to enjoy pretending and losing ourselves in the fictional world and believing in the setting or the dramatic scenario laid out for us in moving images and sounds. But how does a filmmaker begin to depict people, places and events in films? The task of depicting the main character of *Titanic*, that is the ship itself, was huge – enormous amounts of money were spent on simulating the effects of great volumes of water gushing into the ship and its subsequent sinking. Special effects companies like Industrial Light and Magic are part and parcel of high budget films, which have many spectacles and large-scale scenes and settings.

The American Dream

The American Dream is a concept springing from the ideals expressed in the charter created by the first politicians to create the independent American states, from the political discussions stemming from the Declaration of Independence in 1776.

'We hold these truths to be self evident: that all men are created equal, that they are endowed by their creator with certain unalienable rights; that among these are life, liberty and the pursuit of happiness. That to secure these rights governments are instituted among men, deriving their just powers from the consent of the governed.'

In political terms, this belief was that every citizen has equal rights to obtain happiness – and the government is responsive only to the electorate and should not dictate the people's will. The ideas about what America's people believe in have been discussed and fought over in the history and cultural debates of America, since that time.

Though, some critics say that no one in America actually discussed it anymore – they just act it out. (Elizabeth Long in *The American Dream and the Popular Novel*)

The American Dream suggests that if an individual works hard, is self-denying and god-fearing then they will achieve success. This has conventionally meant achieving wealth and/or power. The ultimate exemplars of the American Dream have been self-made millionaires such as John D. Rockefeller, the oil tycoon and Henry Ford, the car manufacturer. In 1880 at the age of seventeen, Ford began work as a $2.50 a week machine-shop worker. By 1926 his Ford Motor Company had assets valued at $1000 Million. American presidents, who have come from humble roots to become the most powerful man in the Western world, are also presented as showing that 'everything is possible'.

The American Nightmare

Malcolm X said: 'I don't see an American Dream – I see a Nightmare.' During the 1800s, the mass importation of black people from Africa and the Caribbean to work as slaves for white cotton plantation owners contributed to a social inequality that was one of the main contributory forces that led to the Civil War (1861–1865) between the Northern and Southern states. Even Abraham Lincoln (American President 1860–65) called America the 'almost chosen people'.

'The lesson of Lincoln's life was that the quest for prosperity is no remedy for melancholy. But that a passion to secure social justice by erasing the line that divides those with hope from those without hope can be.' (*The Real American Dream*, Andrew Delbanco, Harvard, 1999)

Biographical films such as *Malcolm X* represent the inequalities between black and white, which do not match the ideal of 'equal rights for all' message of the American Declaration of Independence.

Key historical and social factors such as immigration, migration and mobility are explored and symbolised in American poetry, literature and films. Other social factors present a level of contradiction and conflict such as:

- dual identity represented by groups such as Cuban Americans, Italian Americans and Jewish Americans
- pursuit of shared community goals versus individual success, status and respect
- social responsibility and law-abiding citizenship versus deviancy/non-conformism

In social terms the values for achieving success combine with a sense of 'being the chosen nation' and these might include views concerning democracy, capitalism, individualism and service to others. The successful arrival on and exploitation of the fertile and mineral rich American soil has led to a core belief in homespun virtues such as hard work, reliability, self-discipline and inventiveness.

Power/powerlessness

In either social system, a useful way of analysing the idea of class or status is to think about power. When studying society, families or individual lives, who holds the power? In films, who is represented as having the power to control and who is controlled?

ACTIVITIES

Study any American film, identify who has the power in the programme:

1. in the domestic settings
2. in the workspace.

How can power be defined?
Is it through social status (i.e. position in the family or firm, police, army or government)?
Is it through emotional control (i.e. through seniority, maturity, manipulation, selflessness or greed)?

Textual analysis and Social Class

With reference to the two films you have chosen to study, identify where relevant the different types of:

- Family – domestic unit
- House
- Job
- Family
- Possessions
- Clothes

- Relations within the family
- Main characters status, class or power position in society
- Talk
- Life events
- Aspirations, dreams and opportunities
- Power

ACTIVITIES

Use these headings to make a list of how the main characters and their family or domestic unit is represented.

Repeat this for your second film selection.

Analyse how your two films are similar or different.

ACTIVITIES

Narrative

Research on the internet (e.g. imdb.com) or a film journal such as *Sight and Sound*, published by the British Film Institute for a detailed outline (synopsis) of the plots of your two films. Make a numbered list of the key elements in your films' narratives.

ACTIVITIES

Themes

List the main themes in the films that you have chosen e.g. heroism, corruption. Compare similarities and differences between the two films.

Key Moments: cinematic ideas

The following activities will enable you to analyse key elements in specific scenes to bring out the cinematic qualities and techniques of construction.

ACTIVITIES

Describe (denotate) four or five frames in one significant and dramatic sequence as though each was a still frame. For each of the frames, explain briefly:

- Camera shot types, and angles of each character, and the perspective contained within the shot: foreground, mid-ground and/or background.
- Camera movement: tracking, zooming, static
- Lighting: source (artificial or natural), direction and spread (dark or bright etc)
- Clothing
- Body posture and position in relation to other people or space
- Diegetic and non-diegetic sound and music (identify genre of music and instruments/sound played)

ACTIVITIES

Write an analysis of the connotations of the following elements within your chosen films:
Perspective (view point of camera)
Lighting (effects)
Clothing (signifiers)
Facial expression, body posture, and gestures (meaning)
Positioning and relationship of characters in the scene/melodrama, e.g. Power relations/good and bad
Mise én scène: background, setting, colour, furniture, props (signifiers)
Diegetic and non-diegetic sound and music (associations with genre or music or mood/atmosphere conveyed)
Themes and links with other parts of the film

TOPIC FIVE

Gender and Situation Comedy

What is Situation Comedy?

Situation Comedies are based upon a single context, or 'situation' usually connected with work or the home, or in some cases both. The comedy grows out of the tensions or conflicts between the characters, usually a narrow group of friends or a family. Whereas Soap Operas demand a large number of characters, this is clearly not the case with sitcoms. Where there are characters outside the central group they are usually acquaintances or temporary inhabitants who provide particular comic storylines.

The narrative of a sitcom rarely continues from one episode into the next, although there are, of course exceptions to this rule. This again contrast with Soaps where the on-going narrative is an essential ingredient.

DISCUSSION

Which sitcoms have on-going storylines? Why do you think their narratives are constructed in this way? Compare these with examples of sitcoms whose episodes are completely free-standing.

Even in sitcoms that have on-going storylines such as *Friends* with Chandler and Monica's march towards matrimony, each instalment begins with a situation that is resolved by the end of the episode. Characters may be simple two-dimensional stereotypes or may be more complex and fully rounded, but they rarely change. Their based 'situation' similarly remains the same from episode to episode. Although some of the running stories will resist closure until the end of a series, or, once again with *Friends*, end a series with a cliffhanger, sitcoms are heavily reliant upon repetition.

What, or who are we laughing at?

Sitcoms give us the opportunity to laugh at aspects of ourselves – sitcoms such as *Keeping up Appearances* are successful because Hyacinth is almost plausible and we can all identify with characters like her. *2.4 Children* defines a 'typical' family and then subverts their lives to create chaos – a gentle way for us to reaffirm our own roles in our own families and to feel more secure in our own worlds.

Other key characteristics of comedy are enigma and comic suspense (similar to dramatic irony). Enigma can generate many sitcom plots – not just the obvious such as the 'secret' relationship between Chandler and Monica in *Friends* but also the more subtle, such as the sitcom *Goodnight Sweetheart* starring Nicholas Lyndhurst as someone living simultaneously in two timeframes. Many comedies, such as *Only Fools and Horses* entertained its audience by ensuring that each week the plots hatched by Del would fail, despite his best efforts. This further extends into sitcoms bordering on farce, such as *The Brittas Empire* or *Some Mothers Do 'Ave 'Em* where the comedy comes from watching the chain of events unfold and disaster builds to a climax by the end of each episode.

Are we laughing **at** the characters or **with** them, when watching and sharing their fortunes and misfortunes? Does our laughter derive from our experience of disruptive surprise and its resolution? Is our laughter allowing us to sublimate or rehearse underlying or unconscious fears, anxieties or desires? Comedy and laughter, allows us to stand outside our own ego and be taken over by events or circumstances outside our control. One example of this might be to consider how painful it can sometimes be to watch John Cleese in *Fawlty Towers*, endlessly thwarted in his neurotic attempts to control, stay organised and organise others – in laughing at him are we also laughing at aspects of ourselves? Maybe this is why so many sitcoms remain grounded in the family or an extended family, to enable us to make these comparisons. *Absolutely Fabulous* offered extreme stereotypes but also reversed many typical relationships (such as mother/daughter). It explored typical situations, for example the mother introducing a new boyfriend to her daughter or the loneliness of an older single woman but frequently subverted them to give a fresh perspective.

ACTIVITIES

Using the key features of sitcom referred to above, try to identify three sitcoms that conform to what you consider to be a conventional pattern. Now see if you can identify another five sitcoms that do not conform to the key features you have identified. Does this make them more successful? Why is this? How have they 'subverted' the format to create this comedy?

In terms of the formulaic element of sitcoms it has been suggested that sitcoms share a common ingredient, the comic trap, as Barry Took remarks:

> *All successful comedies have some trap in which people must exist – like marriage. (The perfect situation for a situation comedy) is a little self enclosed world where you have to live by the rules.*

These rules may be those of the mini-community such as that of the Home Guard in *Dad's Army*. Circumstances and limitations may be social learning to live within one's class (Hyacinth Bucket in *Keeping Up Appearances*) or learning to acknowledge that you have to live within the limits of your own body and age as with the characters in *Dad's Army*).

In sitcoms characters transgress against and learn the value of, closely bound ties of the family or the social group – restoration of the family, or what may be called communalisation, reaffirming the stability and importance of the group. Many of the plots of *Keeping Up Appearances*, for example, involve Hyacinth seeking to improve her circumstances, either directly or through self-betterment, but she cannot. Certain critics have suggested that this underlying thematic concern makes the form particularly suitable for the home-based television audience, going on to suggest that the sitcom, as a form, tends towards the reassertion of conservative values of the home and family (in terms of both setting and theme), and the stereotyping of racial, class, sexual and regional differences. Emphasis is also on the inside (of the home or social unit) against which the 'others' are judged, rejected or simply viewed (neighbours or outsiders). In the case of a programme such as *Dad's Army* or *'Allo, 'Allo*, the question of who is the insider and who the outside has all sorts of implications for wider questions of national identity and national self-identification.

ACTIVITIES

Watch an episode of 'Allo, 'Allo and choose five characters to study. Compare their dress, manner of speech, role and function and then consider to what extent they are presented as French/German/English and to what extent they conform to the stereotypes that we associate with each of these groups. Why is this? How is this presented in the programme? Can you suggest how this helps the comedy of the programme?

It is worth noting, however, that we cannot always assert that the sitcom is an essentially conservative genre, teaching people to live within their limits and limitations. In recent years a tendency has emerged towards sitcoms that goes some way to subverting some of the conventions. Sitcoms such as *Cheers*, *The Young Ones* and *The New Statesman*, all play with the themes and norms of the traditional sitcom form. *Blackadder* burlesques them, (and plays on popular misunderstandings of English history). Situation Comedies like *Rising Damp* were, to some extent, already doing this, setting the eccentricities of Rigby's household against familiar bourgeois life. Rigby is doomed to fail, not only in his amorous advances towards Miss Jones, but also in his attempts to become a cultured member of the middle classes. However, in these, as in all sitcoms, the key question is what, or who we are laughing at, and what, we are laughing with.

ACTIVITIES

Watch an episode of *Blackadder* and identify the role and function of each of the main characters. Try to list five ways in which the programme subverts the codes and conventions of sitcoms and identify the humour in each of these. How important is it for the audience to be familiar with the conventions of sitcoms to be entertained by *Blackadder*?

Situation Comedy – The comedy of aspiration and frustration

We might say that frustration is the keystone of sitcom. For all her strivings, Hyacinth Bucket never makes it into the upper class (in spite of her insistence on pronouncing her surname as Bouquet.) Victor Meldrew never succeeds in his endeavours and when Del eventually does become a millionaire he is not entirely happy and regrets having lost many aspects of his old situation.

Nearly all sitcom characters, be they American or British, are frustrated by being caught in a situation from which they cannot escape – hence the name. The situation may be physical, but it is more likely to be emotional. Rodney is trapped by his family, Geraldine by her position as vicar, Edina and Patsy are trapped in the fantasy of the mores of the Sixties. Joey is trapped by the dichotomy between reality and his self-perceptions (or delusions). This is not only built into the psychology of the sitcom but is fundamental to their structure as television products. A situation comedy is, by definition a comedy with a set cast, and a set location that is repeated in each episode. In other words, the tendency not to change is external as well. Although characters may strive to change, they are in a sense doomed to return each time to somewhere very close to their starting point because that is the way the episodes are defined.

The first part of a typical sitcom episode is where the characters' expectations are elevated; the second part is the disequilibrium when their plans are dashed and they fall to a point below that from which they started; the third part is the return to equilibrium.

At the end of the episode the cycle is complete, the situation restored and few, if any lessons have been learnt. We are back where we started, ready to begin next week's episode. The point is that, unless an actor wants to leave the series, or there is a major change of focus, the basic situation never changes. This is sometimes highlighted by the *coda* at the end of an episode, a brief comic moment after the closing credits. For example the short exchange as equilibrium and light-heartedness is re-established at the end of *Friends* or (more explicitly) the 'joke over a cup of coffee' at the end of *Vicar of Dibley* where Geraldine and Alice share a joke over a cup of coffee that Alice never understands.

The more things change, the more they stay the same!

Sitcom stories, therefore, start out at a point of equilibrium, move through disequilibrium and then re-establish the equilibrium while also allowing for some change or progression. A typical episode of *The Cosby*

Show for example might be an argument between teenager and parent, moving through conflict or compromise or concession, demonstrating possible solutions to dilemmas and conflicts with which the audience can readily identify. What we see in each sitcom is the creation of a problem and a complete solution by the end of the programme. Perhaps the most basic appeal of sitcoms (and most TV programmes) is the fact that predictably everything comes out all right. Nothing really changes.

As each episode ends, despite all the embarrassment and disasters, Richard never leaves Hyacinth, Margaret never leaves Victor, Rodney never leaves Del, Saffy never leaves Edina. Sergeant Bilko never gets rich, Roseanne is never free from children, no one at Grace Brothers ever gets a better job. Life goes on as it did before. Even in sitcoms they end with a message such as when Mork sits on the couch talking to Mindy, biting his lower lip and saying, 'I guess what I've learned Min, is that . . .' and when the 'aliens' in *Third Rock From the Sun* sit chatting on the roof outside the window, nothing has really changed.

It is precisely this lack of change that gives a sitcom, for the audience, the sense of real life. The characters on the screen who play out their trapped lives every week, are mirrors of the people who sit trapped in their own worlds, watching them every week. In the typical, family sitcom we see quick-witted but ultimately conservative teenagers running rings around their decent, but rather dull parents. Kids enjoy these shows because that is how they often see their own parents. The parents also laugh because that is how they see themselves. But it doesn't matter. Sitcoms say to the audience, 'Look, it's like this for everybody. This is what life is like, so you're no different.' The message is that life is full of traps and most things you attempt are doomed to fail, but it doesn't matter. Laughter gives a release and reassurance to the audience.

Structure and internal dynamics

Situation comedies have, therefore the same principle characters in each episode and also stock sets with little outside environment. There are usually recurring motifs, running jokes and catchphrases that offer additional continuity.

The situation within the programmes has to be strictly defined – and in the more successful series very easily recognisable, for example in *Last of the Summer Wine, Only Fools and Horses, Porridge* etc. As such, there are three main conventional situations:

- Home and family – [*2.4 Children*, *One Foot in the Grave*, *Butterflies*]
- Work – [*Are you Being Served*, *Drop the Dead Donkey*, *Hi-de-Hi!*]
- Specific (perhaps unusual) situations – [*Red Dwarf*, *Blackadder*]

Some of the better sitcoms allow for a strong sense of both the inside and the outside world. There are internal dynamics going on within the programme to create the humour: conflicts, comic devices and character squabbles in *One Foot in the Grave*, relationships in *Fawlty Towers*. In some, the intrusion from the outside world motivates the plot – this is typical in *Fawlty Towers* where the situation of a hotel makes this logical as guests create comic narrative opportunities.

Mise en scène

Like all TV forms, sitcoms create their own special physical world. In *Roseanne* there is a living room and the kitchen. In *Drop the Dead Donkey* it's the newsroom. In *Cheers*, it is the bar. Without their television and three-piece suite, the Royle family would be completely lost. In fact the sofa appears as an essential piece of furniture in innumerable sitcoms.

Sitcoms are set in particular locations – the shot of New York at the beginning of *Friends* for example, establishes the location, and the action can then be sited in the more intimate locations of the apartments or coffee shop to ensure focus on relationships. This is even more explicit in *Porridge* for example, where the title sequence establishes the distance from the outside world as we follow Fletcher into the prison and hear the story established. Once the episode begins, the audience accepts the simple sets quickly. The sitting rooms of most family based sitcoms are very similar. Usually prosperous, they are carefully crowded with stuffed couches and comfortable chairs, coffee tables on which there are small objects, and walls on which conventional paintings are hung.

ACTIVITIES

1. Watch an episode of *Keeping Up Appearances*. In what ways is the mise en scène of Hyacinth's house set up to establish her character? Can you imagine her in a different house? What does she wear? What do they add to her character? Is she a total stereotype? Compare the representation of Hyacinth with that of her sister, her home and family.
2. Watch an episode of *The Royle Family* and notice the mise en scène. In what ways does it inform our readings of this text? What comic opportunities does the mise en scène offer?
3. Now watch an episode of *2.4 Children*. How does the mise en scène establish that this is a very different family? If this were a real house, would it be this tidy? Why is it presented this way?

Stereotypes

This is one reason why sitcoms depend on stereotypes and conventional settings to establish their environment quickly and allow for more comic opportunities. The characters are central and establish the comedy and the action – sometimes generating comedy because of their character and sometimes through being exposed to situations that lead to comic action. Equally, we expect to see similar episodes every week and we do not expect to see the characters change, age, progress or develop. In *Men Behaving Badly*, for example, although the situations change superficially (for instance impending marriage or children) these changes are explicitly external and do not affect the real dynamics of the relationships in any way, allowing the comedy to continue (an almost direct reversal of reality) where such events are pivotal and substantially change relationships and situations – perhaps a sign of what audiences seek from sitcoms? *Friends* is a good example of this artificiality – all the principal characters are attractive and appealing. All manage to live a prosperous life without working very hard (or in some cases not at all) and although there is talk of needing money, all seem to have sufficient income to enable them to live as overgrown, affluent students avoiding real responsibilities for a great many years.

Watch an episode of *Roseanne* and observe how frequently she uses comic one-liners. How often are these supportive of the other characters and how often do they put the other characters down in some way? How often are the jokes and shared moments gender related? Why do you think this is so? Notice also that there are many confessional and sharing moments between Roseanne and the other characters. Why is this? How do they integrate into the story? Why are these moments used?

Like us, the central characters in sitcoms are surrounded by others, not merely by practical necessity or circumstance, but because their own goals and desires can only be achieved through other people. In their lives, as depicted on the screen, self-interest and social interaction are fused – the latter is a means to aid the former.

In their miniature societies, they scheme and deceive and give themselves away; they tell stories about each other; they misunderstand and reconcile; invent enemies, and make and break pacts and alliances. Most significantly, their interactions are based on various kinds of status and personal territory. As a result, things get out of balance until they are (usually) set right again, so the moral order embodied in the depicted relationships is restored.

But what makes sitcoms successful is the fact that the characters are more than this. What we respond to isn't merely the foolishness of their personal limitations. It is also, and most essentially, the fact that we can identify with the way they are trapped by their own limitations and have to struggle against those limitations to find happiness in their lives.

Representations

As already mentioned above, sitcoms generally depend on stereotypes to establish character. This sustains the security and dependability of the sitcom environment and offers the audience readily grasped 'handles' on characters and situations. Where this is not the case, it is usually because the sitcom is worked around an eccentric, such as Basil Fawlty.

British sitcoms tend to depend on characters who are socially, materially, emotionally and sexually repressed. They are terribly class conscious, with many sitcoms being centred on social position such as in *Keeping Up Appearances*, *Steptoe and Son* and *Till Death Us Do Part*. The upper classes are often presented as civilised, intelligent and slightly dotty. Their humour lies in their formality, their exaggerated correctness and their distaste for the lower class. The lower classes are frequently represented as being loud, crass and shallow. Their humour lies in their bad taste, their bluntness and their distaste for the upper class.

The British comedy industry is highly differentiated but governed by the overall concept that we all have our little niche in society and somehow we all get by. Americans on the other hand are largely not concerned with class but with their own behaviour. Americans are desperately seeking the American Dream (see page 157 Social Class and American Cinema). They are always on the lookout for self-improvement, as shown in sitcoms such as *Roseanne*, *Frasier* and *Cheers*. Their sitcoms are more personality focused using dysfunctional relationships and unsuccessful characters with whom the audience may compare themselves.

These national assumptions control much of the representation within each nation's sitcoms – American sitcoms are far less 'gentle' and plot driven than British ones – it is almost as if the British characters need to be represented as 'more sinned against than sinning' whereas the representation of characters in US sitcoms is dependent on audience neuroses and this generates a particular style of stereotype.

Gender

A key issue for representational studies in sitcom is gender and gender roles. In early sitcoms, roles and function were clearly outlined for male and female characters and these stereotypes were strictly maintained and many remain today. Hyacinth Bucket is totally 'female' and conforms to traditional stereotypes for middle-class women. Perhaps Margaret in *One Foot in the Grave* is a development – she shows independence and frequently needs to sort out Victor's chaos but she still does so wearing an apron. Diana in *Waiting for God* was clearly an independent and forthright woman but she needed to work with Tom to organise the old people's home and eventually adopted a more gender conventional role despite her original protests that she would not do so.

Sitcoms such as *Absolutely Fabulous* and *Vicar of Dibley* have begun to subvert some of the gender stereotypes, although it is worth noting that

Vicar of Dibley depends on audience knowledge of all those stereotypes to generate its comedy. Sitcoms now frequently play upon the fact that they will at one moment accept a stereotype and the next moment subvert it.

DISCUSSION

How far do you think that sitcoms either reinforce or subvert gender stereotypes?

Case Study

The Flintstones and The Simpsons

In dealing with the key issues of representation, messages and values, discussion on this topic can be divided in three areas;

● Gender/status

● Social context

● Situation Comedy

For this case study, we are going to use the example of two cartoon-based sitcoms rather than two sitcoms using actors. The process and analysis is the same but the programmes feature two dimensional drawings rather than actors. In some ways this makes them valuable studies since we can be sure that the decisions about set, for example, were deliberate as the animators will have fully discussed the design, use of colour, movement and layout very carefully before starting to create the programme.

Our first example is *The Flintstones* that was made by Hanna Barbara between 1960 and 1966. It features a typical American family but within a fantasy prehistoric world called Bedrock where the family lives a normal suburban American lifestyle but they have tools/implements/pets and houses that are prehistoric in presentation (although Dino the pet dinosaur is a good example of how sanitised this vision is in its humour).

To compare a contemporary cartoon based sitcom, we can use *The Simpsons*. This is a far more complex text than *The Flintstones*, reflecting how our responses to cartoons have changed as an audience. We now expect a greater level of sophistication in the narrative, theme, treatment and iconography of a supposedly simple cartoon, precisely because the cartoon initially seems so simplistic. *The Simpsons* is especially successful because it communicates on all these levels. On one level it is simply a story about the everyday lives of a typical (yellow headed) American family – just as the Flintstone family – yet it is also able to question moral beliefs, gender roles and audience expectations with the events portrayed and adds a further layer of subtlety on top. It is a 'reflexive' text, in that it frequently makes reference to other media texts with which the audience will probably be familiar (e.g. episodes which made references to various well-known films or television programmes such as *The Prisoner* or *Star Trek*) and uses guest stars such as Paul McCartney, Michael Keaton, Steven King or Tim Robbins to interact – sometimes as themselves and sometimes as characters relevant to the allusions being made – with the Simpson family. Even the titles of the different episodes frequently refer to other texts and thus add another layer of meaning to the events (this is referred to as intertextuality.)

The Simpsons follows traditional sitcom structure and there is usually some kind of moral message at the end of each episode – usually related to the lines that Bart writes on the blackboard at the beginning of each episode. Indeed the complexity of the text can be illustrated by the example that the title sequence changes every episode to be relevant to the events as well.

ACTIVITIES

1. Watch an episode of *Happy Days* or *The Dick Van Dyke Show* or another early sitcom and notice the relationships between parents and children. Make notes about the visual representation of the children and the expectations they seem to reflect.
2. Now watch a more contemporary sitcom with children such as *2.4 Children* or *The Savages* and observe the same things. What differences do you find? Can you account for these differences? Do you think that these contemporary sitcoms are 'representative' about the relationships within families now?

Extension Activity You might also want to look at an episode of *Butterflies* to see how the changes started to happen with 70s sitcoms in this country.

Messages and Values

As you will have read in Section 2, the concept of Representation refers to the meanings in the media text that convey messages and values about people, places, events and ideas. All media texts imply expectations about society's values and belief systems.

A C T I V I T I E S

Carefully consider any situation comedy you have recently watched and enjoyed. What do you think was the main focus of representation? What was the minor focus of the situation comedy? Consider defining the following as having minor or major significance:

- the place e.g. the décor of the rooms in Hyacinth Bucket's house compared to that of her sister Daisy in *Keeping Up Appearances*;
- the social type of characters e.g. The relationship between Rodney and Cassandra in *Only Fools and Horses* (especially the episodes in which he joined her father's company);
- the events e.g. Monica and Chandler's wedding preparations in *Friends*;
- the ideas e.g. the lifestyles of the main characters in *Sex and the City*.

Situation comedy and Representations of Gender

If situation comedies are assumed to reflect the times in which they are created, then the gender representations within them might be said to reflect the gender roles and positions expected in society at the time. If you compare the expectations for men and women in the 1950s to those today, there have been many changes. This is reflected in the representations in situation comedies.

A C T I V I T I E S

The following extract is taken from a genuine textbook from the 1950s – how far can you see these values reflected in an early sitcom (especially the very early American ones such as *I Love Lucy*) and how far can you see them reflected in a contemporary sitcom such as *Men Behaving Badly*?

HOW TO BE A GOOD WIFE

The following is actually taken from a 1950's Home Economics textbook intended for High School girls; guidelines on how to prepare for married life.

1. Have dinner ready: Plan ahead, even the night before, to have a delicious meal – on time. This is a way of letting him know that you have been thinking about him, and are concerned about his needs. Most men are hungry when they come home and the prospects of a good meal are part of the warm welcome needed.

2. Prepare yourself: Take 15 minutes to rest so you will be refreshed when he arrives. Touch up your make-up, put a ribbon in your hair and be fresh looking. He has just been with a lot of work-weary people. Be a little gay and a little more interesting. His boring day may need a lift.

3. Clear away the clutter: Make one last trip through the main part of the house just before your husband arrives, gathering up school books, toys, paper, etc. Then run a dust cloth over the tables. Your husband will feel he has reached a haven of rest and order, and it will give you a lift too.

4. Prepare the children: Take a few minutes to wash the children's hands and faces if they are small, comb their hair, and if necessary, change their clothes. They are little treasures and he would like to see them playing the part.

5. Minimize the noise: At the time of his arrival, eliminate all noise of washer, dryer, dishwasher, or vacuum. Try to encourage the children to be quiet. Be happy to see him. Greet him with a warm smile and be glad to see him.

6. Some DON'TS: Don't greet him with problems or complaints. Don't complain if he's late for dinner. Count this as minor compared with what he might have gone through that day.

7. Make him comfortable: Have him lean back in a comfortable chair or suggest he lie down in the bedroom. Have a cool or warm drink ready for him. Arrange his pillow and offer to take off his shoes. Speak in a low, soft, soothing and pleasant voice. Allow him to relax and unwind.

8. Listen to him: You may have a dozen things to tell him, but the moment of his arrival is not the time. Let him talk first.

9. Make the evening his: Never complain if he does not take you out to dinner or to other places of entertainment; instead try to understand his world of strain and pressure and his need to be home and relax.

10. The Goal: Try to make your home a place of peace and order where your husband can relax.

Power, powerlessness and gender

When comparing representations of men and women on television, who holds the power? In situation comedies, who is represented as having the power to control and who is controlled? For example, in soaps such as *EastEnders* or *Coronation Street* women tend to dominate all the spaces depicted. In *The Dick Van Dyke Show* men go out to work and women stay at home wearing an apron. In *The Savages*, a recent sitcom, the mother goes out to work whereas the father works freelance from home.

ACTIVITIES

Study two episodes from each of your chosen situation comedies and answer the following questions; (Try to choose two contrasting shows again, for example a more traditional sitcom and a less conventional one such as *Absolutely Fabulous*.).

Identify who has the power in the programme:
1. In the domestic settings
2. In the workspace.

How can power be defined?
Is it through social status (i.e. position in the family or firm, police, army or government)?
Is it through emotional control (i.e. through seniority, maturity, manipulation, selflessness or greed)?

Textual analysis and Gender

With reference to your two situation comedies identify, where relevant, the different types of:

- Family – domestic unit
- House
- Job
- Family
- Possessions
- Clothes
- Relations within the family
- Main characters' status, class or power position in society
- Life events
- Talk
- Aspirations, dreams and opportunities
- Power

Use these headings to make a list of how the main characters and their family or domestic unit is represented. Repeat this for your second situation comedy selection. Analyse how your two situation comedies are similar or different.

Case Study

The Flintstones and The Simpsons.

Themes in *The Flintstones* are:
Suburban life, relationships with friends, parenthood, lifestyle, the American Dream, family life, domestic activity and gender roles.

Themes In *The Simpsons* are:
Parent/teenager relationships, dysfunctional families, new mass consumerism, mass commercialism, anti-authority, individualism, the American Dream, modern society, mass media culture, popular culture and social values.

It is clear that both situation comedies share a core of themes; in particular the family-based issues, however *The Simpsons* is a far more complex text than *The Flintstones*.

Characters
In *The Flintstones*, the family is a typical representation of gender roles at the time – Fred (although incompetent) holds down a job, goes to play golf with his friends, looks after his family and is in control. Wilma, his wife, stays at home, brings up the children, bakes and cleans, talks to her friends, gets her hair done and schemes to catch Fred out, although she rarely does so. This representation is easy to demonstrate by looking at typical drawings for each of the characters;

Two scenes from
The Flintstones.
See page 93,
figures 8 and 9.

By the time *The Simpsons* appeared, gender roles had changed in society and the mother figure presented by Marge is very different to that of Wilma. Homer is still the bumbling, largely incompetent but positive representation of a typical suburban husband but Marge is represented very differently as a more typical mother figure in contemporary American society and she is dressed differently, acts differently, speaks differently, lives differently and has very different expectations to those of Wilma, despite living a life with many similarities in the daily activities.

The Simpsons.
See page 93, figure 10.

Even the children are substantially different to the representations of children in early sitcoms. In the same way as the role and function of the mother figure in each relates directly to society at the time, so do the children – although another key change is that all children in early sitcoms were well behaved to ensure the positive message of the show and to keep the light-hearted tone. There were disruptive teenagers (think of the films of James Dean for example) but this

was not part of the sitcom world. Only as we have become more aware of the world have the sitcom characters become more rounded and complex – hence the reason why Bart in particular gets into so much trouble. He is representative of a typical teenager of today (although exaggerated) and thus can be shown to be less than perfect. Compare the image of Bart and Lisa with Richie and Joanie Cunningham in *Happy Days* for example;

ACTIVITIES

Narrative

Watch each of your chosen episodes of your situation comedies carefully and write a summary of the plot of each episode in no more than 500 words.

Make a numbered list of the key elements in your situation comedies' narratives, thinking about the stages in the narrative and how they relate to the segments of the comedy in relation to timing and breaks needed for adverts etc.

Then write a short list of the narrative moments in the comedy, breaking them down into the relevant segments. Now identify the key narrative moment for each of these segments and then one or two key frames that best illustrate these moments. Try to obtain freeze frame still shots of these moments and, if you can, print off in colour so that you can annotate them in detail to help you.

Themes

List the main themes in your situation comedies e.g. trust, corruption.
Compare similarities and differences between the two situation comedies.

Key Moments: cinematography

The following activities will enable you to analyse key elements in specific scenes to bring out the qualities and techniques of construction.

A C T I V I T I E S

Select one of your key narrative moments and describe four or five frames in one significant and dramatic sequence as though each was a still frame. For each of the frames, explain briefly:

- Camera shot types, angles of each character and the perspective contained within the shot: foreground, mid-ground and/or background.
- Camera movement: tracking, zooming, static etc.
- Lighting: source (artificial or natural), direction and spread (dark or bright etc.)
- Clothing
- Body posture and position in relation to other people or space
- Diegetic and non-diegetic sound and music (identify genre of music and instruments/sound played).

A C T I V I T I E S

Write an analysis of the connotations of the following elements within your chosen situation comedies:

- Perspective (view point of camera). Lighting (effects). Clothing (signifiers)
- Facial expression, body posture, and gestures (meaning)
- Positioning and relationship of characters in the scene/melodrama, e.g. Power relations/good and bad
- Mise en scène: background, setting, colour, furniture, props (signifiers)
- Diegetic and non-diegetic sound and music (associations with genre or music or mood/atmosphere conveyed)
- Themes and links with other parts of the situation comedy.

Look at the stills and annotate the images using the notes that you made in the previous activity. When you have done this and discussed the results as a group, do the same thing with the stills that you have selected for your particular sitcom episodes.

Summary

You have been studying the concept of representation through case studies. To be able to compare both situation comedies effectively you will need to consider that:

- Issues of gender and/or cultural values need to be explained by discussing social attitudes and the director's attitudes e.g. sexism in 60s America is countered by the positive portrayal of the female characters.
- Characters convey attitudes which belong to a wider set of views and values held in society i.e. power relations, gender roles.
- Key moments show the progression of a character's development within the narrative of the situation comedy.
- Ideas must be explored through the language of television.

Section 5
Audience and institutions

Media Studies is not purely concerned with media texts; a thorough analysis of the media will include study of both the audience that consumes the text and the institutions that produce it. During your study of these areas you will need to consider the new media technologies used to produce and distribute texts, the production practices involved and the organisations that own media institutions. This chapter aims to aid your understanding of these areas by offering examples and analysis of these key areas. In the OCR examination, for the first two questions you will be asked to read a passage, similar to the Case Studies in this section, and then answer a selection of questions on the passage.

PART ONE
New media technologies

Introduction

Media-related technologies have developed at an incredible rate even within the last ten years. The speed and capacity of computers has increased to such an extent that the standard 10 GB capacity of a computer today is double that of one-and-a-half years ago. Many home computers are now multimedia, allowing the user to access the Internet, play music or DVD films, edit films and manipulate images. The kind of technology we see in the home today would have cost hundreds of thousands of pounds ten years ago and means that many people are now capable of running businesses from a home computer.

The advent of digital technologies had an extremely significant impact on the media world. Television, radio, film and print text producers have all benefited from the speed and quality of digital processes. Again, this development is now available for home consumption, as well as being part of the production process, and means that the consumer has access to a greater choice of media reception types than ever before. We can receive our television programmes via traditional analogue means, via satellite or cable, or via digital transmission.

Means of access and modes of consumption are a particular issue when discussing new media technologies. We could watch a film, for example, on video, DVD, digital projection, on wide-screen technologies such as IMAX cinema, or we could look at clips from a film on cinema websites. Music can also be accessed through different formats, such as CD, minidisc, DAT, MP3 and older formats such as tape, as well as now being available as an audiovisual form on television or, more controversially, as a product to download from a website such as Napster.

The developments in media technologies have meant an increasing number of contexts in which we can consume the media, formats that we can access and modes of consumption.

The technologies available to both the consumer and media industries are forming closer and closer links, with technologies **converging** in order to develop further. Mobile phones are now capable of accessing the Internet, as are games consoles. Home entertainment systems, which work as a network of technologies with a centralised means of control, will soon be widely available. The necessary interrelation of technologies within these kinds of development has meant that media institutions are now converging in order to create all aspects of the new product. A home entertainment system, for example, will need TV, radio, music, computer and telephone manufacturers to work together.

The Internet

The Internet is an international computer network. It provides access for the consumer to the World Wide Web – about a billion pages of information, organised by those who write and produce them into websites. Once you are linked to the Internet, your computer has access to this information. The Internet is a tool of access and allows you to search for information, send mail, offer information to other users or download information of interest. E-commerce is an ever-expanding area and we can now have banking facilities on the net, sell or buy a house, conduct a business or promote a product.

The global network we have today is still in a process of development and is constantly expanding. Conceived originally as a means of ensuring the passage of information during the Cold War (there is no centralised mainframe to destroy in the event of an attack), the research then moved gradually out of the military arena.

In 1986 the US National Science Foundation created NSFNET (The National Science Foundation Network) by linking five university 'host' computers and offering other universities access to their superior speed and capacity. By 1988 there were over 60,000 host computers on the 'Internet'. Since that date the increase in users and means of access to the Internet has increased exponentially; there are now over 60 million people with web addresses. As it stands, the net is a relatively democratic construct. It is not owned by any one organisation and there are few restrictions on who is allowed access to which kind of information. Obviously this can cause problems and we will explore these later in this chapter. **Service providers** vie for a piece of the extremely lucrative market, but the Internet itself (for now anyway!) remains 'unowned' and therefore, some would say, essentially democratic.

In the mid 90s the 'browser war' was fought primarily between Netscape and Microsoft, with Microsoft eventually releasing Windows 95, a new operating platform. In 1999 the First Internet Bank of Indiana provided the first full service bank available only on the net, adding to the already flourishing group of e-commerce businesses. In ten years the number of host computers for the Internet has risen from around 130,000 to over 20 million. The number of sites on the World Wide Web has increased, in the same period, from around 100 to more than 18 million!

The technologies surrounding the Internet are in constant development because one of the major criticisms the consumer has of the net is the speed at which information can be received. Most people connect to the Internet using telephone lines and modems, but because the data-carrying capacity of the phone line, or its bandwidth, is low, the speed at which a computer receives information is often disappointingly slow. Connecting to the Internet using fibre optic lines or via cable TV are two future possibilities that will increase the speed of information reception dramatically. One of the sources of ideas for the next generation Internet is a consortium of universities, corporations and government agencies known as Internet 2. There is no single network within Internet 2, but hundreds of high-speed computers linked by fibre optics, transmitting data at speeds of up to 2.4 gigabits per second.

In the context of Media Studies, the Internet should be seen as a tool for both the industries and the consumer. It can open up our access to media texts and institutions by providing both information and media-related products. For the media industry the uses are myriad: a photographer might use e-mail to send an image to his/her newspaper; an advertiser might conduct market research surveys via a website; and television production companies may use webcams in order to inform the viewer about the latest events in a programme, a recent example being the

Channel Four programme *Big Brother*. Film makers can use the Internet to promote a cinema release or introduce a new product to an audience. The makers of *The Blair Witch Project,* for example, created an Internet teaser campaign, which then turned into huge box office success.

Big Brother 2001

DISCUSSION

- In small groups discuss how you use the Internet. Are there any differences in use? Are these differences connected with gender? What is the context of use (at home, in school, etc.)? What are the subject areas you are interested in?

- What problems do you consider there are surrounding Internet use? Do you think that users are able to use effectively all of the information they can access?

- Do you think that the Internet is becoming a successor to television as a way to spend free time? Is the amount of time spent on the Internet related to the user's age? What effects do you think increased time spent on the Internet have on the user?

Case Study

Read the extract carefully and answer the questions that follow.

From **Spinning the Net** – *Sight and Sound Mediawatch 2000*

OFFICIAL SITES

In the last five years, the internet has become ever more central to the marketing of movies. Now all mainstream films and most smaller ones have a website, saying, at the very least, when the film is out, and what it is about. *High Fidelity's* official site (http://studio.go.com/movies/highfidelity) has a plot synopsis, information on cast and makers, internet chats with cast members, trailers, clips from the film, details of cinemas showing the film, and the chance to listen to and buy the soundtrack album. For the distributors, websites have a number of advantages as a marketing tool:

- Compared to billboard, magazine or press ads, they're cheap. Used to sell merchandising, they can even be partially self-financing;
- Often up months before a film's release, and still helpful for video/DVD release, websites are more durable than conventional advertising;
- Their discussion forums allow the audience to feel involved as no other form of marketing can. *The Mod Squad* site asked visitors to vote which of five posters would be the official poster;
- Teenagers and young adults, the internet's main US and UK users, are the core film-going audience;
- A website which tracks site visits provides its own market research. Downloading a trailer, a slow process, very likely indicates a film-goer;

- For some lower-budget movies, as *The Blair Witch Project's* success showed, the internet could entirely replace print ads.

GOSSIP SITES

When *Ain't It Cool News* first came to the public attention in 1997, it was seen as an alternative to the Hollywood hype machine. Living in Texas, far from Hollywood, Harry Knowles, an obsessive film fan, apparently infuriated the major studios with well-sourced rumours and reviews of early test screenings of films. Even Knowles' appearance – scruffy, obese, bespectacled – contributed to his status as outsider. Media reports claimed that the film companies were going to ban Knowles from screenings, and hunt down his pseudonymous sources. Instead, Knowles has been befriended by the film companies. They realised that Knowles' site helped build an 'early buzz' around a film. Now treated exactly as conventional media by film companies – the occasional exclusive, plane tickets to filming locations – Knowles, who built his reputation on his difference from the existing publicity machine, was accused of compromising his independence, a feeling compounded by his appearance in the film *The Faculty* and his self-proclaimed friendship with various directors. Moreover, since it started, *Ain't It Cool* News has developed from a hobby to a business, depending on advertising for its budget.

   Naturally, this success spawned many rivals, most significantly ComingAttractions.com and Darkhorizons.com, all benefiting from Knowles' increasingly compromised profile. The evidence overall is of a public appetite for film news far greater than anyone had guessed. These sites contain the kind of information that only used to exist in film industry trade magazines. They provide pre-production rumours about the casting of films, on set reports from extras, passers-by or anonymous crew members and reviews of working drafts of scripts. Even if we play down the idea that the studios are 'planting' stories on these sites, they can use them to track the level of anticipation about movies in progress, especially the more cultish ones (*X-Men, Lord of the Rings*).

1. a. List five ways in which websites are used as a marketing tool.

   b. What information would you typically find on a film industry website?

   c. Why does Hollywood not like Harry Knowles' website?

2. a. What is different about sites such as ComingAttractions.com and Darkhorizons.com?

   b. How effective do you think a website is in the publicising of a film?

Digital television

Digital television uses computer technology rather than standard systems to transmit signals. Unlike an analogue mode of transmission, digital television sounds and images are converted to computerised digits before being sent through the air. These digits can be received by aerials, satellite dishes or via cables, but need either a set-top box or a built-in decoder in order to process the signal for your digital television set. All of this means that pictures and sounds can be transmitted much faster than before and will retain a much higher quality. Interactive television is also possible using digital signals and we are, for example, already able to choose camera angles when watching live sporting events or music concerts.

In 1996, the Digital TV Group was established in order to work towards the launch of terrestrial digital television in 1998. There were eight founder members of this group, including the BBC, and the common aim was to establish an effective digital broadcast, providing also a forum for discussion of issues involving broadcasters, transmission operators and receiver manufacturers. Once digital was launched, the market quickly expanded. There are now three 'platforms' through which it is possible to obtain digital TV: satellite (via, for example, Sky Digital), terrestrial (via ONdigital, which includes non-subscription digital BBC channels) and cable (via, for example, NTL).

Digital television has seen many new types of programme and, by extension, programme consumption. Interactive television offers the viewer greater control over the images being received. Video conferencing is also possible using digital transmission and may have a significant impact on the ability of businesses to communicate, as well as an individual's choice of communication means. 'Pay-per-view' television is also a feature of digital channels where the viewer is asked to pay a fee before being able to access, for example, a sporting event. This type of television is extremely problematic, however, and opponents argue that it will encourage the organisers of large events to allow only 'pay-per-view' coverage, thus excluding those who do not have access to the appropriate technology.

Recent television technology developments, such as flat screens, have already hit the general markets and interactive television is already in evidence on digital channels in the form of TV shopping and 'choose your camera angle' style sporting event coverage.

The main recent advancement has been the move from analogue to digital transmissions, but the technology surrounding television is developing constantly – 3D and holographic televisions are in development, as are plasma screens, which use small packets of glowing gas, rather than tubes.

Video recorders may soon be outstripped by DVD as a means of viewing films at home, but the latest in personal video recorders (PVRs) allow personalised recording. TiVo, which is made by Thomson and marketed by BSkyB and ReplayTV, which is marketed in the US, use a hard drive to store programmes recorded from the television. The system has the ability to 'learn' the viewing habits of the household and record programmes accordingly. This kind or recording technology takes the analogue signal from your TV aerial and converts it into digital codes that can then be stored. When you want to watch the programmes that have been recorded, an MPEG decoder translates the signal from digital back into analogue so it can be read by your television. This translation of signal is not necessary with a digital TV set-up.

What will also be extremely significant for television in the future will be the convergence of both the industries and the technologies they produce in an attempt to provide more advanced and integrated systems. Part 2 of this chapter will look at the institutional importance of convergence in more detail, but in terms of technology, we can construct three areas of product that seem to offer natural convergence. These areas are telecommunications, media technologies and IT technologies.

Telecommunications technologies, such as satellite TV and telephones, may provide one area of convergence. Television broadcasting, the film industry, book publishing and newspaper technologies seem to offer another logical group of related industries that would benefit from more integrated systems. The last area of potential convergence is within the realm of IT technologies, and we may see increased links between Internet providers, computer software and hardware manufacturers, and other IT service providers.

DISCUSSION

- How will interactive television affect the average consumer? Do you think it will breed a more empowered/active television audience?

- What effect will the new range of television channels, brought about by digital TV technology, have on the viewer? Do you think the viewing experience will alter? Will the quantity of channels mean that attention span is altered and viewers adopt a fragmented style of viewing?

Case Study

Read the extract below and answer the questions that follow.

From **Now: TV ads just for you for,** Jamie Doward, *The Guardian*. **Guardian**Unlimited **Archive**

Sunday November 7, 1999

The drive to sell digital television to British viewers is about to receive a major boost with the launch of a revolutionary new set-top box that will act as a sophisticated video recorder and allow broadcasters to tailor advertisements to individual households.

The device, which has been developed by electronics company Pace in conjunction with News Corporation subsidiary NDS, will be unveiled to analysts when the company's next set of results is announced in January, and will be in the shops at the end of next year.

Pace predicts the new set-top box will be heavily subsidised by digital broadcasters and should therefore cost consumers no more than a normal mid-range video player.

The new box, currently called XTV, features a hard drive which will allow users to record up to 20 hours of programmes. The company has plans to develop future versions which will also be capable of storing vast numbers of video games. Other applications for the device will include the ability to store shopping catalogues, allowing users to buy through their television sets without having to spend time surfing the Internet.

The device is intelligent enough to know your viewing patterns and to record programmes it suspects you might like – for instance, the final part of a four-part series.

'If you like watching movies with Bruce Willis, it knows this and will record any for you,' said Pace chief executive Malcolm Miller. He predicted that the new device would mean television schedules could change dramatically in the future.

'Television is currently very wasteful,' Miller said. 'This system will allow broadcasters to transmit programmes at any time of the day or night; the devices will know that you want to watch them and record them, so you can view them whenever.'

However, it is XTV's ability to 'target' television advertisements that Pace predicts will prove a major attraction to the UK's digital broadcasters, who now have around 2.2 million subscribers. The device allows broadcasters to vary advertising according to viewers' socio-demographic and regional profiles, which, marketing companies say, improves response levels.

So, for example, instead of the current system whereby audiences from London to Leith see the same set of advertisements, viewers will receive their own bespoke set of commercials during the programme break.

1 a. List the ways in which this new set-top box (XTV) is different from what has gone before.

b. What impact will XTV have on advertisers?

2 a. How will this new system help to 'streamline' TV broadcasting?

b. Can you envisage any drawbacks for the consumer with this type of technology?

Digital radio

Until digital technology became available to radio, all programmes were broadcast using analogue transmissions (either AM or FM). Analogue processes present the listener with the actual sound which is being generated (during a radio play, for example) and thus tend to recreate any interference or distortion which may occur in the studio. Analogue signals can also be affected by hills or tall buildings that might impede their movement. Digital radio signals are translated into digits and carried by the radio waves in a way that stops interference or distortion.

DISCUSSION

Working in small groups, imagine that you have been asked to write a pitch outlining a new digital radio station. How will the fact that the new station is digital enhance the listening experience of the consumer? You will need to discuss some of the programmes you will broadcast and how they will be improved by digital technologies. Having discussed the above, you should then (orally) present your ideas to other members of your media group.

Case Study

Read the extract below and answer the questions that follow.

From **BBC R & D annual review,** April 1997–1998

Digital Radio

Digital Radio (the new phrase used for Digital Audio Broadcasting) is now a public service with around 60% of people already within the coverage area. This technical success has been built on the work at BBC R&D over the past years. Now we are waiting for receivers to come on to the market in large numbers and at affordable prices to complete the commercial success of the project.

Not surprisingly, recent work in this area has been largely one of pulling through existing ideas. We have concentrated on providing a good coverage, helping receiver manufacturers to design working receivers, providing a good base for multimedia on Digital Radio, and resolving one of the remaining technical problems with satellite radio.

Digital radio infrastructure at Broadcasting House
BBC R&D are collaborating closely with colleagues from BBC Broadcast, Radio Production Resources and Project

Management Services to provide the technical facilities needed to broadcast Digital Radio. These facilities include production, coding, multiplexing and distribution to the transmission network of the national network of Digital Radio services now being broadcast by the BBC. During the past year, we have concentrated on the many new system features from the Eureka 147 specification, such as half-rate audio coding, dynamic range control, servicing linking to and from FM radio, and Announcement services. These provide BBC Broadcast with the 'tools' necessary to enhance BBC Digital Radio services with a wide range of added-value features, with which to encourage the take-up of Digital Radio in the UK when it is launched.

A major achievement was the delivery and installation in Broadcasting House, during early December, of the computer-based Integrated Control System (ICS), designed and developed by BBC R&D. After trials and acceptance testing, the system entered operational service in February 1998. Using a central programme schedule database, the ICS allows operational staff to configure and control, from a single workstation, the individual audio encoders and multiplexers used to code and combine the different programme services and data feeds constituting the multiplex. This makes reconfigurations of the multiplex much easier to implement, allowing new and possibly temporary services to be introduced and removed from the multiplex as and when operational requirements demand.

UK coverage planning
The main Digital Radio service is provided by a network of twenty-seven transmitters which have been constructed over the last three years or so. Not all the stations were straightforward designs. In particular, the tower at Emley Moor provided several seemingly insurmountable difficulties. Following protracted negotiations, during which eight alternative sites were examined, space has finally been made available on the spine at Emley Moor for the BBC National services. This station is expected on air in Spring 1998, completing the twenty-seven station network.

Now that the network is in operation, we have studied ways to improve coverage. Efficient measurement of coverage deficiencies and an understanding of the causes will play an important part in planning the expansion of the network in an economical fashion.

Some improvements in coverage are anticipated as a result of a detailed examination of timing issues within the single-frequency network. One significant benefit will be an increase of coverage in Lancashire, achieved by advancing all transmitters in Northern Ireland relative to the rest of the UK.

Planning the expansion of this network requires detailed coordination of many transmitters with surrounding countries. Fifty potential transmitter sites in southern England have been examined.

On Digital Radio, the BBC's local radio services are likely to be carried alongside commercial local radio stations. We have therefore been in close contact with the Radio Authority, regarding their plans for national and local multiplexes.

In order to develop planning techniques for local radio services the Radio Authority has initiated an experimental Digital Radio network using low-power transmitters in the Chelmsford area. BBC R&D provided help to set up this experimental network using the experience we gained from our earlier high-power London experiment. As yet, there are no results available.

1 a. What technical facilities are needed to broadcast digital radio?

b. What are the benefits of the BBC's Integrated Control System?

2 a. What did the BBC do in order to develop planning techniques for local radio services?

b. What do you think the advantages are to a digital radio system?

MP3s

The latest source that has opened up for music consumers is the Internet. Using free MP3 software – which derives its acronym from MPEG (Motion Picture Experts Group) 1, Audio Layer 3 – an Internet user can convert a song from a CD into a computer file and post it on the net. Another user can then download the file and play it. This means that the music being transferred from one consumer to another is free. This is a significant issue that is causing a great deal of debate within the music industry. Fan sites and music industry official sites have fragments of tracks available to listen to or download, but they do not allow complete albums to be downloaded, and they do not release singles/albums on to the Internet before their official release date. Some artists are not concerned that the consumer may be able to download an album free, possibly even before release. They enjoy the fact that their music is being listened to by an increasing number of people. They don't consider MP3s a threat to sales: David Bowie, the Beastie Boys and Fatboy Slim are firm supporters of MP3s. Other artists, such as Metallica, The Corrs and Eminem are fierce opponents and consider this type of access to their music to be undermining and illicit.

In 1999, Shawn Fanning decided to create an MP3 website which would allow free access to music. He created Napster, a site which functions through what some term a philosophy of democracy. Each Napster user has access to every other user's 'catalogue' of available MP3 files. The fact that Napster allows fans to swop music free of charge has caused much controversy; firstly because the copying of music is actually illegal, and secondly because there is no revenue generated for the music industry. Music creates a £38 billion industry and anything which looks to threaten profits is vehemently fought against. It was Napster against whom Metallica brought a law suit in America, claiming that it allowed illegal copying. The law suit was a small victory, but Metallica were heavily criticised by fans who thought that their motivation was greed. For some bands, MP3 sites and the Internet can be an extremely effective tool in their career, allowing them to promote widely themselves and their single for minimal cost. The Napster site is able to sustain 14,000 downloads per minute, but each of these can be tracked.

The MP3 phenomena is described by its critics as a threat to the continuation of the music industry because it diminishes revenue and therefore limits the amount of potential investment in new and existing artists. The counter argument cites the increased exposure of artists which

MP3s affords, the fact that consumers will still purchase CDs and other formats because they want a real and tangible product, and the democracy of music sharing as beneficial factors.

MP3 is not the only software which enables the consumer to 'stream' and store music files. WMA, or Windows Media Audio, was launched by Microsoft in April 1999 and offers a compression system which provides better quality than MP3. Copyright protection is provided by Windows Media Digital Rights Management (DRM).

DISCUSSION

- Do you think that the emergence of MP3 software and websites like Napster will mean the end of conventional music purchasing?

- In what ways might MP3 files help in the introduction of new artists to the public?

Case Study

From **Net takes safety away from CDs,** Fiachra Gibbons, *The Guardian*.

Net takes safety away from CDs

Radiohead are 'totally cool' about tracks leaking out early, and Fatboy Slim is even more relaxed, while the Smashing Pumpkins sought to make a dramatic gesture.

It is the most eagerly awaited album of the year from the "best band in the world". But a month before the first CD has made it into the shops the songs are already freely available on the internet.

Kid A, the album on which Radiohead have been toiling since OK Computer became the epitome of 90s cool, can be downloaded on Napster, the controversial website which the music industry is trying to shut down.

All but two of the tracks on the album, which is officially released in October, were available at the weekend on the site which the multinationals and some pop stars claim has robbed them of $2.5bn (£1.7bn) in royalties.

Sunset (Bird of Prey), the new single from Fatboy Slim, also turned up on Napster last week, long before it was due to be released. And in the most surprising development of all, the Smashing Pumpkins released their latest album, *Friends and Enemies of Modern Music*, on the internet free as a gesture to an industry "poisoned with greed".

Despite the series of multimillion dollar piracy lawsuits hanging over it and its 19-year-old founder, Shawn Fanning, Napster, it seems, is thriving.

Since the first cases were brought against it in the US courts in April by the rock band Metallica and Time

Warner/AOL, traffic on the site has quadrupled, while its prosecutors have seen sales drop.

Guardian critic Caroline Sullivan believes Metallica misjudged the mood of their fans. "They looked greedy. Most fans see it in simplistic terms – that Metallica don't love them enough to share their music with them."

Napster's democratic nature – fans automatically share all the MP3 music files on their computers when they log on – is the secret of its popularity, allowing it to build up a library of 20m tracks while providing a free platform for the music of up to 17,000 new bands in the past year.

Even if Time Warner/AOL and the Recording Industry Association of America succeeded in closing it, two other sites have sprung up. Gnutella, and Freenet do not need host databases, so they are less vulnerable to legal action.

Not all musicians share the views of their paymasters. A spokesman for Radiohead said: "The band are quite flattered. Obviously you have to be concerned how they [the music] were obtained, but the fact that they have turned up on Napster so early shows there is huge interest. Radiohead do not think that music on the net is the threat that the industry seems to think it is. It has all got a little heavy."

Fatboy Slim, real name Norman Cook, is even more relaxed. Napster's share-and-share-alike ethos fits perfectly with his left leaning politics.

Damian Harris, the boss of Fatboy Slim's Brighton-based label, Skint Records, said: "The amount of time companies spend stressing about getting a record on radio, you would think that the idea of some big global listening post would make perfect sense. I don't see why we can't all live in one big happy music sharing world."

Public Enemy are also fervent proponents of what they call "free music". There was less idealism in the Smashing Pumpkins' decision to embrace Napster. Unhappy with how they see the industry sacrificing real content for "bland, packaged" Britney Spears-type pop, they put it in on the net as a dramatic gesture "to a record label that didn't give us the support we deserved".

Shirley Manson, of Garbage is, with Metallica, Alanis Morissette, Elton John and Paul McCartney, among the most vocal of Napster's opponents. She said: "It pisses me off that the entire world believes it's morally OK to rape musicians of their art and their livelihood. If it were Nike, do you think the establishment would sit back and allow it to happen?"

Links
www.radiohead.com
Radiohead
www.napster.com/pressroom/legal.html
Napster legal case documents
www.riaa.com/napster_legal.cfm
Recording Industry Association of America case documents

1. a. Why is the music industry not in favour of the Internet site Napster?

   b. Why was Metallica's law suit against Napster perhaps ill advised?

2. a. List the arguments for and against websites such as Napster.

   b. What impact do you think MP3 technology will have on the future of music sales?

Computer generated images (CGI)

Computer generated images are evident in many media areas. Films, computer games, television commercials and programmes, amongst others, have all 'benefited' from this new technology. Ridley Scott's film *Gladiator* included a computer generated Rome, and the *Ally McBeal* TV series used the dancing baby CGI to represent Ally's ticking biological clock. The ship and many of the characters seen walking on the deck in James Cameron's *Titanic* were produced on a computer, and the latest *Star Wars* instalment was littered with computer generated images. These computer generated effects are used either to approximate reality (to generate verisimilitude), as with the Rome of *Gladiator* or the ship in *Titanic,* or to give a sense of the unreal or science fictional, as with Ally McBeal's baby or the numerous alien characters in the *Star Wars* prequel.

An example of a computer generated image from the film Titanic. *See page 94, figure 11.*

Computer generated imagery of the type in evidence today was first brought to the attention of both the film industry and the general public in 1991 with James Cameron's sequel *Terminator 2*. The 'morphing' of the T–1000 robot was produced through improved hardware and software and was evidence to the film industry that this new form of special effect was popular with the viewing public. *Jurassic Park* proved to be another successful showcasing for this technology, as did the *Toy Story* films. As yet the main products of CGI have been settings and creatures; if human characters are computer generated they are generally seen from a distance because it is extremely difficult to accurately reproduce the movements, gestures and skin quality of people on a computer.

The process of generating a computer image often begins with the skeleton of the shape to be animated. In *Jurassic Park* the ILM (Industrial Light and Magic) animators began by building dinosaur skeletons in their computers. They found pictures of bones, which were then scanned in to achieve a realistic dinosaur shape. Anatomically accurate models were also built and then scanned into a computer. The scanning was done using a Cyberware scanner, which focuses a revolving laser beam on its subject, thus obtaining information from all angles and from all depths. The next stage was to 'fit' the information from the scanner over the skeleton already created in the computer. The T–Rex dinosaur was produced in this way, and once its movements had been created in the computer, using knowledge of the T–Rex's shape and size plus the information gained through moving the models to predict how it would move, it came to life on the screen.

DISCUSSION

● What other recent films have used Computer generated imagery?
  Do you think they have used it to good effect?

● What might be some of the future uses for CGI? Do you think it
  will eventually make location finding and casting redundant
  because places and actors will be generated using a computer?

Case Study

Read the extract below and answer the questions that follow.

From *The animation of Jar Jar Binks*, from *Cinefex* magazine.

Star Wars Episode I

The animation of Jar Jar would be based on the physical and vocal performance of actor Ahmed Best. Throughout principal photography, Best – wearing a Jar Jar suit constructed by Nick Dudman's creature crew – played the live-action counterpart of the computer generated character. Scenes between Jar Jar and the other actors would be filmed with Best on camera, allowing the actors to work out interactions and timings with the character – a far better acting situation than trying to perform with a nonexisting Jar Jar. Typically, once the scene was worked out to Lucas' satisfaction, production takes would be filmed with Best out of frame. In some instances, however, Lucas preferred the performances in the rehearsal takes that included Best. As a result, ILM's digital rotoscope department – under supervisor Susan Kelly – was faced with a number of 'Ahmed-Best-removal' shots to produce a clean plate into which the CG Jar Jar could be composited.

Initially, Lucas had contemplated computer generating only Jar Jar's head, which would then be matchmoved and attached to Best's body. Toward that end, the performer wore the Jar Jar suit, along with a prosthetic head piece – placed on top of his own head to denote the appropriate height for the character. The notion was to retain the live-action footage of Best up to his neck, then replace everything above the neck with CG. "The original thought was that it was going to be much too expensive to do every single Jar Jar shot entirely as CG," commented Rob Coleman. "So they invested the money into building the suit, and we were only going to do the head replacements. One of my first jobs when I came on the show was to do a test of that idea with a team of animators. We quickly realized that the CG head replacement was not going to be as easy as we thought. There were serious problems with things crossing on front of other things, meaning that some things had to be painted out and others had to be put back in. The biggest problem, though was the fact that as wonderful as Ahmed's performance was, his anatomy was not the same as Jar Jar's anatomy. My main concern was that if we did some of the shots with Jar Jar entirely CG – which we were going to have to do for some of the more extreme, Gungan-like moves – and others with him part-CG and part-Ahmed, they weren't going to cut together well at all. So I presented the work to George and brought up these points; and before we even started production, the decision was made to create Jar Jar entirely through CG. The only shots in the film with Ahmed as Jar Jar as those in which you see an arm or foot or part of a knee in the edge of frame."

Though that decision freed Jar Jar lead animator Lou Dellarosa and his team from the physical limitations of a real live actor, Best's performance was still the model for ninety percent of Jar Jar's animation. "There were shots where we literally followed Ahmed's actions frame by frame," acknowledged Coleman. "So Ahmed's performance is certainly there, even though his body isn't. Ahmed created this character."

While the animation of Jar Jar and other prominent CG characters was principally a performance issue, their clothing was a technical one. Having dealt primarily with the computer animation of unclothed animals, the ILM team had seldom come face to face with the difficulties of animating the dynamics of fabric as it moved and flowed on a CG character's form. It was, in fact, an issue that had plagued the entire CG world for years. "The kinds of cloth simulations seen in off-the-shelf packages tend to emulate thin cotton or lightweight silk materials," said Doug Smythe, "but for this show, there were many heavy costumes and burlap-like materials – an altogether different proposition. For Jar Jar, his clothing was a two-tiered operation, one aspect being his bulky outerwear – made of heavy, leather-like material – and the other, his shirt and pants."

In the past, academics had tried to create a workable cloth simulation by dealing with CG cloth the same way one would deal with fabric in the real world – by cutting out patterns from flat pieces and joining them together. ILM's technique was to model the cloth in 3D in its 'at rest' position – that is, the form it would take when it was on a standing CG character – with 2D textures applied to give it the look of cloth. That cloth geometry would then be modeled into specific costumes, and would be driven by the animation of the CG character.

The procedural cloth simulation software was developed in-house by Jim Hourihan and John Anderson, working with Cary Phillips. "John has an amazing intuitive understanding of conceptual physics," said Hourihan, "which saved the day on this project. Cary and I developed the basis for simulation in our pipeline and a first pass at the cloth solver. John later reworked the solver and came up with physics that really captured the look of several different kinds of fabric."

Ultimately, the cloth simulation would be used not just for clothing but also for cords dangling off of characters, and even as a means of animating Jar Jar's floppy ears. This 'secondary animation' was overseen by Tim McLaughlin, who worked side by side with animators whose primary focus was performance. "The animators would work on the action," stated McLaughlin, "get that correct, and then I would work with them to get the rest of the animation done – all the stuff that moves as a result of the character moving. In a perfect world, an animator would only have to concern himself with the performance of a character, the actual acting: and from there, there would be an automatic procedure to deal with the secondary animation that is driven by the initial performance. There would be basic laws of physics in the virtual world that would always play out as they should. We are not there yet, but we're moving toward having those things happen automatically."

The final stop in the pipeline for Jar Jar was rendering and compositing – both complicated somewhat by the character's pronounced, bright coloring. "His skin color was such that he had some very light areas and some color areas that were very saturated," explained 2D composite supervisor Jon Alexander, "and depending on where the lights were, his light areas could be very, very bright. Within the composite, we'd pull different mattes for different areas to bring those down, leaving his more saturated areas as they were. There was no reason to re-render just to make that kind of color tweak – there was a lot we could do in the composite." Casting of shadows onto Jar Jar from live characters within his proximity was also done in the composite stage. "Once we had all the elements together, we could see what the placement of the shadows should be. There are lighting and shadow touches that are much more difficult to deal with in the render – and there's no point in doing them there when we can do them far more interactively in the composite. It's a huge cheat, but it works and it's efficient."

Creating a character as prominent, as complex, as *alive* as Jar Jar entirely through digital means had been one of George Lucas' riskiest decisions – but in the end, his faith in ILM's animation and technical direction teams was wholly justified. "At one point," recalled Coleman, "George told me that, even after starting the show, he'd been very apprehensive about whether or not we were going to be able to pull off Jar Jar, but that we had surpassed his wildest expectations. That comment alleviated a lot of stress in my life."

1 a. How was the actor Ahmed Best (who was the voice of Jar Jar Binks) used before the animators began?

   b. Why did the animators eventually decide to animate the whole of Jar Jar's body?

2 a. Why are cloths difficult to animate?

   b. Why was it 'risky' to create Jar Jar Binks using digital means?

DVD

One of the newest formats for watching films, listening to music or storing information is the DVD or Digital Versatile Disc. As with a compact disc, the DVD uses a laser to read microscopic pits on a disc, gathering information which it then reproduces as music, information or visuals. DVDs and CDs are the same size, but DVD uses a smaller, thinner infrared laser to pick up information and can, therefore, read more closely packed data. Because of this, a DVD has seven times the capacity of a standard compact disc. Moving images, however, take up enormous amounts of space, even on a DVD. In order to make sure that the viewing public were able to view more than just clips of films DVD developers had to find a way of compressing video footage so that a complete film could be held on the DVD. MPEG (Moving Pictures Expert Group) technology, which was originally used for compressing data from satellites, was then brought in to 'squash' the necessary amount of information on to a DVD.

The versatility of the DVD comes from its capacity to store different types of information and the ease with which the consumer can range through what is on offer. If you are watching a film, for example, on a DVD, the disc will contain not only the film, but information such as biographical notes, scene analysis, storyboards, and so on. In order to access this information, the consumer can scroll through menus and quickly locate what is wanted. The future developments of the DVD include a move towards rewritable digital versatile discs – blank discs which can be recorded onto, much like VHS video. This, of course, has caused much debate concerning the copyright of what might be recorded and the film industry is already taking steps to encrypt, copyguard or watermark their products to prevent free copying. Consumers may still be able to copy films, but at a price. As it stands, a video hacker needs only to use a powerful PC and a simple utility called DeCss to gain the file of codes of which a film comprises. He/she can then recompress it using a format known as DivX file to reproduce the film.

DISCUSSION

- In what ways is the DVD a development of the VHS video technology? List the differences between the two.

- A great deal of additional information is offered alongside the actual film on a DVD, and DVD also offers varying ways in which we can explore the film. How do these additional advantages help us to better understand the film?

Case Study

Read the extract below and answer the questions that follow.

From **DVD News,** BBC Online

Recordable DVD
Those of you who remember the VHS vs. Betamax format war will not be impressed with the competing recordable DVD formats announced. A sign of who's going to win this latest waste of our time and money came with the announcement that Yamaha, Phillips, Ricoh and most importantly Sony will all be backing DVD-RW. This format is fully backward compatible with current DVD players and DVD-ROM Drives unlike the competing DVD-R/RW (catchy huh?) from Pioneer. Let's hope that whatever format wins we aren't stuck with another dog like VHS. Anyone seeking a trip down video recorder memory lane will no doubt enjoy the fabulous *Betamax tribute site.*

TV Hard Discs
While you're waiting for the dust to settle on the competing recordable DVD formats you might like to check out the new hard disc recorders from Phillips and Panasonic. Both systems work essentially like a PC hard drive and both can record up to 30 hours worth of TV programmes. They are also capable of learning your viewing habits and will automatically record programmes that might be of interest to you. Those of you who aren't scared by coming home to 30 hours worth of soap operas should check out Philip's *TiVo System* and Panasonic's *ReplayTV*

"Hellraiser" DVD Rebirth
Those of you who recall the dark days of owning a DVD player over two years ago will recall that one of the only discs available in the UK was "Hellraiser". As DVDs go this was one of the most miserable transfers ever with shockingly poor picture and sound quality. Fans of the film will be glad to know that the US company Anchor Bay are to release "Hellraiser" and "Hellraiser 2" with a remastered 5.1 CDS soundtrack produced by Chace Productions in California. Those of you who enjoyed their brilliant surround sound track remix on the recent DVD "The Texas Chainsaw Massacre" will know what to expect.

1 a. What are the benefits of the new DVD-RW format?

b. What are the capabilities of the new hard disc recorders available?

2 a. In what ways have DVDs improved over the last two years?

b. In what ways might the recordable DVD format cause problems for the motion picture industry?

Big-screen technologies

The spectacle of viewing images on large screens is not a twentieth century phenomenon. Audiences in the early nineteenth century had access to a Diorama experience, and one of the most dramatic of the Diorama productions was *L'Arrivée d'un Train en Gare* filmed in 1896 by Louis Lumière. Large landscapes were painted on to a huge transparent canvas and an audience would watch the image as variations in lighting projected through the canvas made it appear to move. Because of the size of the canvas, the audience had the sensation that they were being pulled into the image, thus taking part in the experience represented on screen. This form of early visual spectacle was an attempt to approximate reality by creating a complete viewing experience. Because even the peripheral vision of those watching the Diorama caught what was happening on the screen, the experience was much more realistic.

Cinema continued to experiment with wide-screen technologies and the advent of sound and colour offered even more exciting audio visual experiences for the audience. The next stages of development saw Fox projecting films in 70mm Grandeur. Paramount's equivalent was Magnafilm and Warner Brothers' format was VitaScope. None of these proved to be particularly successful, partly because of the advent of an alternative new viewing experience in the form of television. It wasn't until the 1950s when Cinerama was introduced that wide screen technologies became popular with audiences again. Films in this format tended to be of real events and the realism of the viewing experience caused some members of the audience to run from the cinema! CinemaScope was to be the next major advancement for the big screen and was developed by 20th Century Fox to deliver an even more realistic and exciting film experience.

Modern big-screen entertainment is perhaps best represented by IMAX cinema, a fully integrated system of film production which uses cameras, film stock, screens and projection equipment especially designed in order to recreate a live experience. IMAX digital sound recording is also used and is projected through the screen in order to enhance the live feel of the shows. The Expo event in Montreal, Canada, in 1967 saw the first showcasing of IMAX cinema technology when film makers Graeme Ferguson, Roman Kroitor and Robert Kerr presented their preliminary ideas for IMAX-style films. They offered their ideas for an integrated IMAX system that would use one powerful projector, and introduced the latest and most realistic wide-screen experience. At the Osaka EXPO in 1970, having worked with the backing of a Japanese consortium,

Ferguson, Kroitor and Kerr revealed their first, finished, IMAX film and the technology which had created it. They also formed the IMAX corporation in this year to produce, market and distribute their new system. After this introduction, IMAX cinemas quickly sprung up and are now to be seen all over the world. In 1994 the Sony IMAX cinema opened in New York City and in 1997 the BFI (British Film Institute) IMAX cinema was started in London.

The BFI IMAX uses Britain's biggest screen. It is more than 20 metres high and 26 metres wide. The projector weighs about two tonnes and the sound comes from an 11,600 watt digital surround sound system that has 44 speakers positioned in seven clusters throughout the auditorium. The verisimilitude (approximation to reality) offered within a big-screen cinema experience, generated by both the image and the sound, is different from that of a standard film. Big-screen productions saturate the senses of the audience and place them firmly within the world that is being portrayed on the screen. Whether this enhances the viewer's experience or limits it is something that you will need to debate.

DISCUSSION

- How would a big-screen experience, such as IMAX, differ from watching a film on a standard sized screen?

- What kind of media texts do you think would benefit most from being presented in a big-screen format? Why do you think this is so?

Case Study

Read the extract below and answer the questions that follow.

From **Now the ultimate cinema experience,** Jason Solomans The BFI London IMAX Experience magazine

'As the camera dived underwater, I was tempted to hold my nose, such is the impression of immersion'

Into The Deep is lovely in the way that most wildlife documentaries are (the footage of the lobster struggling to shed its exoskeleton is wondrous by any standards) but it isn't exactly a rollicking Saturday night out or an art-house attraction. Yet it does give a huge pointer as to the future of cinema.

Its opponents point out that IMAX technology has existed for 30 years and that little advance has been made. Large-format films are good for amusement parks and expos, they say, but it isn't cinema. The reasons so far have been financial. The IMAX circuit was not large enough to justify the investment of more than US$6 million for a 3D film. Plus the cameras themselves make such a racket that all dialogue has to be dubbed on later. Let's not forget, however, that Thomas Edison's first camera was a cumbersome thing and that the Lumiere Brothers showed their first films as expo sideshows in 1895 – *Workers Leaving the Factory* and *Train Arriving At Station* could hardly be deemed terrific movies, but they heralded the dawn of the art form we know and love so well now.

Working on the admirable cinematic principle of "if you build them, they will come", IMAX Corporation is setting up a network of cinemas capable of showing the films so far committed to this form of celluloid.

The screen before me is undoubtedly huge – seven storeys high, I'm told – and when I'm treated to a backlit view, the structure behind it is breathtaking, like a Blade Runner cityscape with its network of metal, lights and loudspeakers. Soon, a digital IMAX camera will be available and the world is then your cinematic oyster. Steven Spielberg and George Lucas are said to be considering large-format film and Disney have already completed the first animated feature in the format, adapting one of their own classics to make *Fantasia 2000*.

They said that *Saving Private Ryan's* opening sequence was like being there – WWII Vets have needed counselling for the recall it gave them. But imagine if that was shot on IMAX 3D – one shudders to think.

A narrative movie made for IMAX cinemas was Frenchman Jean-Jacques Annaud's *Wings of Courage*, a beautiful-looking picture from 1995 about a mailman stuck in the Andes and starring Val Kilmer, Craig Sheffer and Elizabeth McGovern. Despite the lacklustre script, Annaud shot awe-inspiring scenery in 3D and far surpassed anything else ever done in the genre, from the first one, *Bwana Devil* in 1952, to the awful *Jaws 3D*.

IMAX 3D is the first time I've ever experienced something that actually feels 3D and makes use of that extra dimension to artistic and even dramatic effect. It is certainly worth a look.

1 a. What do the critics of IMAX technology think are its drawbacks?

b. What does Jason Solomons think is the difference between the IMAX screen experience and standard cinema visits?

2 a. What plans are there to bring big-screen technologies into feature films?

b. What would IMAX and other forms of big-screen technology bring to our viewing of a feature film?

Video games

There is a vast market for video games and the present global market is said to be worth around £17 billion. The market is split between the games available for a PC and those which are played from a games console, with the latter type holding the bigger share of the market. Over a third of homes in the United Kingdom own an advanced games console, some of the most popular of which in the last five years have been the Sony PlayStation, Sega Dreamcast and the Nintendo N64.

The first types of games from Sega and Nintendo used a cartridge system to 'feed in' the games, but with the arrival of the extremely successful CD-based Sony PlayStation in 1995 the technology shifted. In 1997 Nintendo launched the N64 which went into competition with Sony for the console market. With the number of people using the Internet reaching figures of nearly 200 million in 1999, the scene was set for a games console with Internet access, and in October 1999 Sega launched the Dreamcast games console with Internet access.

Games consoles also have the potential to provide a central control mechanism or conduit for other types of entertainment system. Developments in this area have embraced the idea of technological convergence and have focused on the ability of the console to do more than just offer games. PlayStation 2 extends the capabilities of the first PlayStation in more than just its games capacity. It has a range of digital inputs and outputs that, in time, will mean that it can be connected to other entertainment systems within a household. The potential interactivity and convergence of future home entertainment systems is something that the developers of the new PlayStation have incorporated into their design. PlayStation 2 is based on a DVD drive and can play films and music, as well as games. What converges with this type of technology is not just formats and technologies, but different branches of the Sony organisation, such as its websites and its music and film production which will work more closely together and will all be accessible through PlayStation 2.

The advances in this sector of new media technology have been dramatic and will continue to be so. What is interesting, however, is that the new consoles that are brought out by different companies have little or no compatibility. Unlike a television and video recorder/DVD, for example, a games console does not allow for use with other consoles or with those from the same manufacturer which have gone before. Rarely are products offered which extend the capabilities and capacity of an existing console – new products are sold as entire units, which means that revenue generated is extremely high.

One of the most heated areas of debate concerning games consoles is the content of the games themselves. The violence of games such as

Carmaggedon and *Street Fighter II* has caused some critics to blame the games for copycat violence. The issue seems to be whether or not those playing the games are prompted to violent actions. Does a world saturated with violent computer game images encourage players to become desensitised to the effects of violence, and if it does, do they then act out their aggression without conscience? The other side of the argument suggests that we have an ability to disentangle what is real and what is fictional; that the kinds of violent acts which we are shown on computer games may be unpleasant, but are kept (by the players) in the realms of fantasy and not acted upon.

DISCUSSION

- How will convergence affect the games console market? Do you think it will broaden the range of products available and producers of those products?

- What do you imagine will be the next stage in games console development? Will Internet connection open up further opportunities? Will interactivity with other home entertainment system products increase?

- Do you think there should be limitations on the content of games?

Case Study

Read the following extract and answer the questions that follow.

From *Is the game over for online players?* Chris Ayres, *The Times*

Is the game over for online players?

Investors' hopes for video games over the Internet have been severely tarnished.

Investors in video games companies and the baggy trousered teenagers who play their products have at least one thing in common. They both know what it feels like to stare at a glowing screen with the words "Game Over. Insert Coin(s)" written on it. During the past two years, adrenalin-charged investors have been pumping their spare change into all kinds of games companies, from Britain's Gameplay to Japan's Sega Enterprises. They hoped that the Internet would turn the £14 billion games industry – which already rivals the Hollywood film business for size – into a sizzling hot investment opportunity.

Instead, the Internet has simply presented games companies with many expensive strategic headaches. So far, the money made by games companies in cyberspace would barely match the daily takings of a *Space Invaders* machine. This week Gameplay – an online games "portal" and e-tailer whose shares have lost 78 per cent of their value since late February – underlined this problem by reporting a thumping £33 million pre-tax loss.

The company also admitted that the vast majority of its £23 million of sales came from off-line activities. Indeed, Gameplay has been using some of the cash raised through its flotation to acquire physical distribution companies and retailers throughout Europe. It has even dropped the "dot-com" suffix from its name.

Mark Strachan, Gameplay's chairman, is unrepentant, arguing that the company's bricks and mortar acquisitions are part of an attempt to establish strong offline and online sales channels, and "put the Gameplay brand in front of the consumer at every turn". Sceptics, however, argue that Gameplay has no choice, given the snail's pace at which online gaming is taking off globally.

The concerns that many analysts have over the prospects of the Internet games industry are probably best illustrated by shares in Sega, which now trade at a quarter of their price in February. Analysts fear that Sega's daredevil strategy of selling its Dreamcast consoles to US consumers at a loss in the hope of attracting subscribers to its online gaming service will end in disaster.

In theory, the Internet should completely transform the economics of the video games industry. When consumers are able quickly to download games titles, such as the perennially popular *Tomb Raider*, directly on to their home PCs, analysts argue that distributors and retailers will be wiped out.

Meanwhile, the gross margins of games developers and publishers – such as Britain's Eidos and Rage Software, both of which are quoted on the London Stock Exchange – should explode skywards. After all, in the new wired-up future, there should be no room for middlemen.

Paul Finnegan, the Merseyside entrepreneur behind Rage (who once tried to buy Everton Football Club) believes that the "Holy Grail" for developers and publishers is being able to download games directly on to consumers' PCs for about £11.99 each – compared with their current price of about £39.99 each.

Apart from a small commission siphoned off by portals and e-tailers such as Gameplay and America Online, nearly 100 per cent of this price will be gross profit. Indeed, there is no reason why the likes of Rage cannot sell their titles from their own websites, thus totally bypassing any middlemen.

The impact of the Internet on the video games industry is made more exciting by new technologies such as third-generation mobile phones and interactive television services, which should give games companies even more ways to sell their product.

These technologies coupled with fast Internet access also raise the interesting prospect of giving away games free in "episodes" and selling advertising around each instalment. One company, Freeloader.com – owned by the Alternative Investment Market's Pure Entertainment – is attempting to do this already.

There is only one problem. Fast Internet technology such as British Telecom's "digital subscriber lines" (DSL) are taking a painfully long time to emerge, and are not likely to become mass-market for at least another two years. Even then, DSL will be limited to metropolitan areas. Yet these technologies are vital if online gaming is ever to take off. As Sony pointed out recently (while criticising Sega's online strategy) current Internet gaming technology is about as impressive as current Wap mobile phone technology – ie, not very. By embracing the Internet too soon, video games companies risk putting consumers off it for life.

This crucial delay in the rollout of fast Internet technology has caused one games company, <u>URwired.com</u>, to collapse already. The company, founded in 1998 by Mattias Lamotte, a 29-year-old entrepreneur, went under in August 2000, having gone through some £1.8 million of cash. Most of it belonged to Lamotte's father, a City fund manager.

Lamotte argued that URwired was forced to rely on Internet mail order sales (traditional boxed video games ordered on its website and posted out to customers) while BT dithered over the launch of its DSL technology.

This led to huge losses, which ultimately prevented URwired from being saved by venture capital company. Many suspect that this time-lag problem is the real reason behind Gameplay's strategy of buying into physical distribution and retail.

It is a dangerous strategy nevertheless. The suffering of quoted games retailers such as Game and Electronics Boutique (which eventually bought Game in an ill-fated move to gain "critical mass") have taught investors that the "old economy" games industry is characterised by two things: falling margins and dramatic cyclicality.

Margins tend to fall because of ferocious competition on the high street – plus the constant rip-off allegations made against games companies for £39.99 price tags. And the industry is cyclical because demand for games is influenced heavily by the release of new consoles from the likes of Sony and Nintendo.

At the moment, the games industry is going through a lull because consumers are waiting for the November launch of Sony's PlayStation 2 console before going out and buying any games. This is causing misery throughout the industry, and has already led Eidos to issue several profit warnings.

Exposing itself to this kind of investment risk is only one of Gameplay's problems however. The other is that Gameplay will have to start cannibalising its own bricks and mortar distribution and retail businesses when online gaming does eventually take off. It is hard not to conclude that Gameplay is in something of a *Catch-22* scenario.

So is it "Game Over" for the online video games industry? Probably not. But analysts seem to agree that many games companies may collapse even though the industry will ultimately – eventually – thrive. Size will be important, but whether Gameplay's strategy of gaining "critical mass" by going offline works, remains to be seen. Investors will have to think hard before inserting more coins.

1   a. Why do games console manufacturers believe that Internet-linked games will boost revenue?

     b. What are the current technological problems that are impeding the take off of the games on-line market?

2   a. What impact do new games consoles have on the games market?

     b. Do you think there is a future for the on-line games industry?

Mobile telephones

The first mobile telephones were large and cumbersome. There were few people who owned them, so mobile-to-mobile communication was not common. Mobile phone technology has advanced at an incredible rate in recent years and now wide ranging and compact mobiles are a common sight. The lucrative and expanding nature of the mobile phone market means that competition between different networks, handset manufacturers, PDAs (personal digital assistants) and software companies is fierce.

The data-handling capabilities of many phones available at the moment means that the consumer can gain web access, explore the Internet and send e-mails, and it is this market space which is being competed for most intensely. Plans for mobile Internet services are being offered from AOL, BBC, Orange and Vodafone, to name a few. At the moment, the Internet can only be accessed via mobile if you have WAP (Wireless Application Protocol) technology installed on your phone, but with so many different providers coming into mobile phone technology, the next few years should see many different means of access. When phone display screens increase in size, it will be possible to add audio and video to the present mobile phone services.

In the context of Media Studies, mobile phones are an interesting piece of technology. Because of their developing multimedia capacity, they are being used within the media to speed up certain processes, such as the transfer of photojournalistic images from photographers to their newspaper, via the Internet.

DISCUSSION

- What are the present uses of the mobile phone for both the consumer and media professionals?

- How might mobile phones be made more interactive with other media technologies in the future?

PART TWO
Media ownership

Introduction

As is the case with new media technologies, media ownership is in a state of constant flux. Companies merge or are taken over and what was once an autonomous company might now be a branch within a much bigger corporation. **Convergence** is in operation at an inter-company level as well as between different media products. In Media Studies the integration of products or institutions is called **synergy**, implying that what is born out of the newly forged links is more effective than what had gone before. Synergy is in evidence both in the merging of companies and in the release of certain products in unison; for example a film may be released alongside an associated CD to produce maximum revenue. The advent of many of the new technologies outlined in the first half of this section has meant that production practices within media institutions, such as marketing and distribution, have become ever more wide reaching and advanced. We now have the technology to consume our media in a dizzying number of ways, but it is also important to consider how our consumption is affected by who owns the companies behind the products we consume.

Media ownership is becoming more and more concentrated, with vast companies being created in the place of many smaller ones. This concentration is brought about in two ways. Firstly, a larger company may take control of a smaller competitor in the same market or in a market into which the larger company wishes to expand.

The second mode of concentration is brought about when a company wishes to buy into a particular 'branch' of another of equal size in order to utilise the technology and expertise already held by that other company. For example, a company that manufactures hardware programmes may buy into one that produces appropriate software. For media institutions, convergence, in whatever form, has an effect on the products produced and the ways in which the audience consumes them. We may have a product suddenly drawn to our attention because a new parent company has the financial power to market it effectively. We may buy a product that we would not have considered before because of the reputation we perceive a new parent company to have.

Any discussion of media institutions should include analysis of those companies which are involved in cross-media initiatives, those which have a public service remit, those which are purely concerned with one aspect of a product such as production, and those which have been formed as alliances. This part of Section 5 will offer you case studies based on different ownership issues and will also help you to understand the effect that all of this has on the audience/consumer.

The BBC

The BBC is an example of a company that holds a public service remit. Revenue is generated from the license fee paid by the consumer and also from the sale of its products, not from advertising. Originally a private company set up by a group of radio manufacturers, the BBC was then nationalised to become a state broadcasting corporation. The BBC state service was set up in order to provide both radio and television broadcasting, but was intended to be independent of government interference. It was not established to provide a vehicle or means of expression for the ruling political party, and indeed the Royal Charter, which set up the BBC, stipulates impartiality of presentation, particularly in news and current affairs programmes.

Public service broadcasting (PSB) was seen as a way of reflecting the needs of the viewing public by offering programmes that were of interest to a cross-section of society. The impartiality of the BBC is often tested through coverage of such news items as strikes and elections, and as a student of the media you should look carefully at the ways in which events are reported and consider whether or not the BBC remains a 'voice of the nation' rather than a political voice.

Another important fact to consider in any discussion about the BBC and public service broadcasting is the shifts in programming which have occurred because of a widening of the television channel market place. With the advent of Independent Television on 22nd September 1955, Channel 4 in 1982 and Channel 5 in 1997, as well as satellite and cable, the BBC has been increasingly placed within an intensely competitive market place. Given the fact that there is now more competition for viewers, we must consider whether BBC programming has had to change in order to face that competition. It is argued that the BBC schedules contain too many soap operas, chat shows, comedy programmes and life-style programmes and has lost its distinctive nature. Its news coverage has to compete with terrestrial and satellite alternatives. The BBC now has digital channels for the consumer, such as BBC Choice, which means even more programme options. It is essential to consider whether the BBC has maintained its original remit to offer balance, impartiality and a reflection of a wide range of viewers' needs.

In terms of the future of the BBC, plans are being drawn up for two new digital services. BBC3 will be created from BBC Choice, the existing digital service, and will provide entertainment, comedy and drama aimed at a youth market. BBC4, which will be a reconstituted BBC Knowledge, will contain programmes focused on the arts and culture. The BBC plans to spend an estimated £100 million on digital TV channels in 2001 and £140 million per year from 2002. Thirteen million pounds has also been earmarked for radio developments.

DISCUSSION

- What are the differences and similarities between BBC programming and the independent channels?

- Do you think that the schedules of the BBC channels adequately reflect the viewers' interests?

- Watch a selection of BBC news and current affairs programmes. Do you think they are impartial?

- What difference would it make if we did not have the BBC?

- Do you think that we should pay our licence fee?

Case Study

Read the following extract and answer the questions that follow.

From **It's the BBC but not as we know it,** Adam Sweeting, The Guardian Archive

It's the BBC – but not as we know it

Can the World Service, with its lingering image of a bygone empire and announcers in dinner jackets, compete with the raw commercialism of the new information networks? Adam Sweeting reports

The Guardian

Few broadcasting institutions seem less typical of the digital era than the BBC World Service. Steeped in the tradition of offering a public service to the polyglot citizens of a once sprawling British empire, and still playing that scratchy old Lillibulero signature tune, the World Service can't help triggering flashbacks to the days when radio broadcasters wore dinner jackets and Britannia ruled the waves. "Like MI5, the cucumber sandwich and the Boat Race, the BBC World Service seems to define the identity of the British, even if it touches precious few British lives," as *The Financial Times* put it recently.

The World Service built its reputation on being able to reach territories other broadcasters had never heard of, but the explosive spread of new information networks now threatens its existence. While the majority of World Service listeners still have to struggle to tune in on hissing shortwave, CNN has built itself into the Coca-Cola of world media, and prides itself on its "mindshare", or recognisability. Now, CNN Interactive is gearing up to spread its message throughout Europe, Africa and the Middle East via the internet. For anyone who considers themselves a news junkie, cyberspace offers ample opportunities for a fatal overdose. Yahoo! and MSNBC already have their news services on stream, vying with Sky News, ITN, Reuters, Bloomberg and PA's new virtual newsreader, Ananova. Many major newspapers (including this one) are available in comprehensive online versions. Log on to any internet provider, and you're greeted with a splash of news headlines.

Now that news and current affairs have become commodities to be bought and sold by huge media conglomerates such as CNN's owners AOL/Time-Warner, why should listeners still bother to seek out the World Service's faintly eccentric brand? However, the service is acutely aware of the multiple threats to its position, and the internet is at the forefront of its thinking.

World Service online offers a 24-hour service in 43 languages, covering all the topics you can get through the crackling ether and with regular World Service items available as ready-to-play audio files. The BBC is busily forging relationships to make its content available through overseas internet service providers, for instance Brazil's Universo Online. The corporation has developed its own multilingual software, enabling PC screens to display Arabic and Urdu, or Mandarin and Cantonese. The World Service can brandish figures to show that in the past year, listeners have increased from 143m to 151m, while usage of the online operation has tripled in the same period.

But can it match the pace and pizzazz of the opposition? World Service boss Mark Byford has his tonic-for-the-troops speech ready. "The World Service is a public service proposition," he declares. "That's why it gets its money through government to serve audiences, not to make a profit. We believe its values of trustworthiness, accuracy, fair dealing and impartiality, and also the breadth and depth of its international agenda, will still shine through in a multimedia world. We're not saying we want to move from being a radio broadcaster to being a net broadcaster. What we're saying is we want to be the best-known and most respected voice in international broadcasting."

214

Will it still be the World Service as we know it? "The values and purpose of the service will always be rock solid, cornerstone, fundamental and clear," Byford insists. Chris Westcott, who runs the Service's online operation, argues that the public service remit means that "we don't do things because there is a commercial market there. We're responding to the same kind of market forces as a CNN or an MSNBC, but we're responding in slightly different ways."

Meanwhile, its rivals are scheming relentlessly to steal as much of the World Service's international audience as they can. "Anybody who is producing a news and information service in whatever language is certainly a competitor," warms Mitch Lazar, who's in charge of business development, new media for Turner Broadcasting System Europe.

Lazar was also behind the launch of CNN Mobile last year, a foretaste of emerging technologies which brings CNN content to 41m mobile phone users in 18 countries in SMS, Wap and HDML formats. So far, this is a development that World Service online is only thinking about. CNN has also taken giant steps towards turning itself into an international service, instead of the parochially American institution it used to be. It now has several local-language TV news channels as well as websites in seven languages, while European viewers to its TV service can now count on seeing European anchorpersons, presenting locally tailored content. CNN even offered in-depth coverage of cricket's financial scandals, where once the only sport it seemed to have heard of was American college football. "We've worked very hard to change the perception that we are an American product," says Lazar. "If you watch the TV network today, it's completely different to what you would have seen five years ago."

The World Service's future will depend on how effectively it can continue to make its objective, non-commercial voice heard. "It's key to our position that the unique World Service tone is not eroded," Westcott stresses. "It's often underestimated how sophisticated users of media are. I think there is an increasing wariness about 'you're telling me this, but you're also selling it to me, so why are you telling me?' And of course the BBC doesn't have this problem."

Mitch Lazar takes the opposite view, funnily enough. "I believe one thing we have in our favour, where the BBC might get bogged down, is that in some cases they are not able to move in a commercialised way as fast as a CNN type of operation. We have different elements driving our business versus the element driving their business, which are very focused in the UK. We don't have someone who's paying our bills. We have to earn our revenues by various ways of licensing and advertising."

There's plenty of experience and ingenuity lurking in Bush House; but the hard part will be learning how to extract it and exploit it. Westcott hopes he understands how the World Service can promote its distinctive assets.

"Until recently, what we did was make radio programmes," he says. "We can't just take the content from those radio programmes and put it online, it has to be refashioned specifically for that medium. You have to find ways of leveraging the assets of the organisation, its brand and its reputation, across all of the outputs."

The biggest task has been persuading the stately monolith of the BBC to grasp the necessity for change. "The BBC's last new medium was when television arrived at Alexandra Palace in 1947, so the organisation had forgotten how to change. We've got a very large job to explain to people why the future is not going to be the same as the present, and why something they have done successfully for a long time is no longer going to cut it. But I think it's remarkable that we've dealt with it so well, given all the brickbats you see in the press about how the BBC is supposed to be stuck in the 1940s."

The new challenge is to avoid being stuck in the 1990s.

1. a. What is the traditional profile of the World Service?

   b. Which media companies provide a news online service?

   c. What changes is the World Service making in order to compete in this market?

2. a. How is the World Service different from other competitors in the news online market?

   b. Do you think World Service listeners will move from the radio to the Internet in order to receive their news?

News Corporation

Rupert Murdoch's company News Corporation is an example of a multinational player in the media ownership debate. It has constantly expanded, both geographically and technologically, to become one of the most powerful media companies. News Corporation is the parent company for 20th Century Fox films and television, BSkyB, Sky Digital and Star TV (which operates in Asia) and, under the British press 'wing' of News International, Murdoch acquired *The News of the World*, *The Sun*, *The Times* and *The Sunday Times*.

Expansion into Internet technologies has come through the purchase of Delphi On-Line Internet that operates in America and the United Kingdom. There is also a book publishing section to News Corporation that owns HarperCollins in the US and the UK. Rupert Murdoch has built a multimedia and multinational organisation that works to allow him to promote a product from one particular section of the organisation through a company or product within another. Films to be released by 20th Century Fox, for example, can be marketed and promoted through newspapers, television stations, magazines and the Internet.

Because of the vast range of media products within News Corporation, Rupert Murdoch can afford to take risks on new products. If they are unsuccessful there will still be an extremely successful product somewhere else in the corporation to fill the deficit – one product can, in effect, subsidise another. At the moment, News Corporation products are targeted at the US, British, Western European, Asian and Australian markets, but Africa is sure to be of increasing focus.

As with other huge media corporations, fears have often been expressed concerning Murdoch's expansion plans and potential monopoly of the media market. In 1995, for example, a government White Paper on cross-media ownership expressed concerns about Murdoch's bid for the Channel 5 franchise. This was credited with limiting the extent of News corporation influence within British terrestrial television markets. As with many other media companies, News Corporation is expanding, not just through the countries in which it operates or the products which it offers, but by merging with other companies. Its potential consumer group is therefore ever increasing. The case study below looks at one such merger.

DISCUSSION

- Look at examples of the newspapers owned by News International. Do you see any similarities of style or content? Do they look as if they are products from the same parent company?

- Do you think large corporations, such as News Corporation, are good for the media marketplace or do they mean that the products we are offered do not adequately reflect our needs?

Case Study

Read the extract below and answer the questions that follow.

From *All eyes on the movies,* Dan Milmo, The Guardian Archive

GuardianUnlimited Archive

All eyes on the movies

NTL's link-up with US film giant Universal could be bad news for Sky. So why is everyone so keen not to fall out with Rupert Murdoch?

Friday's announcement of a link-up between US film giant Universal and cable operator NTL typifies the market for digital television in the UK: everyone wants a piece. The list of players involved is a who's who of media big hitters. NTL is linked to BSkyB, which is linked to French media giant Vivendi, which is linked to Universal. A winter of manoeuvring is approaching and the question on everyone's lips is, will this circle of convenience hold?

The NTL and Universal channel is to be called The Studio, combining the UK's largest broadband company with a major Hollywood studio which has a catalogue of blockbusters including *The Mummy, Notting Hill* and *Babe*. It's an intimidating team, and sends out the message to Sky, the dominant player in UK digital TV, that the opposition are finally getting their act together.

The deal is open to NTL subscribers at basic tier entry-level at no extra cost, and will be available on all platforms when it launches in the next six months. It is therefore not a premium channel, unlike Sky's movie offerings, and the considerable Universal archive will give it added appeal.

NTL denies it is an aggressive move, pointing out that it recently signed a five-year carriage deal with BSkyB, which is owned by Rupert Murdoch's News Corporation. Its unexpected anxiety about staying onside with Sky relates as much to the other key pay-TV content, football, as it does to the new battleground of Hollywood movies.

Both NTL and Sky hold stakes in several Premier League clubs, both own a slug of the next season's pay-TV screening rights, NTL on pay-per-view matches, Sky on basic. The arrangement between the two is expected to lead to pay-per-view football channels. For the moment, at least, they are allies. Steve Wagner, managing director of NTL, says: "I speak to BSkyB all the time and they understand what we are doing. We are trying to change the economics of the digital business, to let customers benefit. If consumers benefit, then BSkyB will do even better. This is a win and win situation."

Wagner adds that The Studio has been offered to Sky Digital, though no deal has been concluded. Analysts point out that NTL has committed millions of pounds every year to marketing Sky's premium channels, including its movie package, as part of the carriage deal. But NTL saw the potential in Universal's offer and is obviously itching to get its hands on exclusive content and stop Sky from surging ahead.

"Universal and NTL are trying to set up a basic movie channel and see if it works," says one analyst. "Sky will want to see how long they can wait to carry it, which will be interesting to watch, though they will certainly carry it eventually."

NTL knows it has to get its skates on. Sky has 4.5m subscribers, of whom 80% receive a digital service, while NTL has a target of just 500,000 subscribers by the end of the year. But it should not feel too self-conscious – as the third player in the digital market, ONdigital, co-owned by ITV big hitters Carlton and Granada, only has 750,000 users.

NTL's trump card is its cable coverage. Since snapping up telecoms company Cable & Wireless, its broadband network has the capacity to reach 12m homes. If this distribution platform can be married to content – and there must be more joint ventures in the broadband pipeline – then Sky will be looking over its shoulder on a more regular basis.

And Sky's streak into the distance has come at a cost. Moody's Investor Service, a major credit rating agency, recently downgraded the debt rating of Sky due to a "continuing weakness in the company's financial profile". Its aggressive push into the digital market has seen its debts soar from £665m in June 1999 to £1.1bn 12 months later. However, Sky insists that analogue television can be switched off by 2006, and if it stays ahead of the competition, it will reap the benefits.

But the key – and still somewhat shadowy – figure in the NTL and Universal agreement is Vivendi, the French media conglomerate. Vivendi is in the process of securing European commission approval of its £23bn merger with Seagram of Canada, which owns Universal Studios and Universal Music. The upshot is that very, very quietly – there is not a mention of Vivendi or it pay-TV giant Canal Plus on the press release – last week's deal suddenly puts the company nose-to-nose with Sky.

Eyebrows are raised in Isleworth because Vivendi holds a 25% stake in Sky, yet has decided to launch The Studio with another operator. Even though Universal is technically not yet part of Vivendi, it is known that the French company has encouraged the deal all the way.

So why fly in the face of Murdoch? The answer lies with Jean-Marie Messier, the Vivendi chairman, who is determined to make inroads into the UK market. His first steps have been made with the multiple-access internet portal Vizzavi, which has been soft-launched in the UK with mobile phone operator Vodafone, but that is just the tip of the iceberg.

Messier wants access to the digital market not just here but all over the world, and, analysts say, he is anxious to do this with Murdoch rather than against him. However, Murdoch has held off from letting Vivendi fold its Sky stake into Sky Global Networks, the soon-to-float umbrella company formed from News Corporation's satellite operations.

For the first time, Murdoch is showing signs that he is willing to dilute his family's grip on NewsCorp, as underlined by last week's share-swap with US cable giant Liberty Media, Under the terms of the deal, Liberty took a 4.7% stake in Sky Global and increased its holding in NewsCorp from 7% to 18%.

Messier is now waiting for Murdoch to approach his company with an offer and the Australian-born magnate has indicated that he is willing to do so. If Murdoch prevaricates, then Vivendi will continue to take a slice of the UK, and global, digital market by alternative means.

A senior observer close to the NTL and Universal deal said last week: "Sky will be hacked off that the arrangement carries no commitment to them, but it might concentrate their minds towards Vivendi. There is a lot of stuff that they can do together, and a movie channel is the very least they can do.

"That said, if little beginnings can grow to bigger alliances, then they can also lead to bigger bust-ups."

1 a. Why does the British digital television market encourage so much competition?

b. Why is the link-up between NTL and Universal deemed to be an effective one within this competition?

2 a. What is the place of Rupert Murdoch's News Corporation within this market competition?

b. Why do you think companies are linking in the 'war' to secure a piece of the British digital market?

Sony

The Sony Corporation was founded in 1946 and has expanded at an astonishing rate. It is not purely concerned with media-related activities and products (there are some non-media subsidiaries, such as Sony Life Insurance Co and Sony Assurance INC), but the majority of its operations do have a media focus. It is a global corporation and, as such, has a major influence on the production and purchase of media-related products.

There are few households now that do not either own or use something produced by Sony. Its major products can be split into the following categories: audio (e.g. minidisc systems, CD players, hi-fi components, recordable minidiscs), video (e.g. VHS and digital video players, DVD players, digital stills cameras), Televisions (e.g. projection TVs, flat panel display TVs, personal LCD monitors), information and communications technologies (e.g. computer displays, satellite broadcasting reception systems, cellular phones) and electronic components (e.g. semiconductors, LCDs, Internet-related business in Japan). This diversity of media-related products means that we may use more than one in a particular household.

Sony has also been at the forefront of the development of media technologies (although not all of them have been successful).

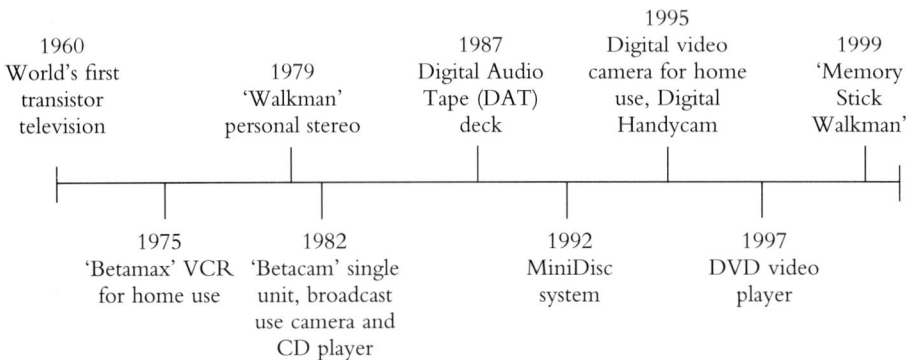

1960 World's first transistor television	1979 'Walkman' personal stereo	1987 Digital Audio Tape (DAT) deck	1995 Digital video camera for home use, Digital Handycam	1999 'Memory Stick Walkman'
1975 'Betamax' VCR for home use	1982 'Betacam' single unit, broadcast use camera and CD player	1992 MiniDisc system	1997 DVD video player	

From a Media Studies perspective this is an interesting list of events because it charts trends in media technology development. The movement towards digital technologies is evident, as is the translation of industry standard equipment into a home context.

The Sony Corporation has six main business areas: Electronics, Games, Music, Pictures, Insurance and Others (includes credit card business), which means that even if you do not have a physical product in your household, it is likely that you will have access to one via, for example, the Internet. The potential for internal synergy is enormous. Sony Pictures could join with Sony OnLine Games to produce a 'tie-in' game/film, for example, and in this way create a much greater market exposure for both products. Sony has not, as yet, merged with other media giants and this may be because of its ability to use different parts of the corporation or different products to enhance market exposure. The breadth of the corporation also enables developments to be gambled upon. 'Betamax' was obliterated by VHS as the domestic standard for home video technology in spite of being able to provide superior picture quality, but the success of other branches of Sony were able to stop this from becoming cataclysmic.

DISCUSSION

● Which recent Sony products have been released in the media marketplace? How have they been advertised? What impression do you get of the Sony Corporation through this advertising?

● Apart from the products that Sony develops and markets, how else does the corporation retain its high consumer profile? Does it sponsor sporting events, for example? How does Sony brand itself?

Case Study

Read the passage below and answer the questions that follow.

From *PlayStation2,* The Sony website

PlayStation2

SONY COMPUTER ENTERTAINMENT ELEVATES ITS ROLE IN THE DIGITAL ERA WITH PLAYSTATION2

New Computer Entertainment System to debut on March 4, 2000 in Japan, Fall 2000 in Europe and North America

TOKYO, September 13, 1999 – Heralding in a new age of digital entertainment, Sony Computer Inc. (SCEI) today announced the launch details of its revolutionary computer entertainment system, PlayStation®2. Building on the success of the worldwide best-selling PlayStation® game console with hardware shipments exceeding 60 million units, PlayStation2 is designed to bring together movies, music and games to form a new world of computer entertainment. PlayStation2 will launch in Japan on March 4, 2000 with an unprecedented initial week's shipment of one million units. Supporting both the audio CD and DVD-Video formats, PlayStation2 offers consumers a wide range of music and video entertainment options. The new system is backwards compatible with the original PlayStation, bridging the gap between the two systems while legitimizing consumers' investment in their existing PlayStation software libraries. Sony Computer Entertainment announced the following details of the new system:

Product Name: PlayStation2
Suggested Retail Price (Japan) 39,800 Yen
Available: March 4, 2000
Accessories included: "Dual Shock"2 analog controller
High capacity 8MB Memory Card
PlayStation2 Demo Disc
AV Multi Cable
AC Power Cord
Dimensions: 301mm (W) × 178mm (H) × 78mm (D) (12″ × 7″ × 3″)
Weight: 2.1 kg (4 lbs. 10 oz.)
Media: PlayStation2 CD-ROM, DVD-ROM

PlayStation CD-ROM
Formats supported: Audio CD, DVD-Video
Interfaces: Controller Port (2)
Memory Card Slot (2)
AV Multi Cable Output (1)
Optical Digital Output (1)
USB Port (2)
I.Link (IEEE1394) (1)
Type III PCMCIA Card Slot

"PlayStation2 is charting a path toward the future of networked digital entertainment," said Ken Kutaragi, president and CEO, Sony Computer Entertainment Inc. "Just as PlayStation brought interactive gaming to an unprecedented mass market, PlayStation2's combination of breathtaking digital graphics, superb sound and DVD video will open the doors to a new computer entertainment experience in the home. "The PlayStation2 computer entertainment system will be available in Asian markets in Summer 2000 and in Fall 2000 in Europe and North America. Sony Computer Entertainment America, a division of Sony Computer Entertainment America Inc., markets the PlayStation game console for distribution in North America, develops and publishes software for the PlayStation game console, and managers the U.S. third party licensing program. Based in Foster City, Calif., Sony Computer Entertainment America Inc. Is a wholly-owned subsidiary of Sony Computer Entertainment Inc.

PlayStation®2 Basic Specifications and Features
CPU 128 Bit "Emotion Engine "
System Clock Frequency 294.912 MHz
Main Memory Direct RDRAM
Memory Size 32MB
Graphics "Graphics Synthesizer"
Clock Frequency 147.456MHz
Embedded Cache VRAM 4MB
Sound SPU2
Number of Voices 48ch plus software
Sound Memory 2MB
IOP I/O Processor
CPU Core PlayStation CPU+
Clock Frequency 33.8688MHz or 36.864MHz (Selectable)
IOP Memory 2MB
Disc Device CD-ROM and DVD-ROM
Device Speed CD-ROM 24 times speed
DVD-ROM 4 times speed

1. In what ways is the new PlayStation2 a multimedia product?

2. How is PlayStation2 different from PlayStation?

3. How are customers reassured that the money they invested in the first PlayStation is not entirely lost when they purchase the second?

4. Why do Sony claim that PlayStation2 heralds 'a new age of digital entertainment'?

Cross-media ownership

Many media companies are involved in expansion processes and one of the areas we need to consider is cross-media ownership. Literally this means that a company might have a significant stake in several different media organisations, for example, films and newspapers. We have already looked at one example of this type of organisation in the form of News Corporation, and have also considered the restrictions which can be placed upon it – because Rupert Murdoch already owns 20% of the British newspaper market, he is prohibited from holding a terrestrial TV licence.

In 1962, the Royal Commission on the press, using the language of the Department of Trade and Industry, stated that, 'action should be taken to regulate the increasing concentration of newspaper ownership which could threaten the freedom and variety of expression of opinion and perhaps even the unbiased presentation of the news'. There are a variety of restrictions on cross-media ownership in Britain that attempt to halt any movements towards monopolies, and perhaps the most significant piece of legislation to date has been the 1996 Broadcasting Act, which forbids any company that owns 20% of national newspaper circulation from having more than a 20% share of an ITV company or Channel 5. This was the legislation that halted News Corporation's move to purchase a larger stake in British terrestrial television.

Many media companies, however, believe that these types of restrictions are unhelpful when trying to compete for a share of the global media market. This is something that is beginning to be recognised also by the British government, which published a White Paper in Autumn 2000 that aimed to consider reforms of broadcasting and telecommunications regulations.

Cross-media ownership issues impact on the audience in a number of ways. First of all, we may consider the ways in which cross-media products owned by the same company or alliance of companies can become 'branded': in other words they may begin to take on a group identity that is the construction of the parent companies. Is it possible for a product to retain its individuality within a market controlled by cross-media companies? The second area for consideration involves issues of bias and partiality. The more companies expand and the more powerful they become, the more products are at their disposal through which they can communicate their own ideological viewpoint. We therefore need to consider whether media products that we study (and consume) can remain ideologically balanced and unbiased within a climate of ever-increasing cross-media ownership.

On its own News Corporation is involved in cross-media expansion, but there have also been many alliances and mergers formed between media companies in order to expand the possibilities of cross-media ownership. One significant example of this is Viacom, which owns MTV and Paramount Pictures and has merged with US television group CBS. The new company is now worth $66 billion. This produces a business generating sales of $21 billion, which is greater than any of its rivals except Disney.

DISCUSSION

- What effect do you think cross-media ownership has on the consumer? Do you think it achieves a greater range and quality of products, or does it tend to prescribe what we consume and how we consume it?

- What other cross-media mergers have you noted in the news?

- Choose one company that is involved in cross-media ownership. How has it used 'synergy' to market a particular product?

Case Study

Read the extract below and answer the questions that follow.

From *The AOL Time Warner deal,* Patrick Barkham, The Guardian Archive

GuardianUnlimited Archive

The AOL Time Warner deal

What is all the fuss about?

The merger of AOL and Time Warner is massive by any standards. It is the biggest US corporate merger ever, creating the fourth largest company in the world, worth $350bn (£220bn), more than the output of Russia or the Netherlands. The new company will have more than 100 million subscribing customers across the globe.

The deal is even more hyped because it will create the world's largest media company from the first significant merger of an internet company with a traditional firm.

Who is the dominant partner?

AOL made $4.8bn in revenue in the 12 months to June 1999; Time Warner made $26.8bn in 1998. AOL employs 12,100; Time Warner 70,000. Despite this, AOL earned four times the net profit of Time Warner in 1998/99 and the stock market values AOL 1.5 times higher than Time Warner. So, although it has been heralded as a "strategic merger of equals", AOL shareholders will be given 55% of the new company to Time Warner's 45%, giving them effective control of the new company.

What is in it for both of them?

Much has been made of traditional media companies failing to get the net. With a media empire embracing TV news (CNN) film (Warner Bros) and magazines (*Time, People*), Time Warner had set aside $500 million to invest in new online efforts. Now it has a ready-made internet strategy and a vast new media platform to distribute its content. Its films, for instance, could soon be downloaded from the internet by AOL subscribers.

AOL, America's leading internet service provider (ISP) which also owns web browser Netscape, wasn't short of content, although Time Warner will provide it with more: Warner Bros offers the potential to "broadcast" thousands of films over the internet.

More importantly, the merger will end AOL's bandwidth problems. The company has struggled to find ways to speeding up its dial-up internet service for American households. Now it can now provide a far quicker, broadband internet service, carried on Time Warner's Roadrunner cable modem service. Time Warner has 13m cable subscribers, who also present AOL, which already boasts 22m internet subscribers, with a vast new market.

How will they work together?

The buzzword is "convergence". At the start of the 1990s Time's publishing empire merged with TV, film and music giant Warner. Ten years on, this merging of a traditional content provider with an online operator appears to make a lot of sense.

AOL will give Time Warner much-needed internet savvy and an established internet platform for its content; Time Warner will grant AOL high-speed cable access to households. The integrated company will be able to provide integrated media services, so that customers can get films, music, magazines and the internet all through their digital TVs.

There will be difficulties which come with forcing together two giant companies of contrasting cultures, personalities and locations. Time Warner are based in New York; AOL in Virginia; the new company will be split between the offices. AOL chairman Steve Case admitted "there are a lot of cooks on stage", with his Time Warner counterpart Gerald Levin, as well as high-profile CNN chief Ted Turner at the apex of the company.

Lower down the food chain, Warner employees may resent working alongside AOL workers made rich by their internet stock options. In turn, the AOL net millionaires may resent the value of their shares being held down by its merger with Time Warner, a traditional media firm with slower growth.

Could there be any problems with the deal?

The deal has not gone through yet. It must be subject to regulatory scrutiny. Legal experts don't foresee any significant problems in America, although AOL's alliance 50–50 joint venture with German media giant Bertelsmann in Europe and Australia could be questioned. Previous proposed mergers between internet and traditional media have collapsed, such as last year's attempted merger of internet portal and search engine Lycos with USA Networks.

What are the implications here?

British consumers will be able to take advantage of a bigger range of Time Warner content services through AOL Europe, which is handed a competitive advantage in its battle with Freeserve, Britain's biggest free internet service provider. Its share value fell yesterday.

The stock market believes this deal is the first of many. That a traditional media company, Time Warner, accepted the higher value of an internet company, AOL, also suggests that the market's high valuation of many internet companies is no chimera. More than £8bn was added to the value of London-listed media shares yesterday.

"Temporarily, maybe it leaves them in the dust," said internet analyst Dan O'Brien of Time Warner's traditional competitors. These media giants, such as Rupert Murdoch's News Corporation, Sony or Disney, all with a significant presence in Britain, may consider striking similar deals with dedicated online companies such as Yahoo, Lycos, AT&T and Microsoft.

What about the future of the internet?

AOL has fiercely campaigned for high-speed cable operators to open their lines to a variety of providers, which would help ensure competitive pricing and consumer choice. It insists that its privileged access to Time Warner's cables will not change its position and both promised to promote open access on their cable network, forcing AT&T to do the same.

Critics argue AOL will surely reduce its campaign for open access. And even if they remain committed to open access that does not necessarily mean they will grant outside providers with equal access to their broadband services. AOL's services are likely to enjoy preferential services on Time Warner's cable system.

Internet idealists argue it is a massive step in the multinational corporate takeover of the Internet and web content. Other internet–media mergers cannot be far behind.

1 a. Why is the AOL/Time Warner merger of such significance?

b. What will each take from the merger?

2 a. What place does convergence have within this deal?

b. Is the fact that AOL is the company that generates more revenue significant to the merger? What does it say about the value of different media technology areas today?

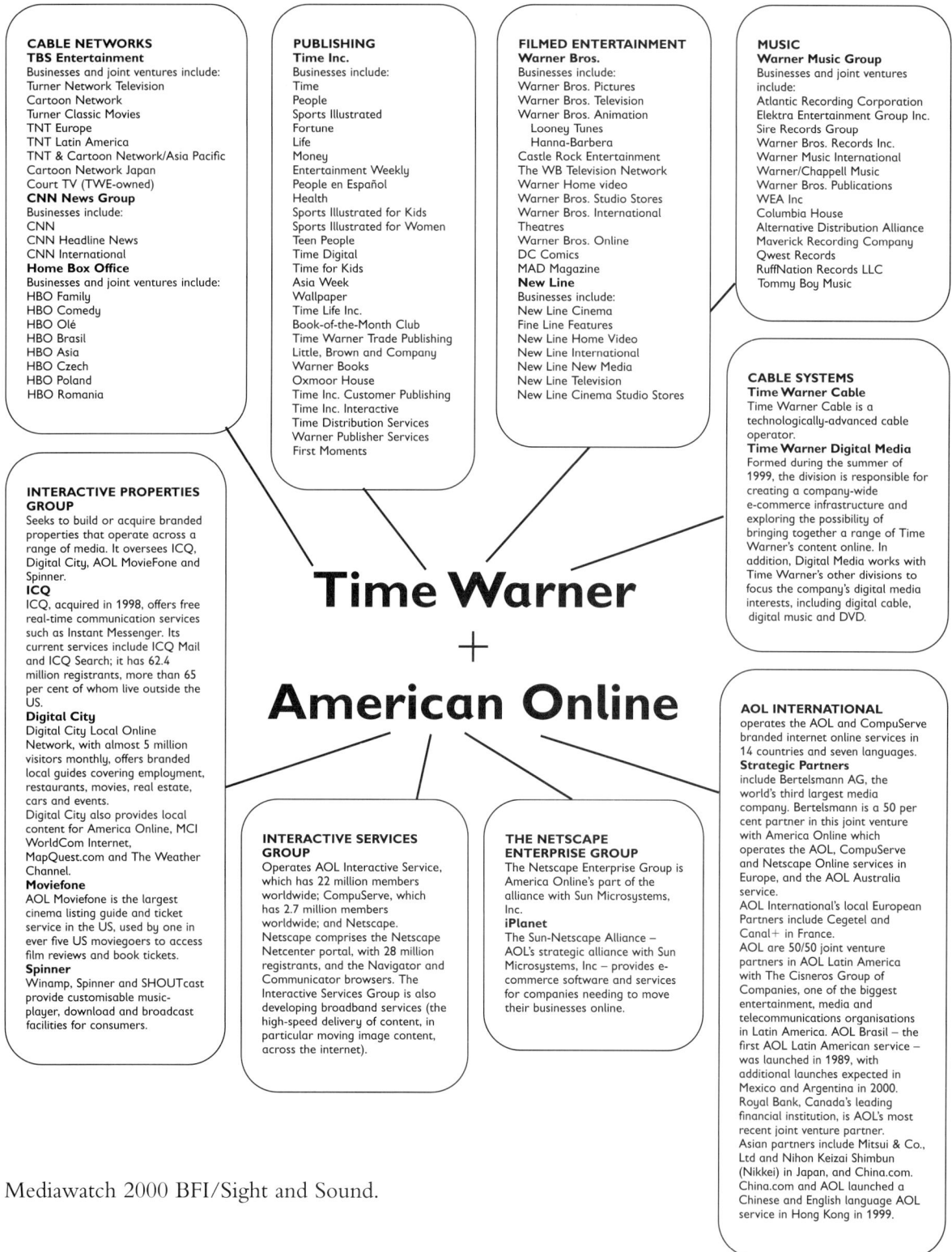

Time Warner
+
American Online

CABLE NETWORKS
TBS Entertainment
Businesses and joint ventures include:
Turner Network Television
Cartoon Network
Turner Classic Movies
TNT Europe
TNT Latin America
TNT & Cartoon Network/Asia Pacific
Cartoon Network Japan
Court TV (TWE-owned)
CNN News Group
Businesses include:
CNN
CNN Headline News
CNN International
Home Box Office
Businesses and joint ventures include:
HBO Family
HBO Comedy
HBO Olé
HBO Brasil
HBO Asia
HBO Czech
HBO Poland
HBO Romania

PUBLISHING
Time Inc.
Businesses include:
Time
People
Sports Illustrated
Fortune
Life
Money
Entertainment Weekly
People en Español
Health
Sports Illustrated for Kids
Sports Illustrated for Women
Teen People
Time Digital
Time for Kids
Asia Week
Wallpaper
Time Life Inc.
Book-of-the-Month Club
Time Warner Trade Publishing
Little, Brown and Company
Warner Books
Oxmoor House
Time Inc. Customer Publishing
Time Inc. Interactive
Time Distribution Services
Warner Publisher Services
First Moments

FILMED ENTERTAINMENT
Warner Bros.
Businesses include:
Warner Bros. Pictures
Warner Bros. Television
Warner Bros. Animation
    Looney Tunes
    Hanna-Barbera
Castle Rock Entertainment
The WB Television Network
Warner Home video
Warner Bros. Studio Stores
Warner Bros. International
Theatres
Warner Bros. Online
DC Comics
MAD Magazine
New Line
Businesses include:
New Line Cinema
Fine Line Features
New Line Home Video
New Line International
New Line New Media
New Line Television
New Line Cinema Studio Stores

MUSIC
Warner Music Group
Businesses and joint ventures
include:
Atlantic Recording Corporation
Elektra Entertainment Group Inc.
Sire Records Group
Warner Bros. Records Inc.
Warner Music International
Warner/Chappell Music
Warner Bros. Publications
WEA Inc
Columbia House
Alternative Distribution Alliance
Maverick Recording Company
Qwest Records
RuffNation Records LLC
Tommy Boy Music

CABLE SYSTEMS
Time Warner Cable
Time Warner Cable is a technologically-advanced cable operator.
Time Warner Digital Media
Formed during the summer of 1999, the division is responsible for creating a company-wide e-commerce infrastructure and exploring the possibility of bringing together a range of Time Warner's content online. In addition, Digital Media works with Time Warner's other divisions to focus the company's digital media interests, including digital cable, digital music and DVD.

INTERACTIVE PROPERTIES GROUP
Seeks to build or acquire branded properties that operate across a range of media. It oversees ICQ, Digital City, AOL MovieFone and Spinner.
ICQ
ICQ, acquired in 1998, offers free real-time communication services such as Instant Messenger. Its current services include ICQ Mail and ICQ Search; it has 62.4 million registrants, more than 65 per cent of whom live outside the US.
Digital City
Digital City Local Online Network, with almost 5 million visitors monthly, offers branded local guides covering employment, restaurants, movies, real estate, cars and events.
Digital City also provides local content for America Online, MCI WorldCom Internet, MapQuest.com and The Weather Channel.
Moviefone
AOL Moviefone is the largest cinema listing guide and ticket service in the US, used by one in ever five US moviegoers to access film reviews and book tickets.
Spinner
Winamp, Spinner and SHOUTcast provide customisable music-player, download and broadcast facilities for consumers.

INTERACTIVE SERVICES GROUP
Operates AOL Interactive Service, which has 22 million members worldwide; CompuServe, which has 2.7 million members worldwide; and Netscape. Netscape comprises the Netscape Netcenter portal, with 28 million registrants, and the Navigator and Communicator browsers. The Interactive Services Group is also developing broadband services (the high-speed delivery of content, in particular moving image content, across the internet).

THE NETSCAPE ENTERPRISE GROUP
The Netscape Enterprise Group is America Online's part of the alliance with Sun Microsystems, Inc.
iPlanet
The Sun-Netscape Alliance – AOL's strategic alliance with Sun Microsystems, Inc – provides e-commerce software and services for companies needing to move their businesses online.

AOL INTERNATIONAL
operates the AOL and CompuServe branded internet online services in 14 countries and seven languages.
Strategic Partners
include Bertelsmann AG, the world's third largest media company. Bertelsmann is a 50 per cent partner in this joint venture with America Online which operates the AOL, CompuServe and Netscape Online services in Europe, and the AOL Australia service.
AOL International's local European Partners include Cegetel and Canal+ in France.
AOL are 50/50 joint venture partners in AOL Latin America with The Cisneros Group of Companies, one of the biggest entertainment, media and telecommunications organisations in Latin America. AOL Brasil – the first AOL Latin American service – was launched in 1989, with additional launches expected in Mexico and Argentina in 2000. Royal Bank, Canada's leading financial institution, is AOL's most recent joint venture partner.
Asian partners include Mitsui & Co., Ltd and Nihon Keizai Shimbun (Nikkei) in Japan, and China.com. China.com and AOL launched a Chinese and English language AOL service in Hong Kong in 1999.

Mediawatch 2000 BFI/Sight and Sound.

Time Warner and AOL

Probably the most significant merger at the beginning of the 21st Century was between Time Warner and AOL. The US company Time Warner, which owns CNN news channel, *Time* magazine and Warner Bros. cartoons has merged with the world's biggest Internet service provider, America Online, in a deal worth $350 billion. The new company is to be called AOL Time Warner, and Ted Turner, who owns $85 billion of Time Warner shares, will be the vice-chairman. This creates the world's fourth largest corporation after Microsoft, General Electric and Cisco Systems. On a smaller scale, Time Warner has also purchased Britain's EMI Music for £12 billion, to increase the share of its music section within the £23 billion global music market. The deal will mean that AOL Time Warner will end up with one of the biggest record companies in the world.

Digital initiatives

One of the most significant developments in media technology has been the move from analogue towards digital systems. Media companies are, of course, aware of both the benefits to product quality and transmission processes which this affords, and are also aware of consumer demand for digital systems. We will now look at some of the current digital initiatives in the media and the companies/organisations that are involved in their development and application.

Within the realms of public service broadcasting, the BBC has been involved in plans to expand the number of channels available to the consumer by creating two new digital options. Earlier in this section the programme profiles of new channels BBC3 and BBC4 were discussed. Digital options, with their range of programme types and means of consumption, provide an interesting debate when they appear within a public service broadcasting schedule. The remit of the BBC, as we have stated, is to be impartial, but also to act as a distinctive alternative to commercial stations. It is important to consider whether this can be sustained within a digital format, which allows a far greater number of programmes and which the consumer may associate with particular types of programme. Sir Christopher Bland, the BBC chairman, countered these concerns when questioned about the place of digital alternatives within the BBC, by stating that, '*The BBC is very clear about its future and will continue to offer a distinctive, valuable alternative to commercial services.*'

The digital television market is extremely lucrative and, therefore, a very competitive area. In order to try and control increasingly large shares of this market companies often develop commercial links. One example in 2000 was between cable operator NTL and film company Universal in an aim to expand further into the digital television market. The NTL/Universal digital channel, called The Studio, provides competition for Rupert Murdoch's Sky within British digital television. In its development it planned to transmit programmes including sports events and films, and with the Universal archive at its disposal provide an attractive alternative. It was the intention of The Studio to be available to basic level entry subscribers at no extra cost, which would make it extremely competitive. This provides another example of cross-media convergence within the media marketplace.

Microsoft is another company involved in digital initiatives and it has recently sought to expand into interactive television through a partnership with News Corporation, in order to create a partner company within .net TV. The link between Microsoft and News Corporation will bring the type of new technologies developed by Microsoft alongside the breadth of media products created by News Corporation.

As is evidenced by these new initiatives and by what we have seen of new media technologies, digital processes and products are becoming more and more common. In order to receive all that is digitally on offer, however, the consumer needs to have the products that can decode digital signals in the home. There has to be a process of updating existing home technologies in order to take advantage of what is on offer, and this has an impact not just financially, but in the way we view media technology in the home. It does not seem enough these days to buy a television set, a computer or a telephone, which will then be kept for years. We seem to be entering a time where our 'equipment' needs to be constantly updated in order to keep up with developments. Referred to as 'built-in obsolescence', this means that the moment we buy technical hardware it is out of date. How consumer friendly is it to market expensive systems which may become obsolete or dated very quickly, when we exist in a time when access to the latest technologies is marketed as an almost essential requirement of everyday life?

DISCUSSION

- Using newspapers and relevant websites, what other digital initiatives are being planned? Which media companies are planning them?

- What impact will these digital initiatives have on the consumer? Do you think they will enhance our media consumption?

Case Study

Read the extract below and answer the questions that follow.

From **CNN unveils European strategy,** Amy Vickers, *The Guardian*

CNN unveils European strategy

CNN Interactive, the digital offshoot of CNN, made a decisive bid to corner the market for pan-European news yesterday with the launch of its first English-language website developed specifically for the international market.

The move is part of CNN's ongoing expansion into Europe and part of a strategy to establish localised online services in a similar way to how CNN International has regionalised its TV channel. In Europe CNN already operates four local-language sites in Danish, Italian, Norwegian and Swedish. It is launching a German site in October.

The launch of CNN.com Europe is backed by £4m pan-European ad campaign, involving WCRS on the creative side, Mediacom on the buying side, Profero on online creative and Firefly for PR.

The new site, accessible from CNN.com or europe.cnn.com is produced and edited from CNN's new European interactive headquarters in London by a team of 30 journalists.

David Brewer, who was poached from BBC News Online to be managing editor for CNN Interactive for Europe, Middle East and Africa, said the site was aimed at people with information overload who wanted a polished product.

"We've got journalists onboard with more than 30 years' experience who'll be explaining the news with real authority. Our core focus is on high quality news without losing the fact that CNN is built around breaking news." He added that Robin Oakley, who was brought in from the BBC, would play a large part in this authoritative coverage.

In addition to written content, the site offers an archive of all CNN TV's video footage and a snapshot of other European news of interest, presented in a way that viewers will be able to understand, pointed out Brewer. Content on the site is split up into general news, weather, business, sport, technology and entertainment.

"We always said we wanted to do this and now the European market is ripe for this, we thought the time was right," said Scott Woelfel, president and editor-in-chief of CNN Interactive. Woelfel declined to give details of how much CNN was spending on the expansion into Europe.

Further details of CNN Interactive's European strategy are still under wraps, particularly its plans to launch an enhanced TV product akin to Sky News Active. Trials are underway and an interactive text service is planned for Telewest's interactive area. A PDA service is also planned to add to the Wap and SMS services CNN runs.

1 a. Why has CNN 'localised' its new online European service?

b. What kind of target audience is the new service aimed at?

2 a. What does CNN Interactive offer apart from immediate news? How might this be attractive to the target audience?

b. How does this digital initiative fit with changes in news consumption that have happened over the last 20 or so years?

Production Companies

Production companies have an important role within the media environment today. They provide programmes for television and radio stations and, through the programmes they produce, may have an impact on the profile of the channel/station. This section will look specifically at two production companies, Ginger and Bazal, and consider not only the profiles of the programmes they produce, but also the impact of those programmes.

Ginger Productions, once owned by Chris Evans and now by the Scottish Media Group, has a wide media profile, including Ginger Television, Virgin Radio and Ginger Online. Some of the programmes offered by Ginger Television have included: *TFI Friday*, *The Priory*, *Red Alert*, *Don't Forget your Toothbrush*, *Models Close-up* and *Carry on Campus*. The broadcasting context for many of these programmes has been Channel Four, which has a reputation for youth orientated programming. Both *TFI* and *The Priory* are music-based programmes hosted by celebrities and aimed at a young, music (or chart) literate audience. *TFI* especially, drew many of its audience members from Chris Evans' Radio 1 programme and in many ways represented 'New Laddism' in a televisual form. It was presented seemingly informally, with music, interviews and comment, in a way that was unthreatening to a young male population which identified with the 'pubs, football and birds' mindset of Chris Evans. The programme was eventually axed because of falling viewing figures, and it is worth discussing whether the show was discontinued because audiences were becoming disenchanted with the 'New Laddist' style of format and delivery.

Bazal, which is now part of the Endemol group, is one of the UK's largest producers of factual and lifestyle entertainment programmes. It is the company that created the *Big Brother* programmes for Channel Four, providing, through the Internet and webcams, a fully interactive programme. Bazal also created *Flatmate*, *Changing Rooms*, *Celebrity Ready Steady Cook* and *Food and Drink*. Programmes have been created for Channel Four, BBC1 and BBC2, giving Bazal a portfolio that covers both public service and independent broadcasting. Factual programmes that use members of the public as subjects are an increasingly popular phenomenon and engage the audience by means of direct identification.

DISCUSSION

- Look at all of the programmes that Bazal produces. Are there any subcategories of programme within the bigger group? Why do you think Bazal is only concerned with creating these types of programmes?

- What are the attitudes concerning age and gender evident within programmes produced by Ginger Productions? Do you think they reflect those of the target audience? Do they challenge or confirm stereotypes?

Case Study

Read the extract below and answer the questions that follow.

Big Brother boost for Channel 4 ratings, Jason Deans, *The Guardian*

Big Brother boost for Channel 4 ratings

Channel 4 looks to be on course to improve its year-on-year audience share figure with a little help from *Big Brother*.

A Channel 4 spokesman said the broadcaster's audience share for the year to date was 10.6%, compared with 0.2% in 1999. Before *Big Brother* went on air in July it stood at 10.5%, the spokesman added, so the show was going to add "0.1 or 0.2% at most". But increasing audience share at all, at a time when most terrestrial channels are losing viewers to multi-channel services, will be an achievement in itself.

Big Brother settled comfortably into its earlier 10pm slot on Tuesday, Wednesday and Thursday last week, averaging 5.6m. Wednesday night's instalment (August 30) was the most watched, averaging 6.4m and a 32% share.

The show, which is produced by Endemol UK subsidiary Bazal, is attracting a very broad, young audience (60% under 34), with a slight female bias (57%).

The *Big Brother* website was averaging 2.4m hits per day prior to 'Nasty' Nick Bateman's eviction, when the number of hits trebled. Since then it has averaged 3m hits per day.

MediaGuardian © Guardian Newspapers Limited 2000

1 a. What impact did the Bazal production *Big Brother* have on television audience share?

b. How does the show *Big Brother* fit with the Channel Four profile?

2 a. Why do you think that 'Nasty Nick's' eviction trebled the number of visitors to the *Big Brother* website?

b. Does a show like *Big Brother* fit with the general production profile of Bazal?

Summary

Any discussion of **new media technologies** should include comment
on the development of the technology, the organisation behind it, how it
might have changed audiences' expectations of certain media experiences,
and the developments that might happen in the future.

Analysis of **media ownership** issues should focus on the profile and role
of different media institutions, the influence they have in the media
market, and how an institution and the products created by it are
consumed by the audience.

There are certain advances and ideas which are relevant to both
technologies and institutions. You should remember to include analysis of
the role of new digital technologies, both in terms of increased
application and mode of consumption, the place of synergy within media
debate, and the increasing evidence of convergence of product and
institution within the media arena.

Section 6
Key Skills and A Level Media Studies

Introducing Key Skills

You will probably have heard the term Key Skills in your school or college, but might not have understood fully what the term means in relation to your own study. Key Skills are not specifically related to a subject area but are **generic**, which means that they can help improve your learning and performance in all of your study areas. The Application of Number Key Skill, for example, is not only relevant within Mathematics, and the Key Skill of Communication does not exist solely within English. These skills allow you to show employers or academic institutions that you have basic skills in key areas such as Communication, Application of Number and Information Technology. You can study the Key Skills in isolation or practise and present your Key Skills knowledge through activities based around one of the subjects you are studying.

This section aims to provide you with activities you can use to enhance your understanding of A Level Media Studies and, at the same time, provide you with knowledge and practice of the core and wider Key Skills listed below.

Core Key Skills: Communication
Application of Number
Information Technology

Wider Key Skills: Working with Others
Improving Own Learning and Performance
Problem Solving

PART ONE
Key Skill: Communication

Topic of Study: Representation

Representation is one of the key concepts within Media Studies. As we saw in Section 2, representation is the process by which images, sounds and words take on meanings beyond what they initially appear to include. The potential meanings within representational analysis may be

Case Study

Margie in the Coen Brothers' film *Fargo*

Frances McDormand played Chief Marge Gunderson in the 1996 film *Fargo*. The character of Margie is of particular interest because she offers comment on both the representation of women and the police within the crime genre (we must remember, however, that *Fargo* includes elements of many other genres and should not be read solely as a crime film). Margie is the central figure in the film and is the character who solves the murders. She brings stability back to the narrative and re-establishes safety for the other characters within the film.

As a police officer she represents the law, and the progress of the film is towards her re-establishment of law and order. The way in which she does this, however, sets her apart from many other cinematic police characters. Her methodology and manner are a counterpoint to the violent world established by the criminal characters, Carl Showalter (Steve Buscemi) and Gaer Grimsrud (Peter Stormare). She is persistent, unflappable and peaceful in her approach. She solves the crimes through systematic police work, using procedure and deduction rather than dramatic action or sudden discovery of key evidence. The police officers around her are largely portrayed as slow and dependent on her greater powers of deduction. Her representation as a female detective differs from someone like Jane Tennison in the television drama *Prime Suspect* because the officers around her do not impede her. She is not a 'fledgling' detective like Clarice Starling in *The Silence of the Lambs* and neither is she under threat, as Jamie Leigh Curtis' police woman is in Kathryn Bigelow's film *Blue Steel*. Margie represents organised, systematic, even dull police work, but is effective. Law and order are not reimposed in a dramatic or maverick way in *Fargo* – they are the outcome of process and a desire to protect peace.

Possibly the most significant fact about Margie is that she is heavily pregnant throughout the course of the film. Her pregnancy is presented to us in scenes showing her constant need to eat and her morning sickness, as well as through her physical presence. She is not constructed as an object of desire for either the other characters within the film or for the viewer, but as a woman who balances the needs of her body with those of the situation she confronts. Her pregnancy de-eroticises her and the way in which she is represented promotes her as a member of a happy, developing, domestic unit. We are often shown scenes of Margie and her husband, Norm, which establish her home life as dull, but peaceful and contented.

Margie differs from the other women in the film because she is not the victim of men (as with Jerry Lundegaard's wife Jean) or there to provide them with a service (as with the prostitutes who Carl and Gaer pick up). She uses her intelligence and calm to bring sanity to the madness which has been imposed by Jerry's plan and Carl and Gaer's violence.

The character of Margie offers an interesting dimension to the representational debates concerning women, the police and female police officers. Our response to her is complex because she avoids the usual stereotypes of female characters in crime-related films. She is not a victim, a *femme fatale*, a novelty maverick or a woman working in opposition to the officers around her. Margie's representation adds to the realism of the film. She refuses to be stereotyped and (gently and persistently, just as in her police work) challenges our preconceptions concerning the reading of female police officers in cinema.

the intention of the text creator or may be a product of the shifting contexts in which the text is viewed (or listened to). Representation is most commonly associated with both the positive and negative depictions of social groups. When you are commenting on the processes of representation, try to avoid restricting yourself to character analysis. Representation deals with the values, ideas and beliefs (or **ideology**) indicated by the depiction of an individual character or group of characters. The process of analysing representation may begin with a study of the gestures, mannerisms, attitudes, costume, associated *mise-en-scène*, narrative place and language of the character, but should extend to deductions concerning the wider social group of which the character may be part, social attitudes towards that group and the attitude of the film or television programme towards that specific group.

DISCUSSION

Discuss in class groups how masculinity is represented through Margie's husband and one other male character.

Representing a specific group: the police

A useful place to begin when considering representation is a study of specific groups of people. If you consider the way a group's depiction changes over time, it is possible to make effective comments about the shifting attitudes towards them. The representation of the police has changed markedly over the years and we should see this as representative of changes in attitudes and beliefs. Remember, however, that representations can confirm established attitudes, as well as challenge them.

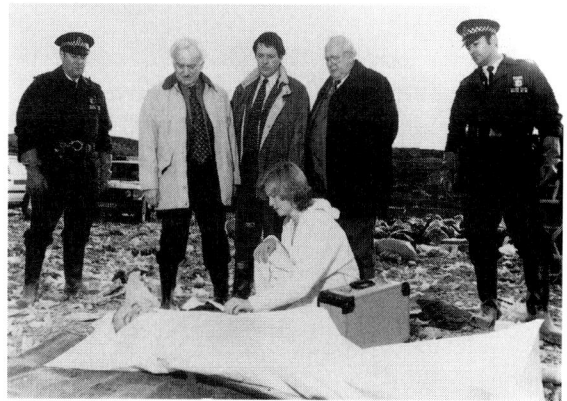

The main characters from Starsky and Hutch *and* Inspector Morse

ACTIVITIES

Look at the illustrations on this and the following page, taken from a selection of past and present television police dramas. For each of them you will need to make notes answering the questions that follow.

1. Look at the police officers shown in the illustrations. What is indicated to us by their body language, facial gestures and costumes?
2. Analyse the *mise-en-scène* of each still. What does it tell us about the way the police are being represented?
3. What do you think has happened in the scene directly preceding each of these stills? What do you think is going to happen next? What do you think the position of the police is at this point in the narrative? Does this help us to comment on the representation of the police?
4. What comments can you make about gender and race from these stills?
5. Do you think the police are being represented as effective in these stills? Do they seem to have a positive social role? What do you think the attitude of the programme creators is to the police?
6. Do the stills help us to comment on changing perceptions of the police? Consider the importance of historical context in the representation debate.

The main characters from Prime Suspect *and* Dixon of Dock Green

238

DISCUSSION

In your Media Studies group discuss your answers to all of the questions you answered in the previous activity.

> **This discussion will provide practice for the Communication Key Skill C3.1a: Contribute to a group discussion about a complex subject.**

Using character to generate representational debate

You do not have to focus on a group of characters in order to make comments concerning representation. The construction of an individual character is of equal use.

ACTIVITIES

1. Watch the scene from Hitchcock's *Rear Window*, which introduces the character of Jeff. Make detailed notes on the way in which iconography (objects) and *mise-en-scène* help us to form a perception of this character.
2. Watch the rest of the film, making notes on the following:
   a) the position of Jeff in the narrative;
   b) his interaction with other characters;
   c) the era of the film and the gender politics evident at that time (you may have to consult history books or your teacher in order to answer this question).
3. Jeff has been described as representing a crisis in masculinity. He is confined to his chair and often seems afraid of a relationship with Lisa. Having made your preliminary notes on the character of Jeff, try to extend your comments to wider representational debate by answering the following questions.
   a) Do you think he represents a period in history in which many men had lost confidence?
   b) Why might this have happened?
   c) How does Hitchcock ask us to consider this debate through the character of Jeff?
4. Choose another film that you think asks us to consider the position of men in society (possibilities may include *Lock, Stock and Two Smoking Barrels*, *Deliverance*, *The Last Seduction* and *High Fidelity*).
   a) Watch the film and make notes on the way in which iconography and *mise-en-scène* are used in order to establish the central male character(s) and then later to develop them.

239

b) Make detailed notes on the ways in which the characters' body language and costumes inform our ideas concerning their representation.

c) What is the position of the characters within the narrative? Do they motivate the plot? How would you describe their role within the genre of the film?

d) How is masculinity being represented through these characters? Does their role indicate a situation of crisis? What is being discussed about the place and expectations of men within the era of the film? Would you consider representations in the film to be radical or challenging to dominant values and beliefs?

> **The following activity should be done in class and the presentation will provide practice for the Communication Key Skill C3.1b: Make a presentation about a complex subject, using at least one image to illustrate complex points.**

e) When you have completed all of your notes, plan a presentation of your material for the rest of the class. You will need to select clips from your chosen film to illustrate some of your points. Make sure that you practise the presentation, and aim to speak clearly. Organise your information in a way that is clear and systematic. You might also consider your presentation materials. You could produce handouts for the class that will consolidate any notes they take.

Using sound and words to inform representation

The majority of discussions surrounding representation deal with visual images, but sounds and words can also be instrumental in helping us to understand wider debates. The values and beliefs being discussed within media texts can be informed and expanded upon through an analysis of the aural (heard) part of the text. Sounds and words can help us to engage with debates about social groups, places and ideas.

ACTIVITIES

1. Watch one of the scenes in *Taxi Driver* where Travis is wandering through the New York streets. Make notes on all of the sounds you hear in the scene – make sure that you note both the **diegetic** sounds (those which form part of the story world) and **non-diegetic** sounds (those which are part of the film's soundtrack). What do the sounds we hear tell us about:

    a) Travis as representative of social outsiders?

    b) New York as a place of chaos and confusion?

    c) alienation and loneliness?

2. Choose a scene from *The Royle Family* where the whole family is together (including Nana). Make detailed notes on the following:

    a) the topic of discussion and the differing attitudes to it amongst the characters;

    b) the amount of time each character speaks, and who seems to have most focus within the discussion;

    c) the position of each character in the set and what this indicates about their place in the conversation;

    d) the attitudes of each of the characters to each other;

    e) the types of language each character uses to express their opinions.

Once you have made your notes, work with a partner to make comments about how words and language interchange can inform us about the representation of the family offered in this programme. Does *The Royle Family* discuss stereotypes through its representation?

> **The following two written activities will provide practice for the Communication Key Skill C3.3:**
> **Write two different types of documents about complex subjects.**
> **One piece of writing should be an extended document and include at least one image.**

3. Choose a scene from a film or a television programme. You are going to create two pieces of written work that illustrate the importance of sound and words within representation. You should use the examples given above to guide your analysis.

    a) Your first writing task is a piece of critical analysis, which your teacher will assess. You should discuss in detail how the sound (diegetic and non-diegetic) and the words in the scene you have chosen represent social groups, places or ideas. Your analysis should be about 1000 words in length and should include a still from the scene you have chosen to illustrate your points.

    b) The second part of your task is to produce a worksheet for other members of your Media Studies group asking them to analyse the scene you have chosen. Try to construct a worksheet that begins with textual analysis of sounds and words, and builds towards questions concerning wider representational issues (use some of the questions we have already discussed in relation to *Taxi Driver* and *The Royle Family* for guidance). You will need about 30 minutes of classroom time to show the scene, ask your classmates to complete the worksheet and then chair a discussion.

Summary

As we have seen, media texts use images, sound and words to encourage us to move beyond technical textual analysis and consider wider issues of debate. The way certain ideas and groups are represented will change over a period of time and it is important to identify historical shifts in representation in your discussions. Don't forget that you are an active participant within this process and can challenge the way a social group or an idea has been represented by a media text.

PART TWO
Key Skill: Improving Own Learning and Performance

Topic of Study: Genre

Groups of texts that have similar elements or characteristics are described as being part of a **genre**. We may discuss horror films, cartoons, the news or soap operas, for example, and in doing so we are identifying genres. The producer of a media text may use the elements of a genre (its **conventions**) in a straightforward way, but they may also subvert conventions, mixing elements from two different genres to provide hybrid forms, or creating sub-genres by slightly altering the conventions used. The study of genre centres on the identification of conventions and the analysis of how they are used within a chosen text. The historical changes in the way a text may use the conventions of its genre will be dependent on the ideological climate in which the text is produced. For example, the 1950s science fiction film *The Thing from Outer Space* can be read as using generic conventions to offer a comment on the Cold War. The United States' military and scientific forces are pitted against an alien intruder (Communism) that seeks to disrupt the social order and jeopardise peace. Ridley Scott's 1979 film *Alien* reflects the fact that feminism has a more central role within current modes of thinking, offering us a female 'saviour' in the form of Ripley. It would be a mistake, however, to read *Alien* simply as a piece of feminist film making – it merely offers comment within a wider debate.

DISCUSSION

1. Television Commercials often use social groups to sell their products. Focusing on the use of the family within TV adverts, how does representation differ from product to product?

2. Through a detailed analysis of two newspapers, discuss the ways in which celebrities are represented in the tabloid press.

Case Study

Horror conventions in Wes Craven's *Scream*

The horror genre includes many sub-divisions (or sub-genres). We could discuss slasher films, psychological horror or gothic horror cinema and identify horror conventions within all of them. Sub-genres and hybrid forms (films that merge more than one film genre, e.g. *Alien* which may be considered to be a hybrid of science fiction and horror) take conventions and utilise them in a way that may be amended, subverted or self-consciously commented upon. Wes Craven's *Scream* provides an example of the slasher format, but also offers a commentary on the construction and consumption of the horror film.

A scene from Scream. *See page 95, figure 12.*

The classic conventions of the horror film include: the final girl, a frightening place, brooding or ominous *mise-en-scène*, narratives that move from equilibrium to disturbance and back to a new equilibrium (although, according to structuralist critic Todorov, this basic structure is evident in all stories), a monster/monstrous human, themes of death and destruction, iconography such as knives and masks, and a disorientation/disturbance of the audience. In *Scream* these conventions are employed literally and at the same time self-consciously. The dialogue of the film includes detailed descriptions of the mechanics and effects of the horror film.

Sydney (played by Neve Campbell) fulfils the role of the final girl. Characters are being killed all around her and she is left at the end of the film having to confront the killers. This confrontation allows her to discover the true identities of the killers and find out the truth about her own mother's murder. The final girl re-establishes order by confronting her own past traumas and fears.

In *Scream* the frightening place is not a gothic castle or an isolated house, but the domestic home. From the first killing of Casey Becker in her middle-class suburban home, we realise that the place we would naturally consider to be safe is, in fact, not. Part of the threat and fear generated in this film is concerned with the invasion of the familial and domestic. These killers attack in the home, thus making the invasion that much more intimate.

The opening scene of Casey Becker's killing also provides examples of the ominous *mise-en-scène* characteristic of a horror film. She moves around a house lit by lamps which provide pockets of light and shadow. The darkened spaces are frightening for both Casey and the viewer because they provide places for a killer to hide. The lack of illumination in the scene is both literal and symbolic – neither Casey nor we know what lurks in the darkness. When Casey looks out of the window the mist over the swimming pool also provides an example of disorientating *mise-en-scène*.

In terms of narrative, *Scream* follows the equilibrium-disturbance-new equilibrium pattern of most horror films. The killing of Casey breaks the peace of the small town, and chaos ensues as other characters become victims. The mid-section of the film charts the successive killings and the inability of the local police to solve the crime. It is only with the final confrontation scene that peace is reinstated. This equilibrium, however, is of a wiser and more cynical type.

The monsters in *Scream* are, of course, the killers who bring chaos and death into the world of the film. What is interesting about Wes Craven's version of this convention, however, is that they are not damaged victims who kill because of their own pain. These are bored teenagers with little or no motive (at one point in the film a character comments on the horror genre, proclaiming, 'This is the millennium. Motives are incidental'), and for many viewers this is a far more frightening creation. Death and destruction are what the killers inflict upon the world of the film, but in *Scream* we are made to look further into this theme. We are also asked to confront an important question: Within a media-saturated environment where we are bombarded with images of death and pain, are we becoming desensitised to the reality of killing? Sydney lives with the horror of her mother's murder and, as a character, shows us the reality of what is seen on the screen, but those around her seem not to fully understand the impact of killing (until, of course, they become the killers' next victim). Through the character of Gayle Weathers (the news reporter), Craven debates this point; she has written a sensationalist book about the man she thinks killed Sydney's mother. For many of the characters in the film murder provides either a book deal or part of the horror film genre, and has ceased to be seen as a real threat.

Scream includes many classic icons of horror. We see knives and a mask in the opening sequence and these are used throughout the film to signify the killers. Knives are intimate and violent weapons. The killer must attack from close quarters and often stabs many times, heightening the fear and pain of the victim. *Psycho, Halloween* and *Nightmare on Elm Street* all include the use of knives, with the first two films also including disguises or masks. Horror films use disguise as a means of disorientating the viewer and obscuring the killer's identity until the end of the film.

As already mentioned, the position of the audience is important to the effectiveness of the horror genre. Often we are placed within a scene, and *Scream* includes many scenes in which we are positioned as Casey Becker or Sydney, waiting for the attack. This subjective (or point-of-view) camerawork forces us to enter a scene of a film and experience the character's fear. The dangerous situations we are sometimes forced to experience make the pleasure of the film's final peace and safety even more palpable.

Horror films often have a knowledgeable audience who are aware of horror conventions and have certain expectations of the genre. *Scream* is a film which clearly acknowledges that its audience will have seen previous horror films. It invites us to comment on the predictability of the genre and at the same time offers us a new, self-conscious, at times humorous, but nonetheless frightening example of the horror film.

DISCUSSION

Look at the still. In small groups, firstly identify the genre of the film and then list the conventions of that genre, which are evident in the illustration. Have these films used the conventions in a literal, subverted or ironic way?

See page 96, figure 13.

ACTIVITIES

This is an extended activity and should be completed over a period of about half a term.

Your task is to research the development of a particular genre over a period of four or five decades. You will be looking specifically at how audience expectations and current ideologies affect the production of films within your chosen genre.

1. Choose a film genre and list all of the conventions of that genre which you know of. When you have completed your list you should discuss it with other members of your Media Studies group and add any conventions they suggest.

2. Using IT resources and print-based materials, choose four or five films from your chosen genre from the same number of decades. For example, if you were to study the science fiction genre you might choose *Metropolis* from the 1920s, *The Thing from Outer Space* from the 1950s, *Close Encounters of the Third Kind* from the 1970s, *Blade runner* from the 1980s and *The Matrix* from the 1990s.

> **The following activity (3) will provide practice for the Improving Own Learning and Performance Key Skill LP3.1:**
> **Agree targets and plan how these will be met over an extended period of time, using support from appropriate people.**

3. Write an outline of your research topic that details:
   a) the resources you are going to use;
   b) the genre and texts you are going to study;
   c) the reasons why you have chosen these particular media texts;
   d) what you aim to discover within your project;
   e) the interim deadlines you are going to set yourself and the work you will have completed at these points.

You should then present this outline to your Media Studies teacher and agree realistic aims and objectives.

You should refer back to your outline regularly to ensure that you are hitting deadlines and covering all of the areas you identified.

4. For each of the texts you have chosen, you should begin by watching them and making detailed notes on the conventions that are evident. You should be aware of how these conventions are used and whether they are being employed literally or in a subverted way.

Activity 5 will provide practice for the Improving Own Learning and Performance Key Skill LP3.2:
Take responsibility for your learning by using your plan, and seeking feedback and support from relevant sources, to help meet your targets.

5. This activity requires you to research the attitudes and ideologies that surround the film. Use the following questions as a guide.
   a) When was the film released and what was happening at that time?
   b) How did the critics and public receive the film?
   c) Does the film offer any comment (either through the dialogue, the images or as an analogy) on the ideas or events current at that time?

You may wish to survey older relatives, friends or teachers in order to discover information or use history books, CD ROMs or the Internet.

Activities 6 and 7 will provide practice for the Improving Own Learning and Performance Key Skill LP3.3: Review progress on two occasions and establish evidence of achievements, including how you have used learning from other tasks to meet new demands.

6. At this stage in your research project you should review the progress you have made and decide whether you need to modify either targets or methodology. This is most effectively done in discussion with your Media Studies teacher.
7. Having analysed your films and researched their contexts, you will now need to create a presentation for the other members of your Media Studies class.
   You should use IT to create your presentation and include sequences from the films you have chosen to illustrate your points. You should include information on:
   a) the typical conventions of the genre you have chosen;
   b) the conventions evident in the individual films and how they have been used;
   c) the historical, social and ideological contexts of your chosen films;
   d) the way the individual film text uses the conventions of its genre within a discussion of attitudes current at the time of its release;
   e) the resources you used to research your project, the problems you may have encountered, the extent to which you followed your initial plan and the overall success of your project.
8. Present your findings to the rest of your Media Studies class and answer any questions they might have.

FOCUS

1. Does the audience's knowledge of a particular genre affect their experience of a text?

2. In what ways is the study of generic conventions useful in an appraisal of the intentions of a media text?

Summary

The study of genre allows us both to categorise media texts and to understand their importance in relation to the world around them. Identifying conventions allows the student of the media to bring other texts from the same genre into any discussion. When analysing genre you should work with both the **micro** elements (those implanted within the text itself, e.g. iconography, *mise-en-scène*, sound) and the **macro** elements (those which 'surround' the text, e.g. narrative) of a text to identify conventions, using these to consider the effect of generic codes on the audience.

3 PART THREE

Key Skill: Application of Number

Topic of Study: Audience

Media texts all have a target audience. The target audience may be wide (**mass**) or specific (**niche**), but each media product will be designed to attract and engage that particular group of viewers, readers or listeners. There are many methods through which the producers of a media product can learn about the expectations and habits of their potential audience. In Section 2 – The Key Concepts of Media Studies, it was suggested that you use the terms **qualitative** (connected with opinions) and **quantitative** (connected with data) to describe the two main types of audience research.

The relationship between the audience and a media product is dynamic, which means that there is an interchange rather than merely a one-way deposit of meaning.

[For definitions of different readings of texts, see section 2 page 24]

Case Study

Stanley Kubrick's *A Clockwork Orange*

In 1972, Stanley Kubrick's *A Clockwork Orange* was released, causing immediate controversy. The film was a study of freedom and control and included scenes of sexual and physical violence. It depicted a world where violence was pervasive, and the only means of controlling this was deemed by those in power to be a harrowing method of brainwashing those who followed a violent path.

A scene from A Clockwork Orange. See page 97, figure 14.

For Kubrick, the film was a discussion and not an invitation to imitate. The almost cartoon quality to some of the violent scenes did not detract from the horror of the violence portrayed, but indicated the mindset of the film's narrator. There were many reviewers who sought to blame the film for copycat violence and argued that the audience was at times encouraged to sympathise with and even emulate the actions of the main character. If the central character was presented as a victim, then his crimes were perhaps a legitimate attempt to counter the confinement he experienced around him. This reading of the film would be considered to be so far from its preferred reading that it would be classified as an **aberrant reading**.

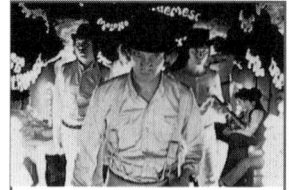

After *A Clockwork Orange's* release, stories appeared in the press in which criminals blamed their actions upon the effects of watching the film. Moral panic ensued, and after Kubrick had received death threats and hate mail he decided to take the film out of general release in Great Britain, with the proviso that it could only be released here after his death. The British Board of Film Classification had passed the film for release, and it was not an institutional decision that forced Kubrick to act in the way he did. It was public pressure and the demonising of the film by some elements of the press.

If there is a preferred reading within this film, then it works as an invitation to challenge what we are shown and not accept dominant ideologies. Neither those in power nor the Droogs are depicted as having found an acceptable means of responding to the world around them. It is a film that demands a negotiated or oppositional reading. Within some studies of audience consumption, *A Clockwork Orange* is accused of encouraging copycat crimes, of helping to desensitise the viewer because of the cartoon, and yet extreme, mode of its violence. On the other side of the argument, we could look to researchers who believe in the audience's essential ability to distinguish between fact and fiction and remain active in the viewing experience.

DISCUSSION

- Do you consider yourself to be a passive or active reader of media texts? Discuss examples of instances where you may not have challenged a text's preferred reading and instances where you have questioned what you have been offered.

- Does your mode of response change from text to text or do you think you have a tendency to always respond in a particular way?

ACTIVITIES

For this exercise you are going to analyse the medium of radio.

> **Activities 1 and 2 will provide practice for the Application of Number Key Skill N3.1: Plan and interpret information from two sources, including a large data set.**

1. RAJAR is the organisation that publishes data concerning radio consumption. Using either the RAJAR website or another available source, collect up-to-date data. Once you have all the available information, answer the questions below.
   a) What types of programmes are most listened to?
   b) On which radio channels would you find these programmes?
   c) What information is given on the profile of these programmes' audiences?
   d) How do you think radio stations use these figures?
2. Create a questionnaire which you can use in order to survey radio consumption. The target audience for your questionnaire will be family members and friends. You should include questions about programmes listened to, amount of listening time, contexts of listening, reasons for listening and changes in listening habits. After your questionnaires have been completed (a good sample will be of between ten and 20 people of different ages), you should make deductions concerning the different audience profiles you find.
   a) What are the similarities in listening habits amongst your sample?
   b) What are the differences?

> **The next part of the activity (3) will provide practice for the Application of Number Key Skill N3.2: Carry out multi-stage calculations.**

3. In small groups, you are going to discuss and interpret your qualitative and quantitative data. Try to complete the following tasks.
   a) Using the group's qualitative research, create statistical data, perhaps in the form of percentages, to illustrate:
   - the genres of radio programmes most listened to and the profile of the listeners;
   - the genres of programmes least listened to and the profile of the listeners;
   - the amount of time that different audience groups listen to the radio and to specific types of programmes;
   - the different contexts of listening you found;
   - the different reasons you identified for listening.

b) Look at the RAJAR data. How do these figures relate to those you have just calculated? What are the similarities and differences?

> **The next part of the activity will provide practice for the Application of Number Key Skill N3.3: Interpret results of your calculations, present your findings and justify your methods. You must use at least one graph, one chart and one diagram.**

4. Still working in your small groups, you are going to present the information you have found to the rest of the class. The purpose of your presentation is to offer information concerning the consumption of radio, but you will also need an introduction to your presentation that outlines your research methodology and its effectiveness. You will need to organise your information systematically, using at least one graph, one chart and one diagram. You should also create a handout for the members of your Media Studies class, which includes the main points and data within your presentation.

Summary

Within any study of the audience you will need to analyse both the theories of audience consumption and the research methods used by media institutions to target the audience effectively. Audience members all have expectations, preconceptions and histories of consumption, which they bring with them when encountering a new text. What is interesting for the media student is how these things affect the consumption of the product and how media institutions attempt to discover and use them to try to ensure success for their product.

FOCUS

1. What methods of audience research do media institutions use in order to help them create effective products?

2. In what ways does American and British research surrounding the audience differ?

PART FOUR

Key Skill: Information Technology

Topic of Study: New Media Technologies

New media technologies are in constant development. The means by which we can consume the media around us are expanding and the processes of media production are developing with the advent of newer and faster technologies. As we identified in Section 5, most households are now saturated with media technologies. We can communicate through landline telephones, mobile telephones, the Internet or even videophones. You might also choose to receive your radio and television stations through digital means, rather than analogue. We have more information available to us now than ever before, but as we have already discussed, this does not necessarily mean that the information is used effectively.

Case Study

The Internet

Many homes now have access to the World Wide Web through the Internet. The web consists of more than a billion pages of information, which can be viewed all over the world. The Internet has provided global access to many types of information, which is being constantly added to or amended.

With the advent of the Internet, e-commerce industries have arisen that allow the consumer to purchase products from the home. Media industries use the World Wide Web to promote their products and to transfer information quickly. Photographers, for example, can send newly taken images via the Internet to their newspapers, thus ensuring a speed of delivery which could result in the all-important 'exclusive'. Within the film industry it is now possible to send sections of film, via the Internet, to production companies. The music industry can build sound into websites and promote the latest singles.

The accessibility of information via the Internet means that information is 'democratically distributed'. The average user can access sites on thousands of subjects. Critics of the Internet cite this as one of the major problems, however, as accessibility means that information can be received by those for whom it is not appropriate. The availability of pornography has caused much debate and, because of the many millions of computers now in homes, it is difficult to enforce legislation on who should have access to it.

Another issue surrounds the quality of information offered by some sites. The vast quantities of information available do not ensure quality. It is left to the consumer to decide the appropriateness and accuracy of information they have found. Our ability to distinguish and differentiate is essential when dealing with large amounts of information and critics point to a lessening of our ability to discriminate, caused by a tendency to be overwhelmed by the volume of information available.

As a new media technology, the Internet has many positive uses and its development will make the potential transfer of images and information much quicker. It is also an effective tool within marketing campaigns and audience research. The problems surrounding the use of the Internet, however, are concerned with the access to and consumption of potentially problematic or inaccurate images and information.

ACTIVITIES

This activity will extend over a period of five or six lessons and will include homework time. The aim of your project is to research and present information connected with the range and application of new media technologies. You will need to work in groups of about four.

> **The following activities (1 and 2) will provide practice for the Information Technology Key Skill IT3.1: Plan and use different sources to search for and select information required for two different purposes.**

1. Each member of the group should opt to research information concerning two from the following list of new media technologies.
   - The Internet.
   - Mobile telephones.
   - Video telephones.
   - Digital television.
   - Digital radio.
   - DVD (Digital Versatile Disks).
   - Games consoles.
   - Big-screen technologies, e.g. IMAX cinemas.
2. Once the selections have been made, each member of the group should aim to research the following:
   a) the development and history of the piece of new media technology;
   b) audience consumption of each piece of technology.
   Research should be carried out using different research techniques (qualitative and quantitative) and sources. Possible research techniques might include: questionnaires given to different households, taped interviews with members of different households, making notes from multimedia sources. The sources for your research may include: the Internet, CD-ROMs, school/college Intranets, print-based publications.

> **The next activity (3) will provide practice for the Information Technology Key Skill IT3.2: Explore, develop and exchange information and derive new information to serve two different purposes.**

3. Once each member of the group has completed the research section of the task you will need to arrange a time to meet in order to discuss your findings. Each member of the group should then present their findings and answer any questions. Information should be

organised by using spreadsheets for data and other IT tools for other information. Individuals will need to give details concerning the sources they used as well as the information gathered. Once each individual has presented the information, the group should try to find links between the different developments and consumption of the new technologies.

> **The last activity (4) will provide practice for the Information Technology Skill IT3.3: Present information from different sources, for two different purposes and audiences. Your work must include at least one example of text, one example of images and one example of numbers.**

4. This part of the activity requires the group to prepare a presentation of all of the material found. You will need to use visual images, text and data to create the presentation. Discuss together what would be the most effective way to organise your materials, decide who will be presenting which sections and make sure that you have all of the equipment necessary. You might decide that the presentation can be split into the two sections outlined in question 2, or you might group certain new technologies together which have similar development and consumption profiles. Try to find two audiences or 'forums' for your presentation: one might be your Media Studies class and the other could be a subject such as Business Studies where students will ask different types of questions.

Summary

The technologies evident within the world of the media allow us to gain information much faster than before, to communicate in many more ways and to produce media products that look much more sophisticated. They are in constant development. Your discussion of new technologies, however, should not only concern itself with development and use, but should also analyse what the impact will be on the individual concerning our response to the media and, indeed, to the world around us.

FOCUS

1. Do the media technologies that today's youth market have at their disposal enhance or inhibit their ability to challenge the world around them?

2. How do you think new media technologies will develop in the future?

5 PART FIVE

Key Skill: Working with others

Topic of Study: mise-en-scène

As we have already noted in earlier sections, *mise-en-scène* is a term we use to describe what is shown within an individual shot. Imagine that you freeze-frame a scene from a television programme or film, what are the elements you see which allow you to make comments about the various meanings generated? *Mise-en-scène* includes the study of character positioning and body language, lighting, settings, sets, colour, props and decor. A shot is composed in order to explain narrative or further character development or understanding, to define the film or programme generically, or to add mood and atmosphere.

Case Study

Use of *mise-en-scène* in Tim Burton's *Sleepy Hollow*

Tim Burton's *Sleepy Hollow* is a cinematic version of Washington Irving's 1819 story *The Legend of Sleepy Hollow*. It is essentially a ghost story and in order to have his modern day audience recognise it as such, Tim Burton was careful to create a very particular *mise-en-scène*, adding to it his own particular style of gothic/horror seen previously in films such as *Beetlejuice* (1988) and *Edward Scissorhands* (1990).

A scene from Sleepy Hollow. *See page 98, figure 15.*

The town of Sleepy Hollow is often shrouded in mist and fog. It is vulnerable and threatened by potential attack from the headless horseman. It becomes an isolated environment, which makes both the characters and the audience feel disorientated and wary. The mists often seem to have a life of their own, curling around houses and, by their presence, often predicting the arrival of the horseman. Many of the scenes, both interior and exterior, are shot to appear darkened. Small pools of light are created by candles in the interior shots and we are left with an actual and metaphorical lack of illumination characteristic of horror. Ichabod Crane (played by Johnny Depp), the detective of the film, gropes around for answers, but the truth is hidden by both the mystery narrative and the disorientating *mise-en-scène*.

The heightened nature of some of the colour saturations in *Sleepy Hollow* adds to the gothic fairy-story feel of the film. The situation is unreal and mysterious. This is a world of nightmares and, as such, the *mise-en-scène* exaggerates shapes and colours to produce the strangeness of a dreamscape. The tree, which provides the focus of the final scene, is huge and knotted, like something from one of Grimm's fairy tales, providing the *mise-en-scène* with another piece of exaggerated Gothic iconography. The scenes with the horseman often frame him with mist, darkness and a blue colouring, which intensifies the chilling nature of his crimes.

The set of *Sleepy Hollow* creates a world of nineteenth-century houses, muddy pathways and woodland; a once tranquil place which has been invaded by fear. As with many fairy stories this is an idyll made horrific by the forces of evil, and the *mise-en-scène* illustrates this through the silence, chill and mist that descend after dark. The houses and costumes of the film are part nineteenth century and part timeless gothic fairy tale. Ichabod Crane's scientific equipment, for example, locates him in a particular period of forensic science history, but also gives his character a strange, almost childlike quality.

The *mise-en-scène* of *Sleepy Hollow* works to create atmosphere, period and genre, as well as indicating a characteristic style of the director. Tim Burton has said of his film, 'We wanted to keep the spirit of the horror movie but be fun with it'.

Gaining information concerning narrative through *mise-en-scène*

Looking at a still image, or **frame**, from a moving image will allow you to make certain assumptions about the place of the action depicted within the narrative of the whole text. You could consider the setting of the still, its lighting and the props used in order to decide whether you are looking at an introductory scene to the narrative or a climactic scene. Certain colours might be dominant that may give you a clue as to the tone and importance of what you are seeing. Consider the last frames of Ridley Scott's *Thelma and Louise,* for example: the Thunderbird is launched from the cliff in a blaze of sunshine, the colours are rich and bright, nothing is evident within the frame apart from the characters, the car and the Grand Canyon below. This is not an image that evokes doom, and therefore we are asked to view it as a climactic moment, a moment of liberation for Thelma and Louise.

A scene from Thelma and Louise. *See page 99, figure 16.*

ACTIVITIES

This activity would provide practice for **Working with Others Key Skill WO3.1: Plan complex work with others, agreeing objectives, responsibilities and working arrangements.**

In groups of about four, each choose a moment that could be considered a turning point in a film. Try to choose films from different genres, and moments that have different significance: you could choose climactic, introductory or dramatic moments. Each of you should then freeze-frame your film and make detailed notes on the ways in which the *mise-en-scène* evident in the still helps to inform the audience about the place in the narrative where the still is found. It is important that you agree in your group to choose very different examples and that you also agree a clear and comprehensive way to make your notes – you could decide on spidergrams, for example. After you have analysed your particular still, present your findings to the rest of the group and together, formulate some ideas as to how different types of film seek to motivate narrative through *mise-en-scène*.

Gaining information concerning character through *mise-en-scène*

When analysing character within the *mise-en-scène* of a particular still, you will need to consider the following:

- the position of the character within the frame;
- the body language and posture of the character;
- their relation to other characters within the frame;
- the relationship of the character to their setting;
- how the character uses the props that surround them;
- how they have been lit.

From a still (a freeze-frame shot) we can make deductions about the importance of the character within the scene and the film, the emotions of the character at that time and their place within a particular genre.

DISCUSSION

Look at the still from *EastEnders* shown below. With a partner, analyse the still for character construction within *mise-en-scène* using the six points listed above.

ACTIVITIES

> The following activity will provide practice for Working with Others Key skill WO3.2: Seek to establish and maintain co-operative working relationships over an extended period of time, agreeing changes to achieve agreed objectives.

In a group of up to six students you are going to 'track' a soap opera character and consider how their status and significance alters over a period of two weeks. Choose one of the soaps that is broadcast two or more times a week and select one character within it for analysis. Each member of the group should opt to record and watch a particular episode, making notes on the importance of the chosen character within that episode. Individuals should also find a still that contains the character, and analyse it for how *mise-en-scène* helps the audience to understand better the character and their status within the episode. During the two weeks you will need to keep each other informed about the work you are undertaking. Don't forget to ask other members of the group for feedback during this period, in order to ensure that you are completing the task effectively. Once all of the individual viewing and note-taking has been completed, your group should meet to discuss how the chosen stills indicate the possibly changing position of the character over the two-week period. You should then present your findings to other members of your Media Studies group and ask them to discuss with you any shifts of character significance you have discovered, and how the *mise-en-scène* you have identified illustrates this.

Using *mise-en-scène* to aid with genre identification

We have identified the main elements that make up the *mise-en-scène* of a shot as character positioning and body language, lighting, props, sets, colour, setting and decor. Media texts can use these elements very effectively to indicate genre. Imagine a still from a film where the lighting created produces pockets of shadow, the character's body language is nervous and defensive, their face is crumpled with fear, the setting is isolated, the set is recognisable but, because of the lighting, takes on an ominous feel. It would be fairly safe to deduce from this that we are looking at a still from a horror film. A still from a fantasy film might be saturated with vivid colours and bright lighting, generating a surreal effect. A Western still might position a sole character amidst an arid and isolating setting to create the impression of questing and loneliness characteristic of that genre.

A still from Coronation Street.

DISCUSSION

With a partner, look at the illustration here, and discuss how the various elements of *mise-en-scène* allow you to comment on the film's genre.

A scene from The Sixth Sense. *See page 100, figure 17.*

ACTIVITIES

In small groups, brainstorm as many film genres as you can. Each member of the group should then choose two of these genres. Your task is to create a still for each which includes appropriate *mise-en-scène* elements. You could draw the still – use a cut-and-paste method or a computer programme. Your still does not have to be elaborate and could include rough sketches or words to indicate a particular aspect of the *mise-en-scène*. Try not to draw your examples from an existing film, but create original ideas. When the tasks have been completed, present your stills to other members of your group and together discuss whether or not they evoke the chosen genre effectively.

Using *mise-en-scène* to analyse mood and atmosphere

The mood and atmosphere generated within a visual image are essential factors for both our enjoyment and critical appreciation of a text. The audience is more likely to be drawn into a visual text if it is engaging. Mood and atmosphere are effects generated by all of the aspects of *mise-en-scène* we have already identified. We discussed earlier how dull or shadowy lighting effects can create an ominous mood within films and we linked this to the genre of horror, but this section does not concern generic identification, and indeed any film may need to express an ominous or portentous mood through its *mise-en-scène*. A visual text may need to express the feelings of a group of people before they enter the scene and this can also be effectively constructed through lighting, sets, props and colours. An atmosphere of confinement might be essential to the themes and intentions of a text and this too can be produced through careful construction of *mise-en-scène*.

DISCUSSION

In what ways can *mise-en-scène* be used to generate the following moods and atmospheres? Make specific reference to films or television programmes to substantiate your points.

Moods:
- depression
- euphoria
- loneliness
- uncertainty

Atmospheres:
- confinement
- ominousness
- liberation

ACTIVITIES

In small groups, look at each of the stills and comment on the *mise-en-scène* evident and how it works to create mood or atmosphere.

A publicity still from Psycho.

A scene from Schindler's List.

A scene from Alien.

The still from the opening sequence of Citizen Kane.

ACTIVITIES

The following activities will provide practice for the **Working with Others Key Skill WO3.3: Review working with others and agreeing ways of improving collaborative work in the future.**

For these activities you will need to work in small groups (these should not be the same groups you have worked with for the other activities). You will need to have in front of you all of the work you have done so far in this section on *mise-en-scène*.

1. Discuss the effectiveness of working with your other groups and together come up with a list of points you think are important when working with others on a common task. You will need to try and implement this way of working within this activity.

2. Plan a way of presenting your findings to other groups which clearly shows the many ways in which *mise-en-scène* functions, and the meanings and effects it is capable of generating. You will need to consider the use of televisions and videos, white boards, overhead projectors and any other presentational tool you think is appropriate. You will also need to decide which member of the group is going to present which section of the material.

3. Present your work on *mise-en-scène* to other members of the group and answer any questions they might have.

FOCUS

1. With specific reference to three films or television programmes, analyse the ways in which *mise-en-scène* can be used as a generic convention.

2. Write a detailed analysis of how *mise-en-scène* can enhance our understanding of the narrative.

3. Discuss the ways in which *mise-en-scène* has been used in two media texts to inform character development.

Summary

Mise-en-scène, as we have seen, is not merely a cosmetic factor within a film. What has been placed within the frame is essential to our understanding not only of a specific moment, but of the text as a whole. You should consider *mise-en-scène* in two ways. Firstly, as a set of elements through which you can analyse visual text moments extremely closely and secondly, as a way of informing your discussions of macro-analysis issues, such as narrative and genre.

261

PART SIX

Key Skill: Problem Solving

Topic of Study: Photojournalism

A photojournalistic image is one that has direct connection to a news story, and has often been constructed in order to represent the story in a particular way. An image may be **cropped** in order to highlight specific sections, or it may be **framed** in a way that promotes a certain reading of the action or person depicted.

There are certain photojournalistic images which have become famous because of their power to represent certain attitudes to a specific event. The Vietnam War produced some powerful visual comments; for example the burned Vietnamese girl running from a napalm attack, or the monk who had set himself on fire in protest against the Vietnam War.

What is important to consider within analysis of photojournalism, however, is not just the construction of the pictures or the event they depict, but the ethics surrounding the process of capturing the image. Intrusive or sensationalist photography, often associated with the tabloid press, prompts us to debate the desire for voyeurism surrounding certain pictures, and stark images of pain or death encourage an ethical debate about the responsibilities of the photographer: should he/she capture moments which will force the public to consider a difficult issue, or do they have a responsibility to help or intervene?

Case Study

Diana and the press

The relationship between Diana, Princess of Wales and the press is one of the most complex of recent times. Possibly the most photographed celebrity of recent years, her life was scrutinised throughout and we have documentary photographic evidence of almost everything she experienced, whether it be her marriage, eating disorders, children, romances or charitable causes.

The use of celebrity images within the press causes much debate. It has been argued that the status of 'celebrity' is created by the public, and therefore celebrities are the property of those who created them: hence the public has a right to know what goes on in their lives. This information may be positive and enhance the position of the celebrity further, but it can also be damaging and defamatory. If it is the latter, then tabloid newspapers argue that infidelities, inconsistencies and problematic behaviour should be exposed and that the celebrity in question is being unfair to the public by hiding details of their lives (obviously the fact that scandal increases circulation figures is an important factor too). The other side of the argument considers press intrusion as inexcusable and vehemently defends a celebrity's right to privacy. Those who support this view often argue that becoming a celebrity does not

*Princess Diana at a formal occasion.
See page 101, figure 19.*

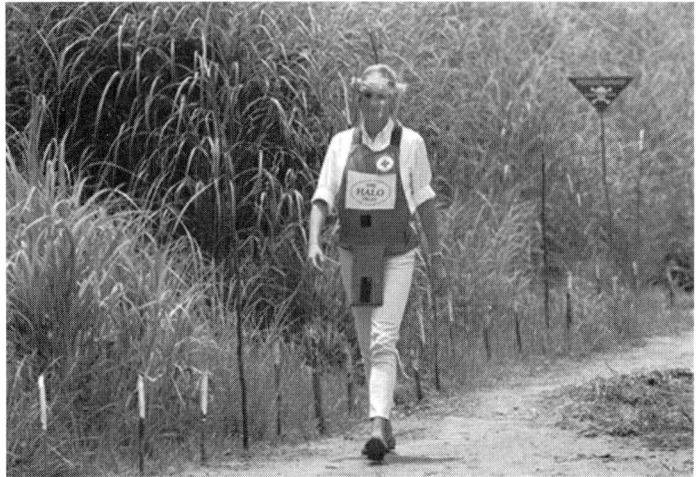

Princess Diana visiting Angola. See page 101, figure 18.

make your personal life public property, that if the individual's fame is a product of their talent in a particular field, then it is only within this arena that they should be judged.

The extent to which Diana understood the complex and dynamic relationship she had with the press is a matter of much discussion and debate. She certainly had a press office, which helped her use media coverage to her advantage at times. Early photographs of Diana show an embarrassed *ingénue*, overwhelmed by the sudden media interest. Later images of an unhappy and desperately thin woman constructed our reading of her as a victim of pressure, and after Andrew Morton's biography she was presented as a product of a loveless marriage and an

The car crash in which Princess Diana died. See page 101, figure 20.

isolating environment. After these revelations, photographs of Diana began to change. She was photographed looking glamorous and happier; repackaged as a survivor. Press coverage of Diana was rarely negative and revelations of her relationship with Dodi Fayed were discussed as a way she might finally attain happiness. Somehow the tabloids justified the intimate photographs, which we were offered of the couple on holiday, because they wished her well. This broaches the question of intentionality as a factor within any debate surrounding photojournalism. If the intention of the photograph is to enhance the celebrity's image then is its publication justified? Should it be the newspapers that decide on what to publish? To what extent are celebrities complicit in the capturing of images that will be to their advantage?

Diana's image, which was recognised internationally, also allowed her to promote causes such as the campaign against land mines. Photojournalistic images represented Diana as a good mother, and she was shown cradling

263

children who had been victims of land mines which further justified both the cause she was promoting and her selection as a spokesperson. As with other celebrities whose lives have had comprehensive press coverage, Diana's image was complex and those who criticised her choice as a spokesperson for particular causes were concerned that the subject of scrutiny would not be the cause itself, but the life of the celebrity used to highlight them.

The last images seen in connection with Diana were of a mangled car in a Parisian underpass. The image became synonymous with tragedy, but also with press intrusion as the crash was initially blamed on an attempt to outrun the paparazzi. Should this image have been shown at all? If we argue that her life was the property of the nation, then perhaps the image was a necessary full stop. It could also be argued that it prompted necessary investigation into the role of the press and the responsibilities of journalists. However, the publication of an image that offered no answers to the tragedy and would be a constant, painful reminder to family members could also be read as the last example of media intrusion into Diana's life.

DISCUSSION

Look at the illustrations of Princess Diana (on pages 101 and 263). What comments on the events which surround them are these images making? What kind of readings of the images are we encouraged to make by the way they have been constructed?

ACTIVITIES

The following activities (1 and 2) will provide practice for the Problem Solving Key Skill PS3.1: Explore a complex problem, devise three options for solving it and justify the option selected for taking it forward.

Your teacher will give you a brief description of three news items (they will include both political and human interest stories).

1. In pairs, choose one of the stories. You should research the story and add detail to the brief description you have been given. You will then need to write detailed descriptions of three images which you think would best represent the main elements within the news item. You should describe:
   - the visual elements of the image;
   - the angles used to take the picture;
   - the framing you would use, i.e. how you would compose the picture;
   - which aspects of the news item your image would represent and why you think these are the main focus of the story.

2. Present your three possible images to another pair and, through discussion with them, decide which image you think would be most appropriate.

> 🔑 **The next activities (3 and 4) will provide practice for the Problem Solving Key Skill PS3.2: Plan and implement at least one option for solving the problem, review progress and revise your approach as necessary.**

3. Your task is now to create the image you have chosen. You could do this by taking a photograph using members of your class and appropriate locations to approximate the people and places suggested in the story, or you could construct the image from 'found' photographs using image manipulation software like Photoshop. Once you have created the image you will need to present it to other members of your Media Studies group and your teacher for comment and review. You might decide at this point that the image is effective or you may amend it.

4. You now have to write the story, create a newspaper page and use the image you have created to illustrate the news item. In order to complete this task effectively you will need to make decisions concerning the following:
   - whether your story is destined for a tabloid or a broadsheet newspaper;
   - the style of language most appropriate to the kind of newspaper you have chosen;
   - the layout of the page and the positioning of your story. Do you think, for example, that your story is worthy of the front page?
   - the caption you will use with your image;
   - the size of your image in relation to the text of the story.

   You may wish to wordprocess your story and then create a newspaper page through a cut-and-paste method, or you may decide to create the page using a desktop publishing programme.

> 🔑 **The next activities (5 and 6) will provide practice for the Problem Solving Key skill PS3.3: Apply agreed methods to check if the problem has been solved, describe the results and review your approach to problem solving.**

5. Before you present your page to other members of your class or your teacher, you need to create a means of assessing the effectiveness of your photojournalistic image to illustrate the story. You might produce a worksheet which asks questions about how the text relates to the image, what the image represents about the story, how the reader is positioned by the image and whether it effectively illustrates the news item.

6. Once the newspaper page and the assessment have been completed, you will need to

present your work to both your Media Studies class and your teacher. You should photocopy your page for the class and discuss with them:

- any problems you had in deciding on the components of the image you have created;
- your reasons for creating your image in the way you have;
- the methods you used to create it;
- your means of assessing the effectiveness of the image to illustrate the story, and the comments/suggestions you received;
- any changes you made during the task;
- the overall success of the image as a piece of photojournalism.

Summary

Photojournalism is, as we have seen, an area that provokes much debate, and the ethical considerations surrounding the capturing of certain types of images will need analysis. You need to consider both the technical means by which the image has been constructed and the intended readings of it which we are offered. Remember also that images have been selected by newspapers to promote a particular reading of a news article.

FOCUS

1. Is it possible to distinguish between tabloid and broadsheet photojournalism in today's press?

2. Are images more powerful than language as a means of commenting on news stories?

7 PART SEVEN
Key Skill: Communication

Topic of Study: Sound

Sound is an integral part of a film and is delivered to the audience in two ways. Firstly, there are the sounds of the story world: radios, street life, traffic and telephones, for example. This type of sound is termed **diegetic**. Secondly, there is the sound that is added to the film after shooting. This is not part of the story world of the film, but acts as a soundtrack. This is **non-diegetic** sound.

Without either diegetic or non-diegetic sound the audience would not be able to enjoy an aural dimension within their cinematic experience. The audience can link the visual elements of the film with what they hear. The linking of aural and visual also helps to shape how the audience interprets the images seen on the screen.

In order to explore how sound is used in film, it is necessary to identify some of the functions of both diegetic and non-diegetic sound. For the purposes of this section we will look at how sound works to generate setting, character and genre.

Case Study

The use of sound in Alfred Hitchcock's *Rear Window*

Alfred Hitchcock's thriller *Rear Window* opens with a 1950s jazz soundtrack, which establishes the period of the film and also offers the only piece of non-diegetic sound evident in the film. The rest of the sounds we hear are generated in the story world. The use of sounds and music in *Rear Window* is sparing and precise and is used to propel the story world. (Interestingly, in Hitchcock's *The Birds*, no non-diegetic sound was used at all. In this instance the lack of background music intensified the tension enormously.)

The use of mainly diegetic sound gives **verisimilitude** (a feeling of reality). We hear radios, record players, children's games, piano playing, street noises and barely audible pieces of conversation, which establish the setting of a cityscape and the apartments that become the main arena of the action. The character of Jeff (played by James Stewart) is confined to his apartment by a broken leg. He is our focus throughout the film and our guide through the thriller narrative. The subjective viewpoint of *Rear Window*, which is evident within the many point-of-view camera shots, is also made clear by the subjective sound within the film. Hitchcock recorded much of the sound from the apartments across the courtyard from Jeff's. There is a hollowness and distance in much of this sound which places the viewer within the subjective aural viewpoint. We need to be positioned with Jeff in order for suspense to build. We are encouraged to make the same discoveries and mistakes that he does.

The characters in *Rear Window* are also given sound themes which help us to understand their position in the film. Miss Lonelyhearts, for example, is associated with the track 'Mona Lisa', and Jeff's signature sound is perhaps the cacophony of the cityscape – a confusing mass of sounds which he needs to disentangle (as he does with the thriller narrative within the film). Lisa (played by Grace Kelly) is a character who is gradually revealed to us during the course of the action and it is, therefore, appropriate that her character theme should be a piece of music constructed as the film progresses. The pianist across the courtyard finishes his composition and we discover at the end of the film that it is called Lisa.

Rear Window is an example of the thriller genre, and the sound within the film helps to define it as such. Our sense of suspense and tension are increased by the confusing fragments of sound we hear, and it is only at the end of the final confrontation scene between Jeff and Thorwald that the tension is broken. There is virtually no sound within this scene except for the dialogue between the characters. Because of this hiatus the suspense builds to a pitch. We are only relieved of tension at the end of the scene when Thorwald ejects Jeff from the window (and, symbolically, from his voyeuristic tendencies) and is caught.

The sound in *Rear Window,* both the musical score by Franz Waxman and the diegetic sound, works to create character, establish genre, motivate narrative and illustrate atmosphere.

Sound and setting

Sound can be used to inform the audience of many aspects of setting. It can evoke historical period, country and character environment. The sound associated with a particular setting can inform us of its hostile, futuristic or idealised nature, for example. Diegetic sound may be used to generate effects such as a sense of chaos, establishing a frenetic setting which is inhospitable to the characters. Non-diegetic sound may be used to promote the idea that a setting is rooted in a particular period of history. Hitchcock's *Rear Window* opens with a jazz track, thus establishing its setting as 1950s America.

ACTIVITIES

These activities will provide practice for Communication Key Skill 3.1a: Contribute to a group discussion about a complex subject.

Non-diegetic sound

Look at the photograph from *Blade Runner*. Discuss in groups the following questions.
1. What kind of setting is presented in this still?
2. What kind of soundtrack do you think could generate a sense of the world you have just described?

A scene from Blade Runner. *See page 102, figure 21.*

Diegetic sound

Listen to the sounds of the city in the film *Se7en*. Discuss in groups the following questions.
1. What kind of environment is this?
2. How do you think the characters in this setting would respond to it or be affected by it?

Sound and character

Sound can be a major component in the creation of character. Non-diegetic sound can act as character theme and can denote either the physical presence of a character in a scene, or it can imply their presence (perhaps in the mind of another character) when they are not visually evident. The soundtrack attached to a particular character may shift in key, pace or volume to establish character's mood at a given moment within the narrative. As with diegetic sound, non-diegetic sound can also inform us of psychological state, whilst providing aural signifiers which we then associate with a particular character.

A C T I V I T I E S

1. Listen to the diegetic sound associated with Darth Vader in *Star Wars*. How is his role within the film confirmed by this sound?
2. Watch the opening underwater sequence in *Jaws*. The shark is not evident, but the soundtrack implies its presence. How does the soundtrack work to create a sense of the shark and its future role within the film?

> **The following presentations will provide practice for Communication Key Skill C3.1b: Make a presentation about a complex subject, using at least one image to illustrate complex points.**

3. Find two more examples for both diegetic and non-diegetic character-related sound. You should prepare a presentation of these findings for the rest of the class. You will need to find clips from four films to exemplify your findings.

Sound and genre

Sound is as essential part of establishing genre. Both diegetic and non-diegetic sound can be used to signify the difference between, for example, a horror film and a Western. Bernard Herrmann's shrieking violins for Hitchcock's *Psycho* magnified the screams of Marion Crane in the shower scene and immediately established the horror credentials of the film. Sergio Leone's use of the whistling pipe sound in his films evoked a hollowness, loneliness and conflict which established that type of sound as synonymous with the Spaghetti Western. Diegetic and non-diegetic sound can also be made to collide in order to establish signifiers within a film.

A C T I V I T I E S

1. Watch the opening credit sequence from the film *Scream*. Write down all of the non-diegetic sounds you hear. One of the first diegetic sounds the audience hears is the telephone in Casey's house. How does the sound we hear on the soundtrack work to establish the telephone as a horror signifier?

> **The written work from activity 2 below will provide practice for Communication Key Skill C3.3: Write two different types of documents that deal with complex subjects. One piece of writing should be an extended document and include at least one image.**

269

2. Find two sections of film where diegetic and non-diegetic sound have been made to collide in order to establish genre signifiers. These clips must be from different genres.
   a) Write an analysis of each of these sections, which discusses how the signifier has been produced, how it evokes the genre of the film and what impact it has on the audience.
   b) Describe, in detail, the opening sequence of a new film. Specify its genre and state how you would use diegetic and non-diegetic sound to establish genre specific signifiers. (You may wish to refer back to the opening sequence from *Scream*.)

DISCUSSION

Choose three other film genres. What kind of soundtrack is most associated with them?

Summary

Sound, as we have seen, is an essential part of the fabric of a film. It can be used to increase the sensory experience and to shape meaning. Both diegetic and non-diegetic sound help to generate many aspects within a film. We have concentrated here on just three: setting, character and genre.

FOCUS

1. With reference to three films, write a detailed analysis of how sound is used to evoke setting.

2. Discuss the ways in which sound can be employed to inform the audience of issues of character representation.

3. Consider the ways in which sound is an integral part of our understanding of genre.

Section 7

So what next?

Looking back and forward

This short section assumes that you are at the end of an AS Media Studies course, and it will therefore take a synoptic view of the studies that you have undertaken with your teacher(s), with other students or on your own. This means that the section aims to help you to tie together all the work you have done so far, the skills you have developed and the knowledge you have gained, and to help you make some connections between the different areas of the AS course. This will enable you to approach a full A Level Media Studies course with confidence and understand how to manage this progression – the A Level course will build upon what you have achieved. If you have decided not to pursue the subject any further, what follows should convince you that the course you have completed has given you some very valuable life-skills, and your future enjoyment of television, films, music, the Internet, radio, magazines and computer games will be enhanced by the experience.

The activities provided in this section do not have any prescribed structure or outcome. There are no absolute 'answers'. This means that it is up to you how you present them. You may decide to make them formal assignments or informal discussions. You may ask your teacher to assess them as preliminary assignments for A Level, or you might simply go through them yourself.

Joined-up thinking

For your AS assessment you will have completed units that have given you a grounding in production work, textual analysis, representation and the ways that institutions operate and audiences respond to texts. However, because of the distinct examinations and coursework tasks that you were working towards, how often were you able to link all this together?

- Have you considered the relationship between your production work and the area of representation studied?
- How would the audience groups you have researched respond to your work?
- What kind of institutions produced the texts you have analysed, and

how do these compare with those investigated for your case study work?

If you continue to the A Level you will do some more production work, but this time you will need to analyse and evaluate your production in a more theoretical way. Rather than analyse single texts, representation, audience and institution separately, you will research topics and make connections between these areas for yourself. You will also start to consider in much more detail some of the debates and issues that arise from the role of media in our society. Even if you are not going on to A Level, it will still be useful to make connections across the work you have already done. It will help you explain what Media Studies is all about. The following activity will help you with this 'mapping'.

Firstly, think about the text you produced yourself (Foundation Production), the two texts you compared for representation (Comparative Textual Study) and the topic you researched for your case study (New Media Technologies or Media Ownership).

- Are the same kinds of audiences involved in each, or are there different audiences?
- More importantly, how are you judging this and upon what information are you basing your ideas?
- How do institutional contexts influence each text?
- What kinds of technology are involved in production and consumption of each text?

Here is an example of a fictional student (who we will call Alex) working through the questions posed above.

Alex produced a thriller sequence, targeted at the 'youth' market, with similarities to horror/thrillers such as *Scream* and the spoof *Scary Movie*. To capture this 'feel', there is an element of parody in the sequence; the audience needs to be able to decode a number of references to films in the same sub-genre. The sequence would be part of a film shown in cinemas and then going to video and DVD (a film like this would, in today's climate, create lots of opportunities for DVD/soundtrack packages, as the soundtrack is a crucial element in targeting the audience). Alex was able to make some interesting connections between working on this Foundation Production and the Comparative Production Textual Study by considering how middle-class America is depicted in two horror films aimed at this youth audience. For the Case Study (New Technologies) it was useful to be able to combine research into the future of DVD consumption with ideas for the thriller.

If it doesn't all fit together quite as easily for you as it did for Alex, then work out why. This in itself may offer some more interesting questions.

- What is the difference between the audiences for your production and the textual analysis area?
- What different issues are brought to light by considering ownership and technology with regard to your own production and those studied for representation?
- What different representational issues are at stake in your production?

You are now thinking in a joined-up way about the work you have done.

Every media text is influenced by ownership, uses technology, has conventions, can be analysed using the core media concepts, has an audience, is consumed in particular contexts using particular equipment, and most importantly of all, is interpreted in different ways by different members of its audience.

Now, having tried to map it all together, look at the following list of study areas and see if any are relevant to your AS work.

- **Media and gender** – how gender is represented in texts, how different gender groups are targeted, how different gender groups might respond differently to texts.
- **Youth culture/the youth market** – youth as an audience, the representation of youth in media texts, youth and consumption/technology.
- **Media and politics** – the political issues arising from ownership of the media and the development of new technologies.
- **Media's effects on audiences** – debates about violence, sexual imagery, language, and so on in media texts.
- **Media texts as products** – the ways in which media texts are sold to audiences and related commercial issues such as merchandising, tie-ins, and so on.
- **Audience research** – ways in which media producers research target audiences and research into how audiences respond to texts.

If you have survived AS, you should find one of the above that relates to your work so far. Make some notes on how what you've learned so far will help you study one of these areas. Again, you need to think 'synoptically' to do this, which means making connections across the different lessons you've had and work you've done so you can draw up a 'bigger picture'.

Celebrating the slippery nature of meaning

It is tempting to try to find the 'right answer' in all educational situations. We know that the capital of France is Paris, that 6 divided by 3 equals 2, that the Battle of Hastings took place in 1066 and that the earth orbits the sun. With 'correct' answers it is easier to know how well you are doing. Media Studies can be frustrating in this way – there are very few absolute answers, but always more questions! Certainly there are facts and figures that, once learned, assist your understanding, but Media Studies is concerned much more with questioning what you see and hear. However, once you become more fully aware of this you will soon start to enjoy this lack of fixed positions. This does not mean that **every** idea is appropriate or acceptable. In any discussion of a media text your point of view must be based upon thorough knowledge and understanding: your opinions must be 'informed'.

A key point to grasp, however is really very simple – no two people are likely to read a text in exactly the same way. We come to texts from our own points of view, which are shaped by our language, background, experience, opinions and friendships. For example, not everyone in your group would necessarily have felt the same way about the quiz shows, game shows and discussion shows you analysed. The reasons for the differences in opinion are as important to understanding media as the conventions used in production. Ask yourself, 'Am I part of the target audience for a text? If not, why not? If so, what assumptions are made about me in the construction of the text?'

Think about your production work. You may have used a camera, either still or moving image and spent a lot of time deciding which angle to use for a shot and how to frame it for a specific effect. You determine what your audience sees and where they view from. Nobody can ask for a different angle on the events. (Even with interactive sports viewing the audiences choices are limited to those selected by the producers of the programme.)

However, even though the entire audience views your shot from the same physical angle, they are all different human beings with different social or psychological positions. Parents and young children may watch programmes like *Thomas the Tank Engine* together, but the ways that they interpret the events on screen are likely to be hugely different. The parents will be able to discuss the programmes in a coherent manner, but at the children's nursery, for instance, the child may watch the same programme with other children of the same age and each has different favourite moments and recognises things in different ways, with different responses. These are not just random; they are influenced by all kinds of things in their life experiences so far, things that are outside of the text. So it is very important in your approach to analysing texts to think of the things that are 'extra-textual' in this way, which influence meaning.

Now imagine a cinema audience of two hundred people watching a film, and the differences between them in terms of age, gender, ethnicity, sexuality, social situation and, most importantly, experience. You soon start to realise that the idea of an absolutely fixed meaning is unrealistic, so it becomes more important to look at the range of possible 'readings' of any text.

Most media texts rely on our understanding of what we consider to be within our world of 'normality'. We have certain preconceived expectations. For instance, how many texts have a disabled hero if the story is not specifically concerned with disability? How many characters just happen to be gay, without this being a major part of their character? Both groups may feel excluded from the majority of media texts, and in a society such as ours that claims to be tolerant and enlightened, this needs to be questioned.

You will have tackled these issues in your studies of representation, but now it is useful to look at the different ways in which different groups of people might respond to the same text, in order to find out who is included and excluded from the messages it provides. The following activity will help you to do this.

ACTIVITIES

Select a media text that you have really enjoyed – think of yourself here not as a student but as a consumer or fan (although these things are always related, of course).

Now consider the key representational issues at work in this text. In other words, which groups/types of people is the text about? Or, put another way, what types of people are the main characters/participants? Who is the primary audience?

Now ask yourself why you like the text so much – write a brief account of this, as little as 50 words is sufficient, and try to describe the kinds of 'pleasure' you find in the text. Next, choose three people you know who you think will fit he following criteria:

- someone who is highly unlikely to get pleasure from the text;
- someone whose reaction you cannot predict;
- someone who you think will share your pleasure.

Without asking them, make some notes on why you have selected them and what assumptions you are making about them as members/non-members of an audience. What is this based on? And how do your assumptions relate to those representational areas you identified at the start of this activity?

Next, if possible, watch/reach/listen to the text with the three others (this may take some organising) and, using a tape recorder, hold a ten-minute discussion about their responses (imagine you are the host of *Late Review*, *Moviewatch* or a similar programme).

Listening to the tape, compare their responses with your predictions. How right were you? Did anything surprise you? If there was disagreement, don't allow yourself to think that you are right and someone else is wrong, but try to account for the difference in opinion. Is it to do with age, gender, opinions, experience, background, intertextual issues (comparison with or knowledge of other texts)?

Finally, and most importantly, think about whether going through this process has made you think any differently about the 'meaning' of the text. This means exposing the necessary responses required from the audience for the text to 'work', and asking firstly why it might not work for everyone and then whether this leads to the possibility that the text might actually mean different things depending on interpretation.

Summary

Let us review what this section has tried to produce in the way of outcomes. For the future A Level student it will hopefully have provided a more 'joined-up' view of the course you have completed, it will have shown how any media text can only send out a set of negotiable meanings, and it will show that you are now ready to construct your own production brief and analyse your own media text using the same critical concepts that you have used for 'real' ones. You should also be thinking about the debates that surround media production and consumption, and hopefully you are looking forward to carrying out some research into peoples' responses to media texts, the institutional influences on media production and/or the importance of the context of consumption, having understood that media learning is rarely classroom-based. Hopefully, for the non-convert, it has convinced you that in a media-saturated world, where reality is always mediated and technology and corporate power merge, being aware of where media products come from, how they are made and how they are differently interpreted is very useful indeed.

Bibliography

A regularly up-dated list of resource linked websites and relevant books can be found on OCR Media Studies website at:
http://ital-dev.ucles.red.cam.ac.uk/ocrmediastudies

Additional useful websites are:
The British Film Institute at http://www.bfi.org.uk
Film Education at http://www.filmeducation.org
The English and Media Centre at
http://www.englishandmedia.co.uk
In the Picture media magazine http://itpmag.demon.co.uk

For research purposes very useful sites are:
BBC Online at http://www.bbc.co.uk
The Guardian and the *Media Guardian* at
http://guardianunlimited.co.uk/

Altman Rick, *Film/Genre*, BFI, 1999.
Arroyo José, *Action/Spectacle Cinema*, BFI, 2000.
Balnaves Mark, Donald James and Hemelryk Donald Stephanie, *The Global Media Atlas*, BFI, 2001.
Barnard Stephen, *Studying Radio* Arnold, 2000.
Blandford Steve, Grant Barry Keith and Hillier Jim, *The Film Studies Dictionary*, Arnold, 2001.
Bunten Peter [Ed], *York Film Notes* series (a series on individual films) Pearson, 2000.
Burton Graeme, *More than Meets the Eye,* Arnold, 1997.
Bordwell David and Thompson Kristin, *Film History, an Introduction*, McGraw-Hill, 1994.
Bordwell David, Staiger Janet and Thompson Kristin, *The Classical Hollywood Cinema*, Routledge, 1985.
Brierley Sean, *The Advertising Handbook*, Routledge, 1997.
Buckingham David, *Public Secrets: EastEnders and its Audience*, BFI, 1987 – O/P.
Buckingham David, *After the Death of Childhood: Growing Up in the Age of Electronic Media*, Polity 2000.
Buckingham David, Grahame Jenny and Sefton-Green Julian, *Making Media: Practical Production in Media Education*, The English and Media Centre, 1995.

Buckland Warren, *Teach Yourself Film Studies*, Hodder & Stoughton, 1998.

Cook Pam and Bernink Mieke, *The Cinema Book*, BFI, 1999.

Creeber Glen, *The Television Genre Book*, BFI, 2001.

Crisell Andrew, *Understanding Radio*, Methuen, 1986.

Curran James and Seaton Jean, *Power Without Responsibility*, Routledge, 1997.

Downes Brenda and Miller Steve, *Teach Yourself Media Studies*, Hodder & Stoughton, 1998.

Dyer Richard, *Stars* BFI, 1998.

Dyer Richard, *The Matter of Images: Essays on Representation*, Routledge, 1993.

Dyja Eddie, [Ed.] *BFI Film and Television Handbook*, BFI Annual publication.

Ellis John, *Visible Fictions*, Routledge, 1982.

Fowler Roger, *Language in the News,* Routledge, 1991.

Gauntlet David, *web.studies*, Arnold, 2000.

Geraghty Christine, *Women and Soap Opera*, Polity, 1991.

Goodwin Andrew and Whannel Gary, *Understanding Television*, Routledge, 1990.

Hartley John, *Understanding News*, Routledge, 1982.

Hayward Susan, *Key Concepts in Cinema Studies*, Routledge, 1996.

Holland Patricia, *The Television Handbook*, Routledge, 1997.

Jackson Kevin, *The Language of Film: A Dictionary of Film*, Carcanet, 1998.

Julius Marshall, *Action! The Action Movie A-Z*, Batsford, 1996.

Katz Steven, *Film Directing Shot by Shot*, Michael Wiese, 1991.

Keeble Richard, *The Newspapers Handbook*, Routledge, 1994.

Lacey Nick, *Image and Representation: Key Concepts in Media Studies*, Macmillan, 1998.

Lacey Nick, *Narrative and Genre*, Macmillan, 2000.

Lewis Lisa A, [Ed] *The Adoring Audience: Fan Culture and Popular Media*, Routledge, 1992.

Martin Roger, *Television for A Level Media Studies*, Hodder & Stoughton 2000.

McKay Jenny, *The Magazines Handbook*, Routledge, 2000.

McKee Robert, *Story: substance, structure, style and the principles of screenwriting*, Methuen, 1998.

McLeish Robert, *Radio Production*, Focal Press, 1997.

McLoughlin Linda, *The Language of Magazines*, Routledge 2000

McQueen David, *Television: A Media Student's Guide*, Arnold, 1998.

Neale Steve, *Genre and Hollywood*, Routledge, 2000.

Nelmes Jill, *An Introduction to Film Studies*, Routledge 1996.

O'Sullivan Tim, Hartley John, *et al, Key Concepts in Communication and Cultural Studies*, Routledge, 1994.

Peak Steve and Fisher Paul, [Ed] *Guardian Media Guide*, Guardian Books/Fourth Estate, Annual publication.

Phillips Patrick, *Understanding Film Texts*, BFI, 2000.

Price Stuart, *The Complete A-Z Media & Communication Handbook*, Hodder & Stoughton, 1997.

Scarratt Elaine, *Science Fiction Film: A Teacher's Guide*, Auteur, 2001.

Selby Keith and Cowderey Ron, *How to Study Television*, Macmillan, 1995.

Shingler Martin and Wieringa Cindy, *On Air,* Arnold, 1998.

Silverstone Roger and Hirsch Eric, [Ed] *Consuming Technologies – Media and Information in Domestic Spaces*, Routledge, 1992.

Stewart Colin, Lavelle Marc and Kowaltzke Adam, *Media and Meaning: An Introduction*, BFI, 2001.

Stokes Jane and Reading Anna, [Ed] *The Media in Britain: Current Debates and Developments*, Macmillan, 1999.

Strinati Dominic and Wagg Stephen, [Ed] *Come on Down? Popular Media Culture in Post-War Britain*, Routledge, 1992.

Tasker Yvonne, *Working Girls: Gender and Sexuality in Popular Cinema*, Routledge, 1998.

Watson James and Hill Anne, *A Dictionary of Communication and Media Studies*, Arnold, 2000.

White Rob, [series Ed.] *BFI Modern Classics*, a series on individual films BFI.

White Rob, [series Ed.] *BFI Film Classics* a series on individual films. BFI.

Wilby Pete and Conroy Andy, *The Radio Handbook*, Routledge, 1994.

Yorke Ivor, *Television News*, Focal Press, 1995.

Glossary

The following glossary offers brief definitions of key words and should be used in conjunction with the index and more detailed definitions of key terms within the book as a whole. Some of the terms have not been used in the book but you may come across them in your further reading.

ABC (Audit Bureau of Circulation) – an independent organisation that provides circulation figures for magazines and newspapers.

Aberrant readings – when a reading of a text is entirely different from the intended meaning. Such a reading may be mistaken or deliberate.

Aerial shot/bird's eye view – shots filmed from aircraft or helicopter, extreme high angle.

Advertorial – in a magazine or newspaper this is an advertisement that has the appearance of an article.

Ambient sound – natural background noise on television, film or radio. In the same manner **ambient light** refers to natural, available light that is not enhanced in any way.

American Dream – the belief that anyone in America can succeed and achieve their dreams, regardless of their social background.

Anchorage – Roland Barthes suggested that all images are open to a variety of interpretations or meanings. He referred to this as **polysemy**. However, if an image is anchored by written text, or sound, then this restricts the possible meanings.

Artificial lighting – is any lighting that is used to light a film or television programme that is not available from a natural source of light.

Audience – all those who receive or interact with any media product. A **target audience** is the group of people to whom a product is particularly aimed. It may be identified as either **mass** (or **mainstream**) if it is targeted at a very large number of people or **niche** if it is targeted at a smaller, more specific group of people.

Auteur – a French term meaning author. It is used to refer to a film director who may be said to direct his or her films with distinctive personal style.

BARB – (The Broadcasters' Audience Research Board) is an independent organisation that is used to measure audiences for television companies. BARB is jointly owned by the BBC and the ITCA (The Independent Television Companies Association).

Binary opposition – where texts are organised around sets of opposite values such as good and evil, light and dark.

Broadsheet – the term strictly refers to the size or format of the newspaper although the term is frequently used as a synonym for the quality press.

Camera angle – this refers to the position of the camera in relation to the main subject. It could be a high angle, low angle, worm's eye view or aerial view. The relevance of each angle is dealt with in more detail in the Section on Textual Analysis on page 74.

Character – the Russian critic and folklorist Vladimir Propp examined hundreds of folk tales and presented an analysis of characters and their specific roles in narratives.

Chiaroscuro lighting – a term originally applied to painting and drawing, it comes from the Italian for light and dark. It applies to high contrast lighting that gives deep shadows and bright highlights.

Cinematographer – the person in filmmaking who is responsible for camera and lighting, often referred to as the director of photography.

Connotation – Roland Barthes refers to this as the meanings that words, images and sounds suggest beyond the literal description or **denotation**.

Continuity editing – sometimes referred to as invisible or academic editing, this is the unobtrusive style of editing developed by Hollywood and still employed in most commercial productions. The basis of continuity editing is to cut on action so that the whole sequence looks natural.

Convergence – this is the coming together of different communication devices and processes. With the aid of a modem, the telephone and computer converge to give access to the Internet that is the new means of communication. Convergence is often made possible by alliances between or mergers of different companies, but the terms are not synonymous. Alliances are when separate individual companies work together in a business venture and mergers/takeovers are when separate companies become one larger organisation as with the merger of AOL and Time Warner.

Cover lines – information about major articles given on the front page of a magazine.

Crane shot – a shot filmed quite literally from a high angle using a crane.

Cross-media ownership – is when corporations own different businesses in several types of media such as News Corporation that has interests in other areas of the media, television, film and the press.

Demographics – demographic data refers to the social characteristics of the population, studies according to groupings such as social class, gender and age.

Denotation – is the simple description of what can be seen or heard (see **connotation**).

Depth of field – the distance between the furthest and the nearest points that are in focus. A wide-angle lens will have a much greater depth of field than a telephoto lens.

Diegetic/non-diegetic sound – diegetic sound is what appears to come from a recognisable source within the narrative of a film, radio or television text. Non-diegetic sound would include a film musical score.

Digital – the conversion of sound and visual to transmit information in a code using the numbers zero and one.

Discourse – A discourse offers a set of statements about a particular area for discussion and organises these statements and gives specific structure to the way that the subject is discussed. Discourses therefore give expression to the meanings and values of institutions or social groups. This can refer to the way in which a particular social group may construct discussion, as in a feminist discourse.

Dissolve – this is a form of **transition** in editing when one image gradually begins to fade and the second image begins to appear. For a brief time the two images can be seen simultaneously. This is not to be confused with **fades** or **wipes** that are different forms of transition.

Dubbing – is a process whereby sound is added to film. This may take the form of adding music or additional sound to dialogue, or it may refer to the addition of an entire soundtrack including dialogue.

Editing – is the selection of material to make a coherent whole. It may refer to the editing of copy and still images for a print product, or sound for radio or images and sound for television or film. In film and television an editor will use a variety of methods of moving from one sequence to another, this is referred to as a **transition**.

Editorial – this may refer to a statement by the editor in any publication or it may also refer to any feature material, that is, not advertising.

Enigma – is a question or puzzle that may be posed at the beginning of and throughout a text. It refers to one of Roland Barthes codes of narrative that he called The Voice of Truth: also called the **hermaneutic** code. These puzzles work to maintain the interest of the audience: they are there to be solved or to delay the pleasure of reaching the end of the story.

Equilibrium/disequilibrium/restoration of equilibrium – these are tensions within a narrative. A secure and balanced state is often used to begin a narrative but this is soon disrupted by tensions or events that cause disequilibrium. A typical happy ending will result in a restoration of balance and restoration of equilibrium. The Bulgarian theorist Tzvetan Todorov is most frequently referred to in relation to this narrative theory.

Establishing Shot – is a **long shot** or **extreme long shot** that establishes the location, general mood and the relative placement of main subjects within a scene.

Fade – is when the image gradually grows dim or faint and then disappears. This form of editing **transition** is not to be confused with a **dissolve**. A fade is usually to a blank black screen, hence fade to black. This is the most common fade although fades to white or red are used for special effects. If an image gradually appears from a blank screen this is referred to as a fade up or fade from. Fade to and from black is commonly found as a standard feature in camcorders.

Form – this term means the structure, or skeleton, of a text and the narrative framework around it. For example, a feature film commonly has a three-act structure. Some structures are determined by a genre and its corresponding codes and conventions.

Frame – as a noun this refers to the single area on a strip of film that holds a single image (or a single still image on video). As a verb it means to adjust the position of the camera or to adjust the camera lens to compose the required image. You would frame your image to construct a close up, **long shot** or medium shot. These are dealt with in greater depth in the Textual Analysis Section on page 79. If the framing of a shot is at an angle this is referred to as a **canted frame** or **Dutch angle**.

Gatekeeping – is the process by which news stories are selected or rejected. A gatekeeper is a journalist, usually the editor who filters the news stories in order to present them in the most successful way possible to the audience. The term is also applied to other major decision makers in media industries.

Genre – this is the classification of any media text into a category or type, e.g. news, horror, documentary, soap opera, docu-soap, science fiction, lifestyle etc. Genres tend to have identifiable codes and **conventions** that have developed over time and for which audiences may have developed particular expectations. Media texts that are a mixture of more than one genre are called generic **hybrids**.

Hegemony – the process by which **dominant ideology** is maintained is called hegemony. This concept owes much to the work of the Italian political theorist Antonio Gramsci. It is a form of consensus that is initially constructed by institutions that wield social and political power, such as government organisations, the mass media, the family, the education system and religion. It is a form of consensus that is frequently re-negotiated between the powerful and the dominated.

High/low key lighting – high key lighting is an even lighting scheme that emphasises bright colours giving a cheerful effect and is often used in comedies and musicals. Low key lighting is where the scene appears under or dimly lit. The overall appearance is of darkness and shadow. This style of lighting is characteristic of thrillers, horror movies and film noir.

Horizontal integration – is when an organisation owns different companies of the same type, for instance Rupert Murdoch owns several newspapers. This occurs when a company takes over a competitor at the same level of production within the same market sector (see **vertical integration**).

Ident – in broadcasting this refers to a jingle or logo that identifies the channel, station or programme.

Ideology – often referred to as the system of ideas, values and beliefs which an individual, group or society holds to be true or important; these are shared by a culture or society about how that society should function. Ideas and values that are seen to be shared, or perpetuated by the most influential social agents (the church, the law, education, government, the media etc.) may be described as **dominant ideologies**.

Intertextuality – often related to **post-modernism** and its culture and criticism. The notion being that we now understand texts by their relationship or reference to another text, or that a text is successful principally because of its intertextual references (e.g. *The Simpsons*, *Scream*). One of the effects on the audience of recognising intertextuality is that it flatters their ability to recognise references and feel superior, or to feel part of a group who share the same joke.

Jump cut – is a break in the continuity of editing. The cut goes from one shot to another in such a way as to disorientate the viewer. This may break the continuity of time by leaping immediately forward from one part of the action to another even though it is clear that they are separated by an interval of time leap in either space or time. Jump cuts can also break the continuity of space in the same way.

Lenses (telephoto, wide angle) – a telephoto lens enables objects to appear closer to the camera without moving the camera itself. It is the camera's equivalent to a telescope. A short telephoto is flattering for faces in close up. A long telephoto can also give crowded streets the appearance of being even more congested. A wide angle lens offers a range of more than 60 degrees. It offers a certain amount of distortion magnifying the foreground and reducing the size of images in the background. Used for close ups this lens will distort the image.

Masthead – the title of a magazine or newspaper usually placed at the top of the front cover.

Mise-en-scène – literally everything that is put in the scene, or frame, to be photographed (appropriate to the time/era portrayed). This usually

286

includes production design, set, location, actors, costumes, make-up, gesture, proxemics/ blocking, extras, props, use of colour, contrast and filter. Lighting is often included within mise-en-scène. Camera shot composition/framing/angle/movement is sometimes referred to as mise-en-shot.

Montage – is taken from the French, to assemble. It has several meanings in the context of film and is not exclusively used to refer to **Soviet montage**. (1) As a synonym for editing. (2) In Hollywood cinema to edit a concentrated sequence with a series of brief cuts with a series of transitions creating the effect of the passage of time or movement over large distances or for expressionistic moods. (3) **Thematic** or **Soviet montage** was developed by Sergei Eisenstein by arranging striking juxtapositions of individual shots to suggest an idea that goes beyond meanings within the individual shots. He called this collision montage. (4) Any sequence that creates a particularly significant effect mainly through its editing. The shower scene in *Psycho* would be such an example.

Narrative – the way in which a plot or story is told, by whom and in what order. Flash backs/forwards and ellipsis may be used as narrative devices. Tsvetan Todorov, Richard Branigan, Bordwell and Thompson and Robert McKee all have interesting points about narrative development.

National Readership Survey (NRS) – an organisation that sets out to provide information on the number and nature of magazine and newspaper readership.

Newsgathering – the process by which news is collected from its source in order to be treated or packaged for presentation.

News values – the process by which news stories or features are selected and their priority and style of presentation (also referred to as gate keeping). These are sometimes categorised as hard or soft. Galtung and Ruge's definitions (recency, currency, negativity etc.) are commonly used to categorise news values in greater detail. The news values are usually determined by the producers and editors to reflect the values of the target audience, what they are interested in reading about or looking at. However, it could be asserted that they also influence and determine the agenda of the readers.

Oscar – this is the popular name for an Academy Award but actually refers to the trophy itself. The gold plated statuette is awarded by the

Academy of Motion Picture Arts and Sciences and is so called, it is claimed, because an early librarian of the Academy, Margaret Herrick, thought that it looked like her Uncle Oscar.

Pan and tilt – a pan is to turn the camera from a fixed position horizontally on the axis of its mount. **Tilt** is to move the camera from a fixed position vertically on the axis of the mount. A **whip** or **zip pan** is the movement done rapidly rather than the usual slow and smooth movement.

Plugs – information about the contents of a magazine or newspaper given on the front cover.

Point of view shot (POV) – is a shot that shows the point of view of a character. This will often be shown as an over the shoulder shot. A **subjective point of view** is when the camera functions as if it were the eyes of the character.

Polysemy – is the possibility of a sign to have several meanings. (See also **anchorage**).

Pre-production – the entire range of preparations that take place before a film or television programme can begin shooting.

Production – is either the product itself or the actual process of filming.

Post-production – the period and the processes that come between the completion of principal photography and the completed film or programme that will include the editing of a film or programme including titles, graphics, special effects etc.

Post-modernism – is a movement or phase in twentieth-century thought. The term is complex and difficult to define in simple terms. It is applied to all the arts and at its most basic refers to the way that new products can be constructed by making reference to already existing ones.

Preferred reading – this term describes the way in which a media text offers a reading or meaning that follows the intentions, either conscious or unconscious, of the maker, or the reading preferred by the dominant forces in society (See **ideology**).

Primary research – is research information or data that you collect yourself. Sources for this may include interviews, questionnaires, analysis of original photographs or other media texts that you undertake yourself (see also **secondary research**).

Properties – are more commonly referred to by the abbreviation **props**. The terms refer to any object that can be carried and used by the actors, as opposed to the larger items of furniture that are considered to be part of the décor of the set itself. In the singular, **property** is also used to refer to any copyrighted text – anything from a complete novel to a song title or synopsis of a plot.

Proxemics – is the study of the way people approach other, or keep their distance from others. What we do with the space between us is seen to be a form of non-verbal communication. It also refers to the way we inhabit our own space, including extensions of ourselves such as rooms, houses, towns and cities.

Public Service Broadcasting – broadcasting that is intended to entertain, educate and inform but does not have a primary commercial intent.

Puff – words or phrases on the cover of a magazine used to boost its status.

Pyrotechnics – are all explosive devices used in films, television or in theatrical stage productions. They are commonly referred to by the abbreviation pyros. In common usage pyrotechnics is a term more narrowly applied to fireworks.

Qualitative research – is research undertaken through observation, analysing texts and documents, interviews, open-ended questionnaires and case studies. It is reasoned argument that is not based upon simple statistical information. Overall qualitative research enables researchers to study psychological, cultural and social phenomena.

Quantitative research – is primarily statistical data most frequently obtained from closed questions in questionnaires or structured interviews. Quantitative research may estimate how many 15–25 year old males watch *EastEnders* but qualitative research is necessary to determine why they watch it.

RAJAR (Radio Joint Audience Research) – this is an organisation involving the BBC and commercial radio, similar to BARB, that is responsible for controlling the system of calculating audience figures for radio.

Ratings – are the estimated number of people who watch or listen to broadcast programmes and can be seen to be a guide to the relative success of broadcast material (See also **BARB** and **RAJAR**).

Readership – this does not simply refer to those who buy a newspaper or magazine, but to the total number of people who are likely to read the publication: usually considered to be three or four times the number of copies actually sold.

Realism – is the dominant mode of representation in television, mainstream films and print. The term usually implies that the media text attempts to represent an external reality: a film or television programme is realistic because it accurately reproduces that part of the real world to which it is referring. The concept is, however, much more complex than this brief definition.

Representation – the process of making meaning in still or moving images and words/sounds. In its simplest form, it means to present/show someone or something. However, as a concept for debate, it is used to describe the process by which an image etc. may be used to represent/stand for someone or something, for example, a place or an idea. Inherent in this second definition is the notion that there may be a responsibility on the part of the producer for any representation, with regard to accuracy, truth and the viewpoints and opinions that such a representation may perpetuate.

Scheduling – is the process by which programmes are broadcast at particular times and in particular sequences to maximise their potential audiences.

Semiology/semiotics – the study of sign systems and their function in society.

Shot-reverse shot – is a standard technique for filming a conversation in which shots from one character's point of view are intercut with those of the second speaker.

Stereotype – is an over-simplified representation of people, places or issues giving a narrow set of attributes. Stereotypes are frequently thought to be entirely negative but this is not necessarily the case.

Storyboard – the planning of a moving image by using a series of drawings with written instructions for the methods of filming.

Stripping – (also occasionally referred to as **stranding**) is the form of scheduling on television whereby the same strand or genre of programme (e.g. sport, soap opera, consumer programme) is offered at the same time every day, every week.

Style – this refers to the look of a media text, its surface appearance. It can be recognised (according to the medium), by the use of colour, typography, graphic design and layout, vocabulary, photography or illustration, mise-en-scène, lighting, music, camera angle, movement, framing, dialogue, editing, etc.

Synchronous/asynchronous sound – synchronous sound is where the sound matches the action or speech in film or television. Asynchronous sound is when there is a mismatch – the most obvious example is when **lip-synch** is out, in other words, when the words spoken and the lip movement of the actor on screen do not match.

Synergy – is the establishment of the relationship between different areas of the media for mutual benefit. This may or may not be within the same organisation, although conglomerates such as AOL/Time Warner and News Corporation are in very enviable positions to make the most of such opportunities. An example might be when the launching of a new film is accompanied by the promotion of a wide range of merchandise, or just a CD of the music. Synergy between films and music is quite common. A rarer example occurred in 2000 between a novel and music. The success of the best-selling novel by Vikram Seth, set in the world of classical music, *An Equal Music* led to the production of a CD featuring all the music referred to in detail within the novel.

Tabloid – a tabloid is a half-sized newspaper. The term is strictly speaking related to the size only, but is frequently used critically, referring to newspapers such as *The Sun* and *The Mirror* (these are also referred to as **red-top tabloids**). *The Daily Mail* and *The Daily Express* are referred to as mid-market tabloids. It should be pointed out that several broadsheet newspapers have tabloid supplements.

Take – a take is a single run of film (or video) as it records a shot. In commercial filmmaking several takes of the same shot would be filmed until a satisfactory one has been achieved.

Teasers – short phrases on the front cover of a newspaper or magazine to tempt a reader to buy the publication. **Teaser trailers** are short film or television trailers shown before a full length trailer is shown.

Terrestrial – transmissions of radio and television that are from land-based transmitters.

Tone – the overall impression that is given by a media text such as serious, comic, romantic, sensationalist etc.

Tracking shot (also referred to as a **dolly shot**) – originally when a camera was moved along on rails or tracks so as to follow the action. When the camera was removed from the rails and placed on a platform with wheels or castors the platform was referred to as a dolly, hence a dolly shot. These shots are also referred to as **trucking** or **travelling shots**.

Typography – the typeface or font that is used in print texts.

Two-shot – literally a shot with two people in the same frame.

Vertical integration – is a term used to describe how one company owns all stages of production and distribution (and in the world of film, exhibition). The Hollywood Studio System from approximately the late 1920s to the 1950s was organised in this way. In print publication it could refer to a company that owns the paper mills that make the paper, through to chains of newsagents who sell the magazines and newspapers.

Voicer – a scripted report that is presented by an additional reporter within a main news bulletin.

Vox pop – the opinions on current issues or topics recorded from members of the public. From the Latin *vox populi* meaning voice of the people.

Wide shot or **wide angled shot** – is a shot that takes in more than 60 degrees of vision rather than the normal range of the camera at 45–50 degrees.

Wipe – a transitional device for editing in which one scene appears to push another off the screen. In early filmmaking the only possibilities were the vertical or horizontal wipe, but with developing technology a wipe can be in an almost infinite variety of patterns.

Wrap – (1) the conclusion of a day's filming or for the entire production. (2) an item in a news programme that begins with the newsreader, cuts to a location reporter and/or an actuality sequence and then returns to the newsreader.

X-Certificate – in the United Kingdom the X Certificate was originally introduced to restrict entry to cinemas for certain films for those under the age of 16. In 1970 that age limit was raised to 18 and in 1983 the X Certificate was superseded by the 18 Certificate. The term Certificate has now been superseded by the term classification. In America the term rating is used.

X – as a prefix is used as an abbreviation for extreme, as in XCU – Extreme Close Up.

Zoom lens – is a lens of variable length used to give the illusion of moving the camera closer to or further away from a subject without moving the camera itself. A zoom shot should not be confused with a **dolly** or **tracking shot** where the camera is physically moved.

Index

Abbreviations are used as follows: [F] films; [M] magazines; [N] newspapers; [R] radio programmes; [T] television programmes